SEDUCTION OF THE SEDUCER OF SEDUCERS

—ANOTHER PLATITUDINOUS UPANISHAD

: A MEMENTO
FOR AN
ETERNAL LIFE

INDERPREET KAUR

DESCLAIMER

ANOTHER PLATITUDINOUS DESCLAIMER
FOR YOU TO SKIP
AHEHEHE...

This is a work of fiction. All the characters are mere tools, created by the Author to bring out the importance of our choices in real-life Scenarios.

Any similarity to actual persons, living or dead, or actual events, is purely coincidental.

TABLE OF CONTENTS
A MAP FOR NAVIGATING THE LABYRINTH OF LIFE

PREFACE / WELCOME

Namaskaaar! *** AaaHeehehehe ***

On hearing my wild laughter, see how your eyes sparkle with the possibility of some wild one-time rendezvous with a nymph from the forest, however the use of a word from an advanced ancient civilization, puts some cold water on your hot expectations as now your intrigued eye sees in me some smart woman with the blood of Rishi's running in her veins, who might lead you behind the dark bushes and then bashfully disappear! However, since I am indeed smart, I understand the language of your silence. Your silence reveals to me you are intrigued enough to start. Feeling encouraged I read out my disclosure: For me to guarantee you a fruitful and meaningful journey together ahead till the end of this Volume will require to promise me of your full focus on me and only me! In the beginning it might seem boring but still stick with it, as I promise that the interesting part starts from the line that comes after the next line!

All these lines appearing on your forehead like a philosopher, show to me all about the turmoil going on inside! Your thoughts are vacillating between either continuing to serve your jail sentence, serving the needs of your numbskull wife's insatiable mortal needs for a boring life until eternity, or else leave all your near and dear ones behind you to come start a new journey with me to Planet Venus, where your insatiable appetite for entertainment from every moment to the next, is a requirement on which we never compromise! You - who still does not know that he is already a slave for the wine that only I serve!

Now I come a step closer to you, just enough to dispel any doubts over me being regular with my shower routine or not.

Clicktiiclick, I snap my fingers to bring you back here from your deep thoughts. I ask you coquettishly, "I said, Namaskar! Are you ready to begin?" With a roguish look you ask me quite phlegmatically, "Is there a happy ending in the end?" As I understand your question, my head bends shyly. With heaving breasts, I say nothing. Seeing the high passion in my response to your desire, you grin. Seeing yourself entertained and a potential for the same ahead, you are ready to do anything I want, so as is befitting a king, you royally lift your hand and say the popular saying in Sanskrit, 'Subhasham Shighram! (Sanskrit Language, meaning, any beneficial task: execute it at the earliest possible)! (A good task should be implemented at the earliest!)'! ...

A PRAYER AT START OF THIS ENDEVOR, WITH EXPECTATION OF NO EXPECTATIONS FROM IT IN RETURN

O, The Knower of Knowledge of all Knowledge, my only prayer to you is to never grant my prayer! Not because you always do things your way regardless then what is the point of me asking, but because now I realize that you know better what is best for me with this instance of my existence from the many other life-forms that I have gone through...

When I fall, my faith in you shakes but then thank you for giving me the reasoning ability to understand that I fell not because you are not there or that I am all alone fighting my daily battles, but because I doubted your existence, because I disobeyed or failed in interpreting Your command, Your laws! Thank you for punishing me in time so now whatever I do, I try to do it in a way that is as close as possible to the way that you would have executed, in the way which will maximize my overall gains ...

A NARRATOR RESUME FOR GAINING THE POST OF NARRATING THIS EPIC TO YOU

INTRODUCTION

Truth itself is one, but what gives meaning to the Observer is only when viewed relatively! For instance, take the solar system as an example. In the Solar System, the Planet Earth is constantly revolving, is a Statement that is an acceptable fact for us to use as base for our own tautologies to build upon. However, this truth holds meaning for the observer only when viewing it in relation to the sun, while when viewing against oneself, the truth that has meaning, is that it is static. Just as capturing truth as a fact is a scientist's job, capturing truth that is relevant to the observer is a poet's job. Since this book is an attempt to capture a Poets perspective the stories are structured in a way that we experience reality compared to the events happening in the Universe of our Heroin Mayuri. What is the essence that makes one a Mayuri? Well first, this name means a Peafowl in Sanskrit. Like a Peafowl when dancing in the rain, excited spreads its tail as a fan displaying vast palette of rich colors in its divine glory, the Heroin too has a deep belief of preparing oneself for all different possibilities in this labyrinth of snakes and ladders every step of life! Enough chatter over the name of the Heroin of this Drama, when this name is just a label for the values that are also present in all people as we all are sailing in the same boat - Earth as her, so wisely we now jump on to the next topic!

QUALIFICATION

Why you should choose me over my competition is because I am not just blessed with the power of the tongue but unlike most authors who have never given birth themselves but write about labor-pain experienced during a delivery, I write from my experience that comes from being exposed to both the eastern and western style of living, where in the first half of my life it was east while the other half of my life in the west, which means it puts the burden of being that **missing link** that is needed to unite the east and the west!

OBJECTIVE

What we need is that child's eyes, who could see what is the Obvious,
as he laughingly shouted, 'The Emperor is naked!'...

Why even bother gathering knowledge from varied sources when all of them must tell the same lies just wrapped in different flowery words? Knowledge received from such sources is not just mis-leading but outright dangerous! Unfortunately, the work of most authors is like that pot-bellied Priest teaching other's lessons in austerity and thus here is another Platitudinous Upanishad to fulfill that void! This work is an attempt of saving human from this great fire of low-frequency forces that is mercilessly devouring any and everything that comes it way! This fire is unlike the regular fire which reduces everything to ash but is cunning as it consumes the inside while deceiving the individual of not even the one be aware of its losses!

The behavior of most characters in scriptures mimics real-life challenges that most of us must go through. Most people like to believe they are in a situation unlike any, but once they start looking as a third person, they are incredibly surprised to know how wrong they have been! They can now see how the behavior of characters in similar situations behave the same way, just the names have changed! The only case we find exceptions is when we are dealing with people who refuse to compromise with their Freedom of living their lives that is true to their essence, their ethical self! This literary work will help you find those compromising situations and then use the techniques that will help you safeguard your heart, in this age where every heart is getting targeted by replacing them with stones, at a frighteningly alarming pace!

This piece of literary art attempts to bring awareness toward uniting the east and the west literally and east and west metaphorically where east is referring to inside while west is referring to outside, uniting to fight all the issues that are threatening this beautiful creation now based on Vedic Principles, else it is not there...

EXPERIENCE

To deliver this message, to quest my thirst for Eternal Truth, like a serpent I shed these mortal skins of gender, color, nationality, taxonomies to experience nothingness, the concept of 'shunya'/zero in Sanskrit, to see the obvious ...

ARCHITECTURE

You are in me, and I am in you, so who better than me to not understand your constant insatiable appetite for entertainment from every moment to moment so therefore unlike most narratives who like to structure their presentation as it progresses with time, I too use this approach, but just not in the traditional monolithic style. I add Masala spice in it by making it a hybrid by crossing it with an event-driven structure!

PHASE ONE OF LIFE: WHEN THE HEART IS KING

A song sung by a solitary nightingale,
When heard by People they think it is for the lover who forgot her,
Not realizing that this melancholy in the song is for every heart that
resonates with the sweet pain.
and yet it is for nobody ...

FOUNDATION

What better structure for me to lay the foundation of my Family than the sacred Banyan Tree!
The secret behind its immortality? Unlike its pears who are unable to go past their limitations of going downward only they can go upward too...

LISTEN TO THE SONG OF THE NIGHTINGALE - 'TU TA TU TA TU'

The song of the nightingale must be the hallmark of beauty,
as my feet get aroused,
dancing to the immortal song- Love,
when played by the magic flute...

CHIRP-CHIRP!
"Maaaaaammmmmie.... We just finished the internet!"

Poor Mommie! Often shudders in dread at the thought that if ever her elder daughter Mayuri now eight, and younger son Chandrashekhar now four, were to run out of their roguish games and tricks that are coming out magically from some bottomless well of imagination and curiosity that has no beginning nor end! And when that day of reckoning comes, she will be facing their firing squad alone! Like Ouroboros, the snake that eats its own tail, their questions too show the circular nature. Example? "Mommie, what came first, the chicken or the egg?" Sounds simple to the child, but for Mommie it is a do-or-die situation, because now her whole reputation as a wise lady is at stake! If she fails, her children may never take her seriously and if not, they will forever obey her every word as gospel! Now that she has finished making all the chapatis - the special Indian bread with it fortunately all the lines of stress on her forehead coming from her little philosophical digression also have vanished!

While mother Aditi was busy in the kitchen making food ready to serve them to her little devils and the father of the little devils - the Satan Incarnate himself the kids were also busy at the roof, rejoicing once more at the happy event of retiring their old rag doll and replacing it with another toy. Mother does not distribute any funds towards toy-purchases, but this time she thought by choosing quality over quantity will help keep her children busy with it for years to come, so this time she bought an expensive toy-nightingale. The craftsman must have spent many sleepless nights to make this mechanical wonder, who's high cost-price justified the product - a sleek nightingale with a beautiful tail, beautiful colors, and a sparkly body. And to make it even more special, it has a little button at the bottom, which when pressed sings.

It soon became a source of great entertainment for the kids and all kids in the neighborhood alike. After having played with the nightingale in several ways, exhausting all new possibilities, little Chandrashekhar heaved a sigh, throwing the bird in his elder sister's lap, exclaims with a bored expression on his face, "I'm so done! One more time she sings, I am ready to bang my head against the wall!" Little big-sister Mayuri takes the threat seriously as she herself has reached that threshold, so starts scratching her head, find some new game to play with the toy which will satiate their monstrous appetite for fun and more importantly also save her brother's life! The eureka moment has arrived as she starts clapping her hands and with her usual enthusiasm and exclaims: "I have a brilliant idea, but for me to disclose the plan you will first have to take an oath of secrecy to be kept hid from mother. Needless to tell you why, when you have been as much a victim as me from her un-predictable volcanic eruptions!"

Wide-eyed, he keenly asks, "Okay then! What is the plan?" She whispers the secret plan in his ears, fearing the real nightingales might hear their evil plan and then destroy it by complaining about their mischief to their mother! "Listen then! Why not throw the bird from the topmost point on the roof to watch the flight of our dear birdie hurtling down and then making a loud crashing sound!"

The plan intuitively appeals to his mischievous mind. He gives his nervous consent by contributing to the plan by making it more thrilling by mutilating its body. Mayuri is now doubly pleased, one from the joy of seeing an actual demolition while the second reason is secret from her partner in crime also, as it is from the joy of having validation of her persuasive powers, even if it is over her own brother, who is much younger!

Without telling any details of their plan to anybody, especially to all kill-joy Ma, as silently as possible, the little monster's race as fast as possible to reach at the top-most area on the roof while making a sport out of their mini-race to the top itself! Little Chandrashekhar rips off the wings to see if it still flies before it meets its fate of death and dissimulation! He swings his arms and says his command in military fashion, "1 2 3 Go!" As the bird, goes hurtling down, it does not forget to keep merrily sing and tell its last most important words to this big bad world -"chirp, chirp"...

HIDE AND SEEK

The pleasure in destruction by the kids of their favorite and mother is most expensive purchase for any toy, soon evaporates when they hear the voice of approaching footsteps of their mother! They look at each other with gaping mouths, before taking flight to hide behind a pillar. Stand there quietly, wondering why mothers must be so silly? Debating with her is not wisdom but suicide! Since they love their lives, they do not back-talk, as if ever they end up offending her even if by accident, it is their neck at the altar of a narcissistic and bipolar tyrant. They stay silent.

A mom, fully armed with her intuitive powers, which naturally come to a woman once she becomes a mother, comes upon hearing the distant chirp-chirp, confused about whether it's her ears that had started playing tricks with age or it's some other trick of her little devils to have her finally locked-up in a lunatic asylum, as the sound which is expected to come from above is instead coming from below! She quizzically looks down, and really it should have not been that much of a surprise but still apparently it was, as she rubs her eyes again in disbelief on seeing all her worst fears take shape!

She wonders, "My eyes, as an adult, just completely fail to see any beauty in the destruction that these children see! Is a child's brain a big pervert which sees beauty and pleasure in destroying, especially any beautiful object that is worthy of worship and that too in the cruelest way?! Lord has mercy! As this also suggests to me that when I was a child, I must have been a bigger pervert, as I am the Template from which these little perverts were born, afterall!"

"You little monsters!" she exclaims as her eyes are simultaneously scanning the room for her plastic slippers. They are meant for walking, but unfortunately her hyperactive pervert brain produces devious ideas that can only be the brainchild of a very tyrannical mind! However, since the children are her signature and a half, so in anticipation they have already countered it by throwing them safely behind the mountain of stacked trunks and suitcases, ensuring that there enemy never returns! On finding that she has been outmaneuvered, she now gets doubly angry. Not someone to go down quickly she switches her weapon to her hand instead. So, she switches her weapon to her strong hands as a spanking instrument, and runs after her children, screaming obscenities that are very unbecoming of any religious and pious lady! She starts spanking them mercilessly with a strength that is simply good enough for hurting a fly. The children pity her as this punishment seems more for her as their skin is now too thick to feel any pain while her fragile hands start feeling pain from her own beatings! ...

A sincere advice: Why any sane mother will want to kill her own creation? Well, the answer lies in your question, my friend, that they are NOT SANE. They are bipolar. So, make your house oceans away from your mother! Fear is not that you might miss her terribly, fear is that she might come there too!

BASE CONSTRUCTOR FOR THE
BIRGHI-GHAI BANYAN TREE

A MOTHER IS SAWED /
1947 INDIA-PAKISTAN PARTITION

When the Devil had its way...

What a travesty, for the Ghai and the Birghi Families for having to see the episode of their own Motherland being sawed into two pieces!

The Grandfather Shri Ram of Little Aakaash Birghi feels a chill run down his spine on witnessing what must be one of those dreadful events in the entire History of Mankind, when on seeing the spear of hatred thrust right through the heart of Mother India, in one of the most bone chilling and heart wrenching orgy of blood that even the stones must have started shedding tears of blood!

Shri Ram is extremely attached to his birthplace, so much so, that he dies, rather than move elsewhere, yet the moment that he hears about the story of an infant being snatched from mother's lap and then killed in a brutal way, he finds himself reversing his stand! He sees in this news-item the hidden message that the Divine is trying to convey to him, that the time for him along with his family has come to leave, as the Land that he had always loved is because it is fertile for humans to thrive but now it has changed its Nature, as now it is for Savages instead!

He does not forget to thank this news-item as if it were not for this, he would still be living with the false sense of security that misinformation or no knowledge of the facts can create! Fact is that in a Land where law enforcement is either weak or corrupt, all our valuables are at risk! What we are seeing now, is all our worst fears take shape of this demon which will only stop once it has stolen all our land for free, has sold us and our women and children as slaves! ...

On reaching Delhi, he begins his search for any house. Much to his dismay, he finds that all the houses he is meeting are either already occupied by Muscle Men or with earlier Muslim owners who are still brave enough to battle the storm! After, disappointment after disappointment Shri Ram is tired but a voice of hope keeps telling him to not give-up. The Protector of all Protectors will ensure that his efforts will get rewarded! Obeying this voice, he continues his search. He notices a house which looked unkempt. Even the door gave an appearance of being un-locked, as if the Owner were someone who did not value their life anymore! He knows not what comes over him and he straight barges his way in the house! In front of him is an old woman who is around eighty-five years old. Their eyes meet. He starts looking at the door to leave. On seeing him leave, very curiously she requests him to stop and only leave after answering her question. He waits patiently.

Old Lady: "You came here to kill me but now when I am in front of you, instead of killing me, you are turning your back to leave! Why?"

Shri Ram: "It is not as much because of pity on killing someone weaker than me is something that is against my ethical self but more because, contrary to the common conception that the whoever has more muscle strength, is the one who wins, while really it is the one who has the most efficient weapon of destruction in their hands emerges as the winner! So even if you are an old lady who needs aid to even get to the bathroom, still with a gun in your hands, it is you who is the stronger one!"

On hearing this remark, the old lady starts laughing! He is taken aback as he had never heard someone laugh so loud over something so serious!

Shri Ram: Now I have seen people laugh on weirdest things but never so much and that too on something that is so serious! This does not make any sense to me! Will you please solve this mystery before I die, not out of depression from seeing fear and horror written on every face that I see around me, but out of curiosity!

Old Lady: The only regret in my life is that despite knowing that it is only after going through many life-forms, do we get this human Form, I still have not been able to do any work so splendid that I can get any place in Heaven!

So, my humble request to you is to first promise me that you will do whatever I ask you to do, for me to achieve my Goal?

Shri Ram: "With a gun next to you, I will do anything!"

Old Lady: "I do not want any thought of pity over an old lady cloud your judgement! Make sure you kill me as even if I died long ago, my attachment to this wretched corpse has not! So, I want you to do this favor for me! This way so you get good Karma points for mercy killing me and I for my sacrifice of giving something valuable of my own, to someone who needs it way more than me..."

Shri Ram: "A Muslim woman is offering me to sacrifice her life just to help a man who is a Hindu, means the cause behind this war has nothing to do with religion!

This event has helped lift the blind fold of religion biases to see how a false propaganda is busy in distorting the true picture for us, us who are one of the ninety-eight percent who become the victims, mainly because we receive the news after the damage has been done! The Mind behind these conspiracies is punch-drunk on their Power, thinking no one is watching, not realizing that when Yam, The Death Broker wields his stick they will pay the hard way!

Now my aware eyes can see that the problem lies in the teaching which trains people to convert others into adopting their way of living! This teaching is against the way we see that the Creator of All Creators have created this World! All different Religions need to respect everyone else's belief, even if they think that theirs is the right one, just as painting the entire World with the same color will destroy its whole beauty making even the most beautiful the most boring, we let it be! When in Tautology Science, the foundation is found to be false, all assumptions based on it are also considered as False and even if a lot of effort had been put in it, is discarded, so then why is it that we are still following the Books that claim that that the Earth is flat instead of the Books from the Vedic Science whose findings are not just limited to the Earth being round but many more findings which are not possible without the knowledge of advanced techniques?! Now I can see the urgent need of a complete re-structuring in the way that we see our Land, by removing the concept of separate Countries to one Country which represents the whole Mother Earth in its entirety, that is consisting of smaller manageable autonomous units which are self-dependent units, thus helping in minimize the areas of confrontation, as the underlying cause behind most wars have been found to be at the point in time when the dependencies are not fulfilled efficiently!

He closes his eyes, the picture of his little daughter Shivdevi comes in his bhumadhya (the region on the forehead between the eyebrows also referred to as the third eye) as the finger on the trigger gets firmer enough to let go of the bullet! The walls get a spatter of blood stains making a pattern that reminded him of a Trishul, the three-pronged spear that Lord Shiva holds! He tries and tries to erase but still he knows not why his sharp eyes still can detect their dark shadows ...

Later when his little Daughter Shivdevi hears about this incident, she knows not why that she is reminded of the episode of Shri Krishna from the epic Mahabharat stealing butter, so, she too starts calling him Makhanchhor (Butter Thief) amongst many of his other loving names ...

1943 CONSTRUCTOR (AAKAASH, THE SEED)

I am the seed for creating my empire, where every generation hereafter
will carry my signature...

Even higher then Aakash (Sky in Hindi), is the worth of a Father, all wise people since all ages attest for this statement! So, when Shri Kartar Singh Birghi names his youngest Son as Aakash, little did he know just how well suited his name is for the important role he will be playing in the future as a father to his children...

The biggest advantage of being the youngest one amongst eight siblings is that he will never have to go to any unhealthy means to get attention, like that woman who burnt her own house to get attention, as he already gets it in abundance from every family member!

Being a Capricorn Male, he has a well-rounded personality. Black in complexion, strong and well-built, he also has been blessed with a mind that all his pears prayed for! Most of the calculations which his pears cannot even do, he can solve all those long and awkward calculations mentally itself! The only source of earnings is the temple, where father - Sardar Kartar Singh works as the head priest. The mother of Aakaash - Mata Shivdev Kaur is an incredibly beautiful woman and fearing the wrath of the women-lib associations we will not refer to her as a baby-making machine, but once they hear the number chances are that they will immediately rescind their objection as the number is the sum is of all fingers from both hands combined - A big fat ten!

Coming from a strong religious background, he grows with deep knowledge of scriptures. As a youth he chooses to be a social scientist for vocation with the government of India, while for a hobby, as a writer/poet. This way, the prosaicness of a stable job gets offset by his injections of bitter truth in his poems. The irony and sting in the verses of his poems end up ruffling a lot of feathers, especially when the hypocrite targets find themselves with the characters portrayed, which makes his own character more on the equivalent side.

1947 CONSTRUCTOR (ADITI, THE CLAY)

I am the clay, the container, for creating his empire such that, the signature of our union which will be present in every generation hereafter...

Even more seamless than any Ocean is the forgiveness of a mother, all wise people since all ages attest for this statement! So, when Shri Gopal Singh Ghai names his fourth Daughter out of six as Aditi (The Mother of Sun God, The Epic Ramayan), little did he know just how well suited her name is for the important role she will be playing in the future as a mother to her children...

The Father of Aditi ⁓ Shri Gopal Singh (the name comes from Lord Shri Krishna's one of the many names that he had), once retired from his military job, starts a small business of selling motor and cycle parts to support the family needs. He is a tall and well-built man built like a warrior, like a man who cannot just protect his wife and children, but the wife and children of other families from unwanted invaders too. Military training had not just given him strong arms, but also self-discipline and structure needed for leading a meaning full life and serve as an inspiration to his children.

The mother of Aditi ⁓ Ma Agya Kaur Ghai, the cause of her daughter's beauty is an incredibly beautiful woman, blessed with beautiful sharp Indian features and an equally beautiful mind. Her daughter Aditi always feels indebted for beautiful white skin, sharp chiseled facial features, like a swan's face and an even more beautiful mind, which like thorns with a rose flower always helped her in protecting herself!

Being a family where all the members of family take-up the family business for their source of income, there is less emphasis on formal education, than in learning the family business. And therefore, it becomes more creditable for Aditi, when she beat all odds and gets her degree in English Literature and later when she gets her master's degree, studying while her son lay sleeping in her lap!

Aditi is a woman blessed with a razor-sharp mind, which helps her beat everyone in every field and that too with a jaw-dropping margin. That her victory is no fortuitous interjections of fate is clear by the consistency of this occurrence repeating itself year after year!

ULTIMATE PURITY -
A MARRIAGE TILL ETERNITY

O my slave full moon,
You shine up in the sky for me, my sweetheart shines down on earth
for me,
The moon above makes his movements elegantly, my moon down
makes here too movements makes his movements unnoticed towards me,
My eyes wait patiently for the day, when my moon will illuminate me
with his full power just like the full moon above,
I will spend the whole night, looking in his eyes,
My whole body motionless like the night, his body also motionless like
the stars,
I will not let a night like this ever end,
I will tie that night tightly with the ropes of my eyelashes, and not let
the moon vanish!

HER ETERNAL WAIT?

Aditi's beauty forced even the beautiful moon to bow his head in his respect. Her spellbinding beauty is a big blessing, but the same blessing becomes the cause of her curse too! This is absurd, you must wonder, how can anything that is a blessing be also a curse? Well, indeed there is no dearth of handsome young men in the community, but the same beauty becomes a curse because now she must learn how to hide her beauty from the unwanted vultures who can smell blood from miles away and so come swoop her to bring in their castle against her wishes! So, to avoid any unnecessary complications, she dresses simple, minimal jewelry, negligible make-up, so she can focus on her college education undisturbed before she gets married.

Ma Agya (the name meaning Request in Sanskrit), Aditi's mother is a highly intelligent woman. The kind who can count the wings of any bird flying far away! As a loving and caring mother, she wants the best, a highly educated man for her beautiful and well-educated daughter. However, everyone around her had already started laughing at her expectations as she had already challenged the norms by letting her daughter go to college, when most men around in the community were not even secondary school educated, as due to unfortunate circumstances created due to the India-Pakistan Partition most boys had to sacrifice their education needs over supporting men folk in running their businesses. Which is not good news for Aditi's matrimonial prospects as now for an educated woman the number of eligible bachelors from the pool of possibilities is now less than one percent! Upon learning about all these statistics, she is full of dread over a strong possibility of a long, lonely life ahead! The fear starts growing and consuming her inside day and night every-time when she hears of her wise mother's rejection after rejection of proposals due to them being illiterates!

When Ma Agya enters the kitchen, where her daughter is sitting near to the clay-oven making Chapatis (Indian Bread), buried in deep thoughts, she asks her the reason of the lines of worry over her forehead. Aditi voices her doubts, "What will become of me? Will I have to live as a burden on my brothers! Will I have to bear the taunts of people scorning my ability, laughing at me behind my back? Will you ever be able to find a man who is worthy for your well-educated daughter now?" When Ma Agya sees her daughter Aditi showing signs of cracking under pressure of finding a man in near future, she laughs! Then explaining her the big secret behind her calmness over something that was a big cause of worry in her daughter, she says, "My dear lovely daughter Aditi, you yourself tell me, that patience is a virtue but you yourself do not have any! **Have faith! When you pray every day for a good Husband and yet you doubt if you will ever get one negates all the benefit of a prayer, or of your faith!** Have faith in destiny and its mysterious ways, unknown to us how they work the way they work. The man who is meant to be your husband, has taken birth already for this purpose. So, take heart and he will find his way to you himself!"

On hearing Mother Agya's words Aditi now finds new hope, as she says her newly found revelation with joy to herself, "I am like the marijuana weed, whose insanity grows when not allowed to breed and yet, this insanity is precisely what I need, as now, all my senses are at full strength, transmitting invisible, secret messages, meant for my lover to decode and once that good time has come, he will come to my humble abode, which I have been preparing for welcoming him, to start a new future together."

The very next instant the doorbell rings. Aditi's heart skips a beat, she runs to open the door, with her hand over her bosom, saying to herself, "Is it him?" No. It is the mail man. ...

A SWEET MISUNDERSTANDING

As soon as the mother-daughter have ended their conversation that the man meant for her, will come to her himself, there comes a proposal from the Birghi family as an answer to their prayers. However, turns out the proposal is not for our Hero of our story Aakaash's, but his older brother, Mahinder! Aakaash is waiting for his older brother to get married, so according to convention, he will marry only after his brother has been married.

With great hope and excitement, the proposal of the Birghi's gets accepted. Both brothers decide to go there together, on the evening of invitation for tea which snacks. Aditi is happy but too shy to ask her mother for a picture and Agya thought that since it is too late to exchange pictures, it should not much of an issue since they will be seeing each other face-2-face.

On the appointed day, both eligible bachelors together to see Aditi. The guy in question gets too-well-dressed in his best suit he had, with a sparkling tie added for some special effects to seal the deal with the would-be bride Aditi. Aakaash dressed more casually so he does not steal the thunder from the would-be-bridegroom, arming himself with tips which will prove useful when his time comes.

The duo arrives at the tea party at the right time. There is excitement in the air. Mahinder is nervous with excitement. Both are waiting anxiously to see the would-be bride's face. Mother Agya have the duo seated, and once welcome with the customary courtesies are over, Aakaash quips, "when do we see the Eid-ka-chhand?" Agya smiles and says, "Let me ask Aditi to bring tea with some hot

47

Samosas as appetizers." When Aditi enters slowly balancing a tray of tea in her hands and a bent head, they feel their wait well rewarded. Setting the tray, she lifts her eyes only to see the man in front of her, assuming she will meet eyes with the man-in-question. The man in front turned to be Aakaash, the younger brother of the real man-in-question!

Aditi's eyes meet Aakaash's and had feelings that are in-appropriate for a Man to have for a woman who is meant for his brother! He at once shook his head vigorously to come out of the spell that Aditi's beauty had cast on him. Aditi's face blushed a crimson red and betrayed her secret of developing love for Aakaash, that she too is under the same spell! Secretly she accepts Aakaash as her husband.

Now, Mahinder has no idea of the secret communication that had just occurred between the Aakaash and Aditi... Aditi's presence was simply intimidating him. In his excitement, he could barely talk and sat stiff and awkward in his mannerisms. Whenever he opened his mouth to speak, his tongue would betray him and so the closest description to the words that came-out of his mouth is 'incoherent stammering'! In his confusion, he spills tea all over his white shirt and right then a frightful screaming arose! He really looked like a clumsy man, and no one can really blame Aditi for pointing her finger at him and bursting into an uncontrolled laughter, all targeted at him. Mahinder gets very offended and gets up ready to leave.

Now pointing his finger at her in return, he loses his temper and says angry words to Aditi, "You proud woman, your laughter carries seed of your ruin!" Aditi's mother Agya, too gets engulfed in his fumes of anger as he blurts, "Your daughter has insulted me, laughed at me, I will never marry this misbehaved woman!"

Aditi just looked at her mother and then the ground, bewildered at the accusation and more on the big misunderstanding of the switch!

Mother Agya started apologizing for Aditi who did not say any word. Aakaash said everything to calm his brother, but his whole face was red in anger and gets ready to leave. Aakaash comes forward and says "I do not want anybody be offended over a miscommunication. What Mahinder sees as a big issue; Aditi sees it as trivial! From this observation we can conclude that there is a big probability of many more such misunderstandings continuing to happen in the future also! Therefore, it is only prudent that he does not marry Aditi. Now, after saying that I would like to bring a new proposal on the table."

Aakaash then looks towards at Mother Agya to bless her with a permission to marry her daughter Aditi. We do not want to leave the Ghai household with bitterness, and enmities of lifetimes, therefore, if Aditi consents, I would like to step forward and take Aditi as my wife." Agya is impressed with his wisdom and looks at Aditi, whose silent nod seals the deal.

Brother Mahinder also feels relieved with the outcome and feels infinitely grateful to Aakaash for have sacrificed his own future by marrying such a conceited woman, just to save the family name, while Aakaash wonders how beautifully his brilliant mind came to the rescue and made everything fit like peas in a pod. Now both him and his elder brother will get to enjoy the fruit of his little white trickery, till the end of eternity! With that thought a pleased Aakaash himself makes more tea for everyone for a new round of tea, much to the delight of Mother Agya.

They decide on a simple engagement between Aditi and Aakaash and then wait for the elder brother to find himself a bride, so this way they can get married the same day in the same ceremony. Soon enough, elder brother Mahinder finds his match and both couples get married in the same event. Both the couples choose the same Honeymoon package to head to the beautiful mountains in Nainital, Himachal Pradesh, India.

Double the trouble, double the fun!

SPROUTS

When a child is born,
the child cries, possibly because he still has recollection from its earlier
births,
that life is not a bed of roses, but a merciless tyrant that does not hesi-
tate in cracking it is whip when anyone violates the cosmic laws ...

DERIVED CLASS, MAY 17.1973 ADITYA HRUDUYAM (A HYMN WRITTEN IN PRAISE OF THE SUN, FOUND IN EPIC RAMAYANA.)

Just like a child when coming out of the mother's dark womb to light
cries,
we adults too should take comfort now of our breakdowns,
as this moment must be like a message
from the Divine,
that the death of darkness has begun,
making space for a new reality for the awakened eye to sprout ...

The couple is celebrating their Marriage Anniversary, still not knowing that this is an occasion for double celebration as a gift from the Universe has already taken root, binding the couple's future together for many more years of blissful togetherness!

What more auspicious a time than seventeenth of May, at around two pm, when the Life-giving-Father Sun is the closest to the Nurturing-Mother Earth! Under His radiant abundance, a Taurus girl leaps into existence from Mother Aditi's womb reliving her from all the strict diet guidelines that she had been following to protect the developing baby from any discomfort!

Mother rejoices on seeing her victory when she sees the White in her brown-skin daughter, Father rejoices on seeing his victory when he sees the Black in their brown skin daughter, while everyone around rejoices seeing this unique instance of fruit which shouts to the whole world the beauty of that sinful night when the seed took root!

On seeing how their daughter start dancing like some drunken peafowl every time that it rains, they laughingly decide to name her *Mast Mayuri, The Intoxicated Peafowl Dancing in the Rain...*

DATA HIDING

Data hiding for ensuring minimal headaches for
the concerned parties.

One would think that after going through the excruciating pain equivalent of twenty bones breaking together, a mother will not even accidentally the thought of a going through that experience again will fill her with dread but what happens in actual is just the direct opposite of what Logic assumption says! As is clear from all the rice-balls and water they are feeding to the crows every day to bribe The SuperKundalini, to bless them once again with a strong son like the father after gifting them with a lovely daughter like the mother. Why a crow? Because scientific research has shown that crow is one of the very few Animals to have a conscious like us humans and after having a special mention in Scripture Bhagwad Gita. The belief is that our ancestors often come to visit us when going through their life in the form of a crow!

Just as the blessing come once again in Aditi's womb silently and discreetly, she too follows the same protocol by holding-on to the excitement for the next few days just in case it is not one of her wild fantasies taking flight without much content in it! So, it is only after an impatient wait of a natural confirmation that she joyfully breaks this news to her Dear Husband - the equal partner in the crime!

Exited with the news, Husband Aakaash runs towards the phone to share the news with his closest Sister! When Wife Aditi sees him picking the phone, she gets horrified and at once lunges forward to snatch the phone receiver from his hand. She at once ends the impending disaster by slamming the receiver back on the handset with a loud enough thud!

Mother Aditi: "Seems like you do not know us women at all! We all women are still carrying the curse, that King Yudhisthira in the Epic Mahabharata gave to all us women of never being able to keep any secrets and so just because she is your sister does not make her an exception to the rule! For that matter, do not you remember that at the wedding ceremony of my younger sister, beating her chest proudly and loudly she had said in front of to the whole gathering that the other name of her is "A Loudspeaker!" Now you tell me, if there is any chance left that she will not do this job also same as announcers do on the All-India-Radio! A broadcast so wide that it will cover your whole office circle, our neighborhood circle and to whoever who cares to listen to her never-ending ennui! If it were in her power, she would use the Satellite services to broadcast this news from the Moon to the whole universe! In short, "just zip it!" She says this with folded hands as in an Anjali Mudra in Yoga.

Father Aakaash: *rubbing her still flat belly:* "you know all about what information should stay private, protected, or public, then O wise lady, tell me that even if I am successful in hiding this information from people till now but what happens when this belly of yours balloons bigger than ten footballs! Then how will you hide your dirty secret from going public!

Mother Aditi: "Here is the rule of thumb! You are just always saying the obvious. I started with not even showing the News to you, who is like my other half and yet without a confirmation from this natural reproductive system I kept this secret to myself. So, in a way really, I started with nothing, then when more internal changes stared to reveal themselves externally with symptoms such

56

as nausea, vomiting, taste changes amongst many other, did I add more visibility to the circle by adding you. We will start widening the circle by including People on a **need basis** only. By following this scientifically based Encapsulation Model, we are not just protecting our own sanity but also the emotions of our near and dear ones involved and the whole society in many known and unknown ways. In about three months when the baby has taken a firmer shape, we can show the news within our protected circle, which consists of our close relatives and trusted friends. A secret behind the Wisdom that I am going to share now has its inferences from the Vedic Science! As the protective energies in a new-born are still developing it is wise to not expose the babies to any alien touch or the evil eye of wicked and jealous people! I suggest that when the baby comes, we host a religious Ceremony too, where we feed the poor and everyone who wants to celebrate our happiness and good fortune as one of us!

THE COW WHO LICKED HER CALF SO HARD THAT IT BEGAN TO BLEED

When I close my eyes, I can hear better,
When I close my ears, I can see better,
That is why I have now decided to meet people wearing a blindfold
and earplugs so I can understand them better...

When the time for making evening snacks is approaching, mother is walking excitedly towards the kitchen to make some spinach Pakoras, a delicious Indian Delicacy! Not someone who will accept to be left behind daughter Baby Mayuri lunges forward to grab on to the end of her mother's long veil which whether fulfills its promises of keeping the Victoria's Secret a secret but does a good job of sweeping the floor as it grazes past it. Her little baby fingers grip it tight, lest her mother insults her once again by choosing her solitude over her charming company!

Mother starts chopping. Like monkey copies, daughter Mayuri too picks up another knife that is even sharper than her to outdo her in some invisible competition between them! But what a killjoy when Mother takes the sharp knife from her daughter's hand and then with her loving hands puts her back on the sofa which is within her eye-view. On seeing the confused look on her daughter's face, she volunteers her explanation, saying to her loving words in her sweetest voice, "You are Moi-Lidl-Princess! Till you are under my care, you never will have to worry about preparing your meals as this is my duty to ensure that you never go hungry! I will serve you like a slave and all I ask in return is that you just sit right there in front of my eyes, as every time that I see you my body experiences immense motherly joys!"

These 'pearls of wisdom' are received not just received by the intended audience but also by the silent observer - paternal Grandma Shivdevi who is laying in the adjacent room. Her feet spring in action with those words and even when her knees hurt, she comes with a pace that defies all such claims! Once face to face with her daughter-in-law Aditi, she forgets all about her own principle of never giving any advice to others until asked for and begins with her lecture, for which all the future generations will be indebted to her for saving them from a dark future due to the illiteracy of their mothers!

Paternal Grandma: "Like every good Mother I am sure you will not do anything that will hurt your child's development but unfortunately you are also doing the same mistake that most women are doing these days! The reason that I got more cautious and alarmed by your words is because the words of Lord Krishna's forecast in the epic Bhagwad Gita that in Kalyug (The Era of Darkness) it will so happen that Cow will lick her Calf so hard that it will begin to bleed!". Love is to help enable the wings so the bird can fly away from you. This behavior will only make the child dependent on you and disabled for life! As the wisdom from an ancient proverb rightly says, "Rasri aawat jaat se sil par parat nisat," meaning that, "when a rope keeps going repeatedly over the same spot then, even a hard material like stone starts to show signs of wear."

Mother Aditi: "The reason that I can weigh your advice against my own is that I too have been brought up by a mother who being from the same generation as yours, follows the same values as yours. The main reason behind the change in my method from the earlier generation is because time is not the same anymore. At the time when my own mother was of age ten studying in fifth grade, she was not allowed to study any further despite topping the class, which makes sense under those conditions as her value is not in burning midnight oil to get top grades as the system was still not set-up for Women to work in same offices as Men, her contribution is more if she works in the Kitchen! But now when the Time has flipped, really, we need to do a headstand to see the same reality! That does not mean we no longer need to eat anymore but that we need to re-prioritize by shifting it from being a primary goal of the whole family down to a more manageable timeslot!

Ideally childhood should be a golden period of one's life mainly because we could play in the Sun all day long but in this age of never-ending ennui of Homework's and stress of surviving these highly competitive environments, the only sun that the children get to enjoy is in fairy tales! I too have a heart of a mother like yours! Every time when I am packing these Sumo-wrestler-like school bags for my children, I can see all these injustices that little children of this generation are getting subjected to! This is one of the main reasons, that I try my best to pamper them by doing all homely chores myself so that they can have time to play their silly games! Many of my friends are sending their children for working some odd jobs for money but if we are able, we will not do it, as I will let you in on a well-kept secret that the moment you initiate children into this race for money, know that you just introduced them to the devil!"

Grandmother goes silent. ...

PARTIAL GRANDMA!

Little Mayuri and her year older Cousin Sister Cheena are lying in a face-up Cobra yoga position. Sister Cheena is reading aloud from a storybook which she had borrowed from a batch-mate with strict instructions from her to return the same evening. Nothing could stop them from their single-minded determination of keeping their promise, but little did they know that their winning matrix has a small fault! That is that the outcome of any competition does not just depend on the speed and accuracy of the competitors but also the outside factors which are beyond our control which are also playing with us as the third hidden secret player! So then, as if to confirm this hypothesis the speed-reading indeed gets interrupted when the neighbor knocked on the door to give the fatal news which like lightening wrecks all the plans of these two little girls of meeting their targets! The news is that Ma Aditi will be late from school because of the assembly session held every morning in the outside playground went too long! Unfortunately for the children, the school Principal in her enthusiasm of ridding the society from marijuana in one day, went on and on till a poor student fell on the ground from fainting under the wrath of the merciless Sun! Everyone looked at him with great respect and gratitude as if it were not for his sacrifice the future of their own lives was the same as him – laying on the ground senseless! So, since Mother Aditi was chosen to be the one who will escort the child to take him to the nearest Hospital she is forced to give-up her pride which scorns the very idea of taking help from anyone especially given that she is still young and able, to ask her mother-in-law, making her finally acknowledge that having a Mother-in-Law in the house, even if old and high-maintenance still has some benefit after all! With this thought, she requests grandma to take the responsibility of cooking for the children!

When Grandma hears the message, her first thought does not go to her aching knees but of a helpless mother in need and so without another thought she commits to the request but when she looks at the huge pile of beans, she has a fit! "There is just no way that I can peel this entire heap of beans all by herself and then cook the entire meal for everyone in time, unless ... Fortunately that ellipse after the sentence carried the seeds of the answer that she was looking for - Child-labor!" On finding a solution to her problem, excitedly, grandma asks the little girls to leave everything they are doing to help her make lunch for everybody in the house! While the cousin continued to read, little Mayuri quits everything she is doing to help G-Ma. Cousin Cheena's behavior is like a little brat! She immediately voices her refusal with an explanation that suited her behavior, her logic being that only servants do chores, and she is no servant but a princess of her father's heart and that whoever who ever tries to force a child to do things that go against her nature is a tyrant, who is sure to get their due when they face the Ultimate Court of Law above! Now that she has said it all without waiting for any response, she tries to resume her work to completion, but she is unable! Because now all that focus has gotten diverted from constructive of working on reading to destructive of anger over Baby Mayuri. What did Baby Mayuri do to deserve Baby Cheena's wrath? For not becoming a partner in her cause of rebelling against the Tyrant Grandmother while Little Mayuri, still ignorant of the vendetta which is brewing in Baby Cheena's head is pleased with herself for being able to peel all the potatoes by herself! She peels every potato slowly and carefully, after all this task does need a lot of skill for a child her age,

an age where every task minor or major assumes the same importance!

While Baby Mayuri has already forgotten about the old task,
Cousin Cheena is not. She is internally trembling over having
risked her all respect in front of Dear Grandma's eyes towards her.
Now she cannot finish the very task for which she had risked all as
all her focus has now gotten consumed by the fire of vengeance
burning in her over the betrayal of her own like-sister Baby Mayuri
by deserting their alliance and her deception does not just end there
as she rubs more salt to her wounds by joining forces with the tyrant
camp! Such a betrayal is unpardonable! Her own little like-sister
Mayuri has thrown her under the bus. As Cousin Cheena's
thoughts are deepening increasingly so are her suspicions rising pro-
portionally over the whole conspiracy theory cooked by wretched
Baby Mayuri's evil head! She can now see how smartly Baby Mayuri
has become successful in her motive of getting high marks in
grandma's heart while poor Cheena falls in our dear grandma's eyes.
As the time elapses increasingly, her suspicious mind gets increasingly creative in its mean assumptions getting more fueled by jealousy
and the competitive spirit with which we are all blessed with! Cousin
Cheena looks daggers from the corner of her eyes at Baby Mayuri
who is laughing and merrily doing Grandma's work as if both are a
team while she is some evil outsider plotting to divide them!

When grandma notices that the cooking vessel is aluminum
(symbol AL in the Periodic Table) she nearly faints! Recovering
from her temporary stupor the first thing she does is to throw all
the Aluminum vessels in trash and then prepares for her lecture to
her daughter-in-law over all the harmful effects of AL getting in
the body in cooking as fortunately just recently she had read in an
Ayurvedic and another scientific journal that AL is a harmful neu-
rotoxic metal! High levels of this metal can lead to problems with
the Central Nervous System (CNS), including Alzheimer's disease!

When subjected to high cooking temperatures, the probability of the metal infusion into the food and then from the food into the body are remarkably high! When Baby Mayuri hears this alarming piece of information, her big eyes get even bigger. Praising grandma's intelligence Baby Mayuri cannot help but comment over the contrast between the two mature ladies, "Grandma, how is it that grandmothers are so wise while mothers equally ignorant? That is why now my favorite pastime has become to figure out why *mothers must be so silly!?*" Cousin Cheena sees all praise of Grandma from Mayuri's mouth as flattery, an effort to become more dearer to Grandma than herself! She is now fearing the consequences even more. Even worse is that Grandma also has big teeth in her stomach! Which means she cannot digest any such episodes of disobedience and rests only after she has shared it with whoever she meets! Now soon enough she will become the star of all the gossip circles! Then they will make a concerted effort in making her image look like some cold, selfish witch! Then everyone will learn and rejoice from my misfortune at the cost of my image!

Finally, God bless grandma! Any amount of gratitude is enough for this huge favor which has not only helped in saving her future generation's from dying of starvation but also if there is indeed a heaven after death, she was sure to get a spot there! Pleased with the success of her project, grandma wants to share her happiness with her assistant by offering Baby Mayuri a reward of buying any gold earrings of her own choice! On hearing this decision which reeked of favoritism Cousin Cheena cannot let the reward slip from right under her nose without putting a fight! So, to get the prize she starts her own little drama to overturn the tables! For this she starts with throwing a tantrum and a big fuss over the injustice in Grandma's action of rewarding only one and not the other even if both are her own grandchildren. "Partiality! Partiality! This is injustice and once my father and needless to remind is also your eldest son whose words carry most weight in deciding all family matters including the monthly allowance you get from each of your sons! Now dear Grandma, with this new piece of information will you please try once again!?"

Now it is grandma's turn. Grandma not just have the same blood running in her veins but has silver white hair that gives her an edge just enough for her to come out a winner! "First you make your own grandma look like some merciless tyrant who is cracking her whip on poor little children who are completely alive only due to the mercy of their master and then blackmail me to give you also a reward without obeying my wishes! Now dear Baby Cheena, with this new piece of information will you please try to be gracious and accept your loss to come out as a better person from your loss! Looks like your mother has not a good job in teaching you so let me rectify that mistake by letting you know that Obedience of the rightful orders of the elders is the greatest form of Respect that anyone can give. Respect is love. Love is God. Thus, wherever there is love there is God's abundance. That is why it is common to see maids having more physical strength than these women who do nothing! Even-if you get good meals every day, without you breaking any sweat off your back I never see a look of gratitude on your face but now when I have failed in my duty and that too due to reasons that are beyond my control, instead of co-operating with me you are ready to eat me instead! So why should I not reward the person who helped me in extinguishing the fire? A hidden side-effect of my action is also to shame the person who tried to manipulate the system to her own advantage by creating a big fuss. You accuse me of favoritism for another when really my judgments favor you as if indeed, I was being just then I would have punished you! True justice is merciless! If I were to give everyone the same amount of prize money for the same job, then the value of my reward becomes meaningless!

Just then Ma Aditi, hungry herself and stressed over possibly her children also going hungry, enters the door in great rush! On seeing Mother Aditi, grandma forgets all her own lessons in compassion over a stressed mother and instead straightaway begins reprimanding her for all her frightening behavior!

Grandma: I know you have no fear left of this old lady who now hates her life for continuing to live for nothing but at least fear the wrath of God for breaking an ancient tradition of preparing our girls for their future by engaging them in domestic chores!

Ma Aditi: My dear, A survivor is who can adapt to the environment changes! In the earlier generation women were being trained towards becoming efficient homemakers but now when the time has flipped our strategies too will have to change! Now women are also getting their college degrees same as men! Which means women they too will start getting good jobs, they will start having money of their own, which also means then they will be able to pursue any lifestyle of their own choice! And this freedom of living one's life one's way is the best gift that any mother can give! So, to enable my daughter to be able to achieve this goal, I do all the household chores so she can focus on her education while cooking is like swimming. The moment you put an infant in water it automatically turns his head to get its next breath same must be the case for cooking. The moment she is to fly away from me, automatically her survival instincts will kick-in and in no time, she will be making delicious meals according to her taste!

Grandma wants to say some words of agreement with her daughters-in-law statements above but instead knows not why she just jumped on to her next concern:

Grandma: I threw all the aluminum vessels!

Feeling exasperated after a long day, only to hear more "good news," Ma Aditi too responds with equal passion:

Ma Aditi: Hai Hai! (An expression of exasperation in Language

Hindi), you threw them! Is your father now coming to pay for new vessels!? Already you were not even contributing a single penny towards the expenses but as if that is not enough, you have now started to create more losses and problems for me?

Now ma Aditi mumbles incoherently, 'My fantasy is to wrestle you down someday!'

Grandma: "What did you say?"

Ma Aditi(lying): "I said the list of your favors on me keep growing day by day!"

Saying that she bows to her with folded hands and says, "Jai Mata di! (Grandma, we salute you!)!"

When the children see their mother doing a good thing, they too like copying monkeys join her by folding their hands and bowing to Grandma and then singing say:

"Jai Mata di!

Jai Mata di!

Jai Mata di!

(Grandma, we salute you!)" ...

DERIVED CLASS-FEBRUARY 15.1977
CHANDRASHEKHAR

The night is happy with its moon above and my lap is happy with my
moon below,
You play with many toys, but my only toy is you...

Husband Aakash and Wife Aditi are playing the Game Moksh-Paddam, popularly known as (Snakes and Ladders). When they think of adding some more thrill by playing for some prize.

Father Aakash: "I am all about equality with woman, so if you lose you will give me a son, and if you win, I will give you any amount of money that you want. And when you read the fine print, you can see it says, currency will be of fake Monopoly game money!"

Both share a good laugh!

In the start of the king of seasons - spring, when flowers are blooming everywhere a little flower from the Almighty is also getting ready to bloom into the Birghi Household! The arrival of the baby is known by all from his loud cries piercing the silence of the night! The louder he cries, the more everyone's heart rejoices, listening to this sound of life, raw and un-restrained! The moon too whispers his blessings to the Birghi and Ghai households! The SuperKundalini has gifted them with a handsome son who strengthens the family bonds even more. The new sister Mayuri starts jumping and clapping with joy on watching her baby brother in the cradle with his deep Aquarius Man's eyes, a light tan skin complexion, naughty twinkling eyes, mischievous smile, and a shining blue diaper on him that made him look very edible to her. As she is getting ready to put her enormous mouth on it to eat, mother laughingly spanks her, reminding her that he is not some object of eating that she is trying to eat it! Everybody around shares a hearty laughter!

Baby smiles all the time as he greets everyone around him, who were fighting with each other for their turn to hold him in their arms.

To share their happiness with the world, Father Aakaash invites all relatives and loved ones to come and join them in their happiness. He has the whole street decorated with colors, streamers, and fragrant flowers! Food is available in abundance! A band plays joyful songs and put that puts all in a joyful mood. A procession starts from the Birghi residence covering the whole street with people dancing all their way to the Temple!

Holding him in his arms Father Abnash joyously exclaims, "our savior, who will carry the Birghi surname for all generations to come, has arrived! Since my son looks as beautiful as the Moon, from now onwards we will call him **Chandrashekhar** (Sanskrit: Chandra - moon, Shekhar - crest", which is also an epithet worn by Lord Shiva)- The Prince of all Hearts!" ...

I DO NOT LOVE YOU... I LIKE YOU

The cause behind all crimes is either Money or Heart. The thought carrying the seed of solution to this problem must be the right one as I have a smile on my face. Now I have started living like a tree ...

Little Chandrashekhar with his enormous eyes comes in running with wearing a memento of bright red lipstick on his cheeks. When his young cousin brother Karan, who is just hitting puberty, jumps on the opportunity of having a hidden encounter with a lady who gives so generously! He at once extends his big hand to act like a fence, stops Chandrashekhar's excited run! With a naughty grin on his face, he stoops down to look into his immense big eyes and asks him with his usual curiosity and roguishness, "You little rascal, tell us who is kissing you behind closed doors, maybe if we ask her, she will extend her generosity towards us, the lesser fortunate ones too? Then looking back with double roguishness, little Chandrashekhar divulges all about his dirty little secret in an equally devious style: "your mother."

Cousin Karan's laughing face now begins to look like some sucked mango. ...

WHEN HE SOLD HIS MOTHER FOR DAMNED WRESTLING GLOVES

The boys will be boys! Little Chandrashekhar is playing with much older boy than him. To make the games more interesting he suggests they put some *"spice"* in it by raising the stakes. Now they begin playing for rewards. All things equal, needless to mention that the smaller one has lost!

Now the winner asks the loser to pay with him with the most valuable thing he has. He says the most valuable thing I have is my mother while hiding his favorite wrestling gloves behind his back.

Both go to his mother. Older one says to the mother, you are mine now! Give me all the butter you have! Your son has already sold you to me in a match! She starts looking around. Children at once sense danger and children being children, they ask the enemy itself to show her intention! All she had to mention is about her infamous stick, which they had fondly baptized as their witch's broom, both vanish!

TIPS TO THE UNIVERSE

That pure childishness, that absolute decorousness, with which a child behaves has much to enrich one's psychological observations. The midday sun is at its peak strength, which for Mother Aditi is a signal that it is time to feed her little son. Leaving her son alone, she goes into the kitchen to get some bread for her son. When she comes back, she is surprised to see a new little visitor from the sky's playing with his son. Her son was feeding a crow from his own share of the meal on his plate. When Ma sees this scene, her first instinct is to shoo the crow away who is happily eating the meal which she has made with great efforts for her only son. As she lifts her arm in the air to drive away the offender, she is surprised to see the face of horror on her son's face that bore a look of askance. On noticing the contrast between their responses automatically her raised arm drops. Now she can feel a surge of compassion run through her, not just for her son but also for a whole different being from the animal kingdom! This event triggers in her the memory of an eternal secret which her Mother Agya had passed on to her which was a product of her own inferences from the Vedic Literature. She had emphatically told her to be always generous in giving. As our Tenth Guru of Khalsa Religion, Guru Gobind Singh ji also had told us of sharing at least ten percent of whatever you receive with others. When you are giving without any expectations of getting back anything in return, without your knowledge Magic is happening! What you gave comes back mostly with generous bonuses!

Shame on me! Despite knowing all about this Eternal Secret I was miserly most of the time, possibly because I still have doubts over His being merciful or even worse if He even exists!

Then she sits next to her son and affectionately says, "many mothers must teach their children to share their most loved items with all other children too, but now after seeing the sharing streak in you at the level of the character 'Daanvir Karan' from the Ancient Epic Mahabharata, who was famous for his charity as he would not turn down anyone who came to ask for his possessions. Therefore, for me to teach you a lesson in giving is meaningless when you are the one who is teaching me, still me being the more experienced one will teach you a saying which has more relevance in these times."

"Mein bhi bhookha na rahu, aur sadhu bhi bhookha na jai"

(I also do not go hungry, and beggar also does not go back hungry) ...

POLYMORPHISM - MIRROR IMAGES

Tohe mohe mohe tohe
Antar kaisa, antar kaisa...
(You me you,
Where is any difference...)
- Guru Ramdas, the fourth Guru of Khalsa Religion

Wife Aditi: I fight with my husband for no real reasons. It is as if that with time our differences kept driving a deeper wedge between us, so much so that he prefers staying late at office than deal with the constant cold energy in the house! The distance between us seems now just too wide for us to be able to bridge within this lifetime! And yet this statement cannot be true as the memento of or love - my son's face lies a mirror image of my husband for me to cherish minus the entropy of misunderstandings that come over Time - the Great Reverser! Every time, when my heart misses the then Aakaash from the happy courtship days, I play with our son instead as he is another form of you, O dear husband of mine! When I see those similarities, all the love energies in me find their nourishment just the same way if not even more!

Similarly extrapolating this thought at a universal level, when I see your characteristics in someone else, like someone with your name, someone with similar handwriting as yours, someone with similar eyes like yours, makes me have tender feelings reflexively towards them like some mirror images of you! Which makes me wonder if to love my husband for his pure thoughts is the same as loving everything that is pure, is same as loving the one above who is the purest of all?

With this thought I now feel freed from the bondage of what's yours and what's mine, as Guru Govind Singh, the tenth Guru of Khalsa Religion said when he was informed about the death of all four of his sons who died fighting for protecting their freedom of choice, he said something that someone who is very spiritually aware could say that, 'char moae to kya hua, jeevat kai hazzar' (So what if all my blood four sons have died, thousands of other fighting for the same cause who are still alive give me same happiness as my own sons did!)

These thoughts make her kiss her son sitting next to her, engrossed in playing with his army man toy. On receiving this sudden attack of affection, he bends his head feeling shy as he wonders once again, why do mothers have to be so unpredictable!?

CLAY MODELLING

Ek OM kar, Satnaam, karta purakh, nir bbhao, nir ver, akal murat,
ajooni se bhang, gur parsad, jap
One God Ik OM
True Name Sat Nam
The doer is The Eternal - Kurtah Purakh
Without fear - Nir Bhau
Without hate - Nir Vair
Timeless Image - Akaal Moorat
Never born never died - Ajooni
Self-existent - Saibhang
Guru's blessings - Gurprasaad
Worship - Jap
- Mool Mantra (meaning Core Mantra in English), Guru Granth
Sahib

Who are we? The complete signature of a lustful moment shared by two bodies, giving rise to an altogether new unique product! This genius product does not just capture all the ancestral history of the two participants but also reveals many of the secret energies related with passion, which were dominant in exploring new lands and sowing new seed, will yield some juicy fruits! Once this product comes into existence, the parents often get too busy with other social and life obligations that we forget to take a moment of gratitude to marvel at the unparalleled precision which has gone behind this creation! And when the parents find themselves marveling over their creation, they often tend to forget the smaller miracles of orchestrating the meeting of the right people at the right time and with the right energies which happened to create a bigger miracle in the form of a child.

Since the mind of a child takes in all information without the knowledge of consequences, Father Aakaash realizes the importance of exposing them to the Vedic literature. This way, a person brought up with these principles can make the right choices. Since Vedic literature is not a part of the school syllabus, the parents take upon themselves to ensure that they know the value in staying true to the Godliness in them. Always.

VICTORIA'S SECRET

In one of Father Aakaash's secret sneak checks of his daughter room his eyes sparkle on seeing his efforts rewarded upon stumbling on a romantic 'Victoria's Secret' novel hidden carefully under a pile of newspapers! Confronting her directly will do no good as then she will become more cautious and might start destroying all evidence, so now the problem has shifted from keeping his secret a secret to confront the secret without the secret owner know you know their secret. He does attack the topic just in some indirect way.

Father Aakaash: "I am not against my children learning reality through movies and novels as this way is a safe one of experiencing different types of emotions by proxy through the actors, without the stress component associated with such real-life situations! Still, I cannot recommend them to you as they are as further from the truth as can be!

Pleasure is one of the main driving forces behind all actions. Whenever an inexperienced amateur discovers new sources of joy, it becomes extremely easy to lose one's mind and thus become a slave of these momentary pleasures. By no means am I suggesting that you stop all activities that give you pleasure, but that whenever you are enjoying you are doing in a way that you are always in control, that you stay in the driver seat and not the source of your enjoyment.

Keep in my mind, woman is 'XX' the complete set of chromosomes, which carry the complete genetic information; while all biological books refer to man as a set of "XY" chromosomes, is somewhat misleading because it appears to the listener that the "Y" is something that is some alien chromosome whereas really, it's still the same X chromosome, just missing a quarter of the complete leg of the 'X'. Therefore, to avoid all confusion, we should refer to them as X-1/two times! Therefore, it is really the 'absence' of a set of chromosomes that differentiates a people to become a male or female, which is what makes the man more than a woman in some ways and less in some other!" The other male in the room, Little Chandrashekhar, who was intently listening cannot hold his tongue anymore as he feels he has the answer to this age-old mystery, blurts out the answer: "I know where the missing leg went! Right here, in my pants!" Father Aakash smiles his charming smile.

THE PROXY MOTHER / A TWIN PATTERN

Children are dancing as they rejoice the start of their summer vacation and their temporary freedom from controlling teachers and the strict demands of hypocritical classroom rules and regulations! Since the children had never seen any beach in their lifetime yet, Father Aakaash makes all arrangements to change that! So, if anyone were to get the award for the best father, he would for making all sacrifices needed to have his children experience the beauty of playing with the monstrous waves of the ocean hitting the shore and then going back quietly as if nothing had ever happened before!

When the children see the beach for the first time in their lives, their eyes widened and even if they did not any swimming, the gigantic frothy waves of the beach tempt them. Dismissing all these statics on child drowning as something written by the association of protective mothers, who blinded by their love for her children, change the data to use it as a perfect excuse for keeping their children tied to their breast forever, they outsmart her by running so far away that all her concerned voices cannot kill any of their joy in their flirtations with death anymore!

As all children are in the water, playing with the waves, when it comes, they rejoice when riding the wave, when it goes, they scream for more repeatedly! However, like all good things to end their ride also ends when some woman from the crowd loses all her bearings on seeing a snake and worried about the children starts screaming at the top of her lungs, 'SNAKEEE, SNAKEEEEEE, SNAKEEEEEEEEE'! Now if only that over wise mother had been wise enough to keep her mouth shut, nothing real would have happened; the snake itself would have gotten scared on seeing too many people and would have quietly slid away without creating any mischief but now due to the woman's panic call which was meant to save the crowd became the very cause of all the chaos which ensued! All the people, fearing for their lives start running in different directions! In this do-or-die situation, when all thought processes go into hibernation, everyone is mindlessly running in any direction to save their lives, but it is only the sister in the whole crowd who first looks back to find where her little brother is! Fortunately, he was not too far from her and was on his all four from falling on the ground. Leaving all panic from time limitations, she runs backwards again to pick her brother and only once she both are holding hands and she can lead them to safety does she finally rest!

Ma is stretching out so far from the window to watch the whole episode that if she were to have fainted, she could have fallen on her own children's head! Seeing this little son Chandrashekhar says, 'how terrible when the news headlines would say that instead of the snake it was the mother who was the cause of injury to her own little children!" Now both siblings **wonder once again, why do mothers have to be so clueless!?** Now that her children have escaped from death not once but twice, Mother Aditi is doubly happy to see the faces of her children alive and kicking! Mother sinks on her knees and thanks The SuperKundalini over a million times! Brother Chandrashekhar is feeling the love so smilingly he too makes the women of the house happier by fixing the now window's wobbly ledge!

After seeing this rare scene of selfless love, Mother Aditi cannot help but exclaim in wonderment, " Innocence is the mark of childhood. Childhood the mark of purity as the new-born is still how the Almighty wanted, still not exposed as much to evil negative forces ready to destroy one's individuality to make them like themselves - dead! Then is not the bond between baby siblings the purest? Then is not the bond between a baby sister with her baby brother the purest? How rightly someone once said that *an older sister is like a second mother*! When the strength of an elder sister with her younger brother unites, this union has the power of even defeating Yamraj - The Death Broker! In-spite of the fact that both of you are capable of picking-up your own load and yet if ever some unfavorable time comes, there is a faith and trust between you both that the other half will always be there to soften the blow and will not let the other fail! Now I feel confident in saying that whenever God will put them through the ringer of His strictest tests in the future, their bonds of love will pass every test and from which they will only emerge even stronger!"

AVATAR / MULTITASKING

The Curse on a watched pot is that it will never boil!

It is a proven fact now that the whole universe is in constant vibration then it must mean that all these scriptures preaching us about the virtues of patience, the prerequisite of which is stillness, should be burnt in the same fire for spreading lies as their statement contradicts themselves when they also say that even the smallest particle with which that we are made of - the atom, is also in vibration? The only supporting statement which can prevent this bon-fire of our revered scriptures, is this statement that can only come from someone who has the vision of a poet as they seem to be the chosen one to act as mediums for communication with anything and everything including about the knowledge of this curse on a watched pot: 'The Curse on a watched pot is that it will never boil!'! So, to use this secret for multitasking one should first start a task which will take time but none to minimal attention and then instead of watching the pot boiling you switch to another task!

Even in computer science, one of the many Memory structures we have is a famous Stack structure/ (Last-In-First-Out (LIFO). There is a common misconception that a multi-tasking machine can all tasks simultaneously, but the fact is that even the most efficient multi-tasking computers can only process one task at a time. It is the efficiency with which the computer manages its wait times between switching between tasks is the criteria that acts as one of the main deciding factors for the quality of the output! Even the smartest brains be it any computer do only one task at-a-time! They switch tasks once the current task has reached its goal. Similarly, we too can enjoy multiple flavors in life by switching into new roles as per the current task requirement. We first bury the current task in the memory-recesses/ a temporary amnesia which is essential for us to do justice to our present without any disturbances from memories which are like ghosts from the past not letting us enjoy our present to its fullest! This way one can enjoy the present moment to its fullest in the new Avatar. **Thus, by playing this Shuttlecock between Remembering and forgetting one can enjoy every moment!**

A CULTURE BREAKDOWN?

Curse evil time for destroying all the beauty in patience! Impatient Maternal Grandma Agya cannot resist any more from seeing the one daughter out of the three who she secretly loves the most! The secret behind her secret favoritism: In this daughter she sees the most beautiful expression of herself possible, as she reflects all those hidden good qualities in herself which have now found an expression in this fruit which has made it the most desirable and beautiful! In her surprise visit she is feeling happy in expecting to see her lovely daughter Aditi busy in making food for children after her long day of teaching job, while the possibility of seeing her son-in-law is out of the question as the office hours are known to consume almost all of the daylight hours but then when she sees the real time scenario she soon realizes she will have to do a head-stand to see a match to her expectations! Her ideal beautiful daughter who was supposed to be in the kitchen cooking is outside while her son-in-law who was supposed to be outside is inside in the kitchen cooking! Now she is hoping that her next assumption is also wrong as not seeing Mother at lunch hour in kitchen means that the children will now have to go hungry and yet the distinct aroma which can only come from healthy Ayurvedic cooking style makes her hold herself from making any more assumptions and so just straight asks for an explanation behind all her observations as they contradict with everything that she has seen all these long years of her existence in this life-form! Now she is so curious that despite aching knees and little energy from travel she is running towards the kitchen to get all her answers finally before she loses her mind with assumptions built over assumptions! Being sharp minded, it does not take much time to understand that it is her own son-in-law Aakaash who is cooking the meals for her favorite idol Daughter Aditi and the children! She stands there speechless for a moment as she had spent her entire lifetime believing that the day a man starts staying inside to work while the Woman starts going outside to work know that the Dark Ages have begun! What disturbs her even more is that her own daughter to who she had herself dutifully passed on the baton of proven Values that can help make a home a home, run in the most efficient way! As she is venting out her frustration, she cannot see this injustice from continuing anymore in front of her eyes, so without any further delay she lunges forward and then snatches the ladle from Son-in-Law Aakaash hand to finally put an end to this embarrassment moment, that too in front of her dear Son-in-Law, that too the cause of it all is her very own daughter who she always saw as her best representative of her own best self! She says in an apologetic voice: "I apologize on behalf of my ignorant daughter and will surely scold her for making her Man who is worthy of worship, to do all her duties like some unpaid slave! My whole life briefly is a big sacrifice as a mother who did everything to bring-up her daughter as a woman-of-virtue only to find in the end that everything I did was for nothing! What disturbs me even more is that my own conduct could never inspire her enough for her to do everything just as I did! Help me understand, if the day men and women switch roles is it not a sign that time made a flip right under our nose without us even knowing how and when it all happened? If this is not some bad omen signaling a serious breakdown of our ancient culture, then what else can be?!" On hearing her concern, Son-in-Law Aakaash first laughs his laugh which acts like a calming balm on her, then taking the ladle back from his Mother-in-Law Agya's hand begins his address in his soothing voice: "If helping one's wife with her chores makes one a slave then with great pride I say that 'Yes, I am a slave but this statement is not complete as it is dependent on my next clause: 'but I am a slave of your daughter alone and nobody else's! Some men who have some doubt over their own masculinity may feel ashamed in doing tasks that are traditionally by a woman, but because I have no such false-male-chauvinistic attitude in me I go ahead and deliberately do womanly chores to prove to myself that I am comfortable with my masculinity and this attitude has certainly made me a better man! For that matter, to ensure the smooth running of this system I have taken special permission from my work for shifting my hours from the day shift to the night shift instead! This way, me and my wife are not wasting our energies in doing the same task! Means when I am resting, she is working; when she is resting, I am working, and this is the big secret behind our well rested and stress-free faces!

Regarding your other concern regarding the breakdown of our culture and heritage, then my fair lady I agree that your concerns also bother me but try to look at it this way: when one ties a wheel from a Bullock-cart to a bullet train for running then it does not take some genius to tell us that such a Vehicle is bound to fail! The Traditional Domestic Model is where we see the woman as a cow who stays within the confines of the house to nourish the whole household, while the man like a Horse, a hunter who goes outside to get the resources needed for the smooth running of the household. This model of division of labor has proven to work since ancient times but due to the western Influences being more powerful, we too need to meet the demand of the changed environment by going with the flow! The problem now with us middle-service-level class is that we could neither become the wealthy West nor the old spiritual east anymore! The current way that we see the world united is based on national boundaries. Deception! World is united by their Ideologies! When the Air, the Oceans, the Land, and other Natural Resources are all interconnected and the changes occurring in one side of the world also effect the other side of the world, then why should the governing bodies and the rules and Regulations across the globe be different? I am not saying to Paint the whole world in the same color as its beauty is in its diversity! The secret of co-existence is not of converting everybody as we but by respecting the differences in others!

On hearing such wise words from her Son-in-law's mouth, Mother-in-law Agya feels ashamed over the feelings of jealousy come over her! Then brushing off her absurd emotion, she laughingly complements him, "Silly me for envying my own daughter over her good fortune of having a Man whose help is comparable to hiring ten servants combined!"

LONG LONGINGS

O merciful Sun! why do you have to come to end a night like this!
Like an enemy, you will snatch my beloved from me,
do not be so cruel,
I have only my one moon,
the one and the only...

When father does not come back when expected, mother sits like a mad woman, intoxicated on the wine of the in-pain longing and anxiety from separation so now when he now comes, he looks twice more handsome, and the anxiety works as a shot of passion in her belly. Now every footstep she hears puts in her feet so much supercharge that without any slippers or even straightening her hair, her run is beautiful even if her intent is evil! Locking him forever and then throwing the key in some deep well, a place from which no one can ever find...

All this show of affection is meaningless to a Man coming back from travel with an empty stomach. Knowing that the way to a man's heart is through his stomach she heads towards the kitchen and without further delay, makes porridge for him. When mother serves porridge to her children and they put the first spoon in their mouth, they blink their eyes in disbelief! Why? Because every day the porridge that mother cooked was lacking in some way or another. Sometimes the water was too much or sometimes the salt was too little, in short never perfect. The children wonder, if her real intent was to punish 'his' children, just so they begin complaining to him when on the phone, so then he is sure to leave all work and come running back! This is not at all to say that it is his love for his children that really binds him to her and not just herself!

This porridge on this day when he unexpectedly came back had a remarkable taste like never tasted before! The children cannot but exchange mocking glances with each other and remark, "Dear Paapaua Guinea, you should make mother wait more times as this way we can get such an amazing tasting porridge every day but please also keep in mind to not let her wait that long that you knock the wind out of her! And if there is no mommy there is no porridge either - good or bad! In this worst-case scenario we all lose as we all are sure to die with hunger then! Which will not benefit anyone!"

Then the children exchange their secret laugh as they say once more to themselves, '*why do mothers have to be so silly!?*'

Seeing such emotional display of affection, he feels guilty of making her beautiful wife wait like that. So, to make-up for it all, he promises her to take her and the children too with him, whenever the next trip happens.

THE DEADLIEST BLACK WIDOW BITE

Wife Aditi to Husband Aakash: "I need an explanation right now else my mind will explode from not venting it out! All this while, I have been on cloud nine thinking no woman can be luckier than me for getting a man who has the purest heart of all but now after hearing this one statement from your mouth, all my faith in men has vanished! I always felt proud of myself for having an educated Husband and so will never react the same as the illiterate man on the street, only to find that when it comes to raw instincts, the behavior of all men is the same! If only I knew this before marriage, I would have run in the streets warning everybody to never surrender your freedom to any man!"

Now it is his turn to act innocent and not respond to her indirect form of inquiries.

Husband Aakash: "You keep going on and on whipping me with your acid tongue without even letting me know the reason behind it! Is this fair, in your court of justice, my Lord? Why do my ears detect coldness and distance in the voice of my wife that is sweeter than honey"?

Wife Aditi now takes an about turn so that now her back is facing him, sending a message that the matter is indeed serious.

Husband Aakash: "Your voice is always sweet and welcoming like a nightingale. Please try to welcome me again but this time wearing your best ornament that God gave you - your intoxicating smile!"

Wife Aditi now calmer turns from showing her back to front: "Why did you want to see my nails now and felt disappointed when you noticed that they were not looking manicured?"

A word is enough for the wise, and he is more than wise, at once understands the matter, but still, it is of little use as the matters which seem serious to a woman seem trivial to a man! He unsuspectingly shows everything about his new widow friend who he meets at the bus-stop to drop the kids, not realizing that every word he is saying from this point further is making him fall into this vixen's trap!

Husband Aakash: "Oh I had meant to tell you about this lady I just met. She is little Siddhartha's mother whose husband died long ago. It is a duty of all our men to ensure that she never feels the absence of her man! She had a fresh manicure yesterday and just wanted me to be a part of her happiness by touching and feeling her hand for myself. Now you are not just my wife but also my friend, so I feel that it will not mean that I am crossing any limits when I disclose to you this secret, that when I held her dainty hand in mine, it felt very ticklish and soft like plush cushions that tempted me to squeeze them, but I did it just slightly only! Why did I not go to the next level? Because this marriage ring on my finger which is a constant reminder of my allegiance to you and my love for you demands sacrifice and denial from me!"

Now that the cat is out of the bag, all hell breaks loose! She can see dire consequences of this Witch's footsteps nearing her house and then by using her mind-control tricks will snatch everything from her – first her Husband, then her children for using them as child-labor to sweep her floors! To dismiss this enemy as a nobody, will just be more a proof of her complacency than an underestimation of the enemy's strength! And what-if he is still hiding from her many more such so-called harmless incidents! This means, evil lustful desires are already secretly working behind the scenes to unite these potential lovers! Dangerous! Nip the evil in the bud as they say, and this is her duty to do this right away!

Once the awareness of the oncoming battle dawns, there is no time for complacency but only 'forward march'! Attack!

Wife Aditi: "The very reason I chose you as my Husband is that I saw all qualities that make a person great and yet when I see this contradiction in you, puts me back in doubt over my understanding of you! I can understand how even a man of character can also lose his mind when facing a willing woman, but please enlighten me on how such a man can also forget his allegiance with his children who are bound by blood and still fall prey to her advances?"

Husband Aakash knows very well that in a verbal duel with a woman she can easily defeat a man, so he resorts to the only way, say nothing!

By not dealing with the toxicity in the situation, the situation only worsens by every passing day.

The Widow is happy thinking she has a husband-by-proxy. Not content with just enjoying their company outside while dropping off the children at the school bus-stop, she thinks of ways of extracting more from this relationship. She comes to leave her son to Husband Aakash to watch for her child till she can complete some of her errands.

Wife Aditi to the Widow: "Absolutely not! We are not running a charity here! I warn you, even if I see your shadow seven houses away, I will have you arrested and put behind bars for stalking my man!"

Aditi behaves rudely with her. On seeing his wife's rude behavior towards someone who he genuinely cares for, he loses all his temper and instinctively raises his hand that lands hard on her face making a loud sound which sends tremors through the children's heart who were standing close-by! So far, they were silent witnesses to this whole drama but now they step in. In a low and respectful voice, Chandrashekhar says to the widow, "There is no good way to say this, but since only one sword can live in a sword-case, you will have to leave." Mayuri too silently sacrifices all her dreams of a budding romance with her son for greater good for all.

A word to the wise and she is more than wise.

She vanishes.

The End.

1984 CAUGHT IN AN INFERNO
OF A GENOCIDE

Dharmo Rakshati Rakshitah
(The protector of dharm (Ethics),
The Protector-of-Protectors itself protects the protector of dharm
(Ethics))
- Ved Shastr/ Vedic Literature

When the wolf comes wearing sheep skin, wins their trust enough to take the role as their protector then know that the days of the sheep are nearing their end! Same is the condition of the country when the nineteen-eighty-four riots happen!

Little Mayuri to her brother Chandrashekhar: "Caught in this cross-fire is also my dear small family! Now when I read the fear and dread written all over my father's face my face too starts showing similar expressions although on different causes, his is over the mob while mine is over the reaction of my father in handing the mob! My fears find fuel when I see him drawing the only old rusty sword he has had from ages, seeing which, I quickly scan for a hiding place, a place that even if he found it out still could never get to! Now, father is looking here and then there, not smelling the grand foul play devised by his own little daughter. Now when father sees his only weapon vanishing mysteriously, he gives up any further search taking it as some sign from above he that very instant gives up his search! On my seeing him give-up his search for his weapon, I give a silent sigh of relief! Now I can see the signs of dread on the face of Judgmental People who are wondering what explanation a daughter can give for an action which has put her own father's life in danger!? My justification is simple! As from all my observations all such false drama has no legs and lasts for three or four days more or less! Once the dust settles, businesses resume as nothing had ever happened. One will expect the judiciary will punish the criminals and also possibly reward the survivors with some meaningless titles and medals, but instead what we actually see in this real environment around us that is plagued with materialism is that these paid goons from mafia when they kill get paid hand-somely and continue to roam free on the streets, while the same act if by my father, even if it has been for self and family's defense, even if he is a citizen   who pays his taxes same as the majority, will be framed and sentenced with some cruel punishment which is worse than death! This incident taught me an important lesson in survival:

When we are thrown in the middle of a swamp of corruption, nepotism, groups following dirty crowd manipulation tactics to sa-tiate their never ending greed for Money to buy these dangerous mind-altering drugs which might help deaden the screams of res-cue coming from the tormented soul inside rebelling against the life-style which is a complete opposite of their true self, for becom-ing a self who they always despised, like that horse who the horse-trainer could not domesticate because it would get anxious every time it would see its shadow, tells an important lesson that wherev-er hypocrisy is king it is wise to fight it with the tool of diplomacy! To try to become a rebel with strength that is not yet enough to overthrow the giant, also when such an event is fake like some storm that will blow over in little time, then trying to fight this temporary storm is not bravery but suicide! It is like destroying one's long-term goals for one's short-term goals!"

Unlike the wise man who gets petrified from the knowledge of the enemy fast approaching, the little ones in the family are not! He is blissful because he uses his imagination and not his mind, which has already envisioned his victory by defeating the enemy with their clever karate chops! While Mother Aditi from Khalsa Community goes to her Hindu neighbor Mandodari's house to ask her for her help by giving her shelter till these wild winds will calm down!

Mother Aditi: I be kind to my prey, not because of pity or any such silly thing, but because tomorrow when it is my turn as a pray in front of my predator, I am the one with the smile...

Hindu Neighbor, Mandodari: My ethics cannot allow me to give shelter to people who belong to a region which my government is hunting. I will have to live the rest of my life as a traitor who betrayed the orders of the leader of this country!

Khalsa Mother Aditi: Enough is enough! Hearing such deluded words from an educated woman like you is making me extremely nervous about the whole future of this great nation! If you ever get the opportunity to see an Analysis report of our DNA, (deoxyribonucleic acid) you will be surprised to see just the amazingly high extent that all people across the World had interbred, for that matter the report even show links to many other species like with fish, apes, and many other Animals for that matter! Since ages, such injustices have been going on by distortion of facts! The agenda pushers are so effective that they can easily make us believe that the tyrant was loving like God, while all those who stood-up for their Rights were troublemakers! Since ages, religion has served as an excellent tool in the hands of the manipulators to use the love for our ancestors as a blindfold, so we never can see the obvious!

Hindu Neighbor, Mandodari: What you are saying is resonating with me and yet why am I not able to accept it?

Khalsa Mother Aditi: The reason for your inability to grasp this is that you too have fallen prey to the constant brain-washing that has not just started now but from ages ago! How did this question even arise that we and Hindus are separate when all our Gurus were Hindus! If only Guru Govind Singh ji, our founder would have known that this will take us away from our roots he would never would have done it! When his own Father, Guru Teg bahadur ji is a Hindu, how can his intent ever be to not live-in harmony with the Hindu community? Now when I am experiencing this unthinkable moment of shadow seeing itself as separate than its body, I can see just how clever and organized the enemy must be! This makes see the bitter truth, that we are all naked, that there is death all around us, by the time any information percolates down to our level it is too late! When this awareness comes back to me, I hear the words from the scriptures echo loud in me, 'Dharmo Rakshati Rakshitah' (The protector of dharm (Ethics),

The Protector-of-Protectors itself protects the protector of dharm (Ethics)), and this brings my smile back! When have you ever seen the average person like you and me, taking part in arsenal and looting, especially when we have little time left after dealing with their daily battles of supporting himself and his dear family's needs! The Hindus are quiet now because they think it does not affect them, not realizing that time always reverses and then when that happens, know that you will be smiling because the ones who you helped then, will help you now! Even if I can see how tax-structures are more like contributions towards some corrupt pyramid scheme, still I pay and then take some depression medication to deaden the voices of rebellion in me for doing these things that are against my ethics!

Hindu Neighbor, Mandodari: Subhasham Shighram! (Sanskrit Language, meaning, any beneficial task: execute it at the earliest possible)! (Sanskrit Language, meaning, any beneficial task: execute it at the earliest possible)! Please make haste and get your whole family to stay with us if you feel that the outside conditions have become favorable for you!

ENTERING THE MOUTH OF
THE FIRE DRAGON CALLED /
THE EDUCATION SYSTEM

Gururbrahma gururvishnuh,
gururdevo maheshwarah |
Guruhsakshat parabrahma
tasmai shrigurave namah | |
(Guru is Brahma, Guru is Vishnu, Guru is Lord Shiva. Guru is verily
the supreme reality. Sublime prostrations to Him.
- Skanda Purana

If someone wanted to learn some art, then the first thing the person looks for is knowledgeable in the field and has his work to back his work. The more the work highlights advanced skills to create that end-product the more genius of the creator comes to the front! Now knowing the value of quality in products, we too want the best teacher to teach us those skills. So, now that we are ready to pay anything to hire this genius, this teacher/ guru, where is he? Fortunately, you do not have to take another debt from synthetic sources to learn as it is something that you can learn on your own! Where is this guru and how can it teach me? The guru is in every creation in nature. All you need is an eye that sees how the subject of study runs. So, you do not need the best brain here. Suspend all thinking as now you become a dumb machine blindly following the design patterns used by Nature. We are just reverse engineering now! Since the way, the Creator of All runs have proven to work timelessly repeatedly, it must be the right way, it must carry the instructions for us to follow.

The reason the teachings of the Creator of All's creation is not in-sync with the education systems is mainly because the syllabus is more geared towards enabling us to get better situated in our society! Unfortunately for humankind one of the most important topics in the world - The Education System is also one of the most mis-understood! How? Because what is really meant for exercising the brain towards critical reasoning and logical thinking is instead dumbing down the child, by not encouraging any healthy debates. Result: The system got a disposable, dime-a-dozen employee, and in exchange the Employee got a stable job, however what they hide from you is that it is stable only till your skills are in demand. Deception! Thus, little is the Individual aware of his Infinite losses! The irony of the situation is that the very system which killed the genius in the child, that genius who could author a whole new system, feels infinitely indebted to this system for helping in paying for himself and his family needs! A stable job for the individual means parents will never have to stress over their children's going through any tough times. With this thinking the parent kills his self, never learns anything else, thinking his sacrifice will help his child lead a happy life. Now when the same child grows up and becomes the parent, he too goes through this same cycle of fear and false sense of Sacrifice. This cycle keeps repeating from one to the next, without any break!

As a result, Individualism loses to these fake agenda pushers towards lies! That is why because of a bad system, teaching which should have been the most revered job, is so only when the teacher sleeps through the lecture, as all they bring with them is nuisance value, so please do what you do best - sleep!

WHEN I SHED MY OLD SKIN OF BABY MAYURI TO TRANSFORM INTO MY NEW SKIN OF GRANDMA BABY MAYURI / GO WITH THE FLOW

The Water Element in us reminds us that wherever we go, we surren-
der ourselves to assimilate with the essence of the environment
- The Mast Mayuri, Intoxicated Peafowl in the Rain

The scene is of a parent-teacher meeting in Father Aakaash's child Mayuri's school - 'The-model-that-will-ensure-that-the-rich-will-be-come-richer-while-the-poor-become-poorer'! An immaculately dressed, young junior teacher with her enormous eyes, is standing on the stage addressing all proud parents of their now well-cultured children, encouraging them to have an open and honest discussion on all and every issue that their children are facing now. Her en-couraging, eloquent and fiery words make Father Aakaash forget his own main principle in life, which had always helped him stay peaceful when dealing with all kinds of people, which says: 'always stay neutral with people. People are not my enemy, and I am not people's friend either!' As she is speaking, her words are hitting the right spot in Little Mayuri's Father Aakaash. So, Father Aakaash by now is itching in his seat, restless till he has voiced his voice against the injustices that his daughter, who he loves more than himself, subjected to by the teacher referred to as Ms. Fox.

Back in time, when his daughter had told him about the unjust incident, he had controlled his anger just so that the flames of his anger do not engulf his daughter also! He had dismissed it then, as some accidental one-time occurrence and had promised himself to pursue the matter if it ever happens again. Now when this junior teacher, as if some expert in face reading, detects some concern on Father Aakaash's face, she at once pounces on this onetime opportunity for her road to stardom. She encourages him to share his concern with the whole assembly, a concern for one, might be a concern for all too!

The same speech when delivered by a man to a man it does not make as much of an impression while when delivered by the opposite gender the ROI (return-on-investment) skyrockets! Then it is easier for the wall of male pride to fall and have him fall on her neck in gratitude for the great deed of opening his eyes! Even if prudence says, spilling guts to the priest in a confessional does not solve any problems, digs a grave for oneself, still Father Aakaash cannot hold himself any longer and blurts out all the gory details of the secret event simmering in him out in front of this amateur priest! 'Listen, to this injustice that has still not found rest just like an arrow still stuck in my heart! After hearing your words of encouragement, you are the right one who can finally help pull this arrow out so I can then sleep peacefully! The incident is as follows: "the Class Teacher, Mrs. Fox of my daughter little Mayuri, as punishment for a crime that could've been easily ignored - forgetting her notebook in the playground that had her homework! She first unbraided her long hair yanking her hair in the process causing physical and emotional stress, teaching her to suffer injustice which damages the soul. She did not just stop at that. She then asked the whole class to say in on voice together that, 'Mayuri is a loser, Mayuri is a monkey, Mayuri is a fool,' repeatedly, a punishment that does not match the crime! I fear that such toxicity will never let her survive in this environment! Please take the strictest action against her before things get out of hand!"

Hearing just the words that the junior teacher is looking for her eyes sparkle! What a great opportunity for getting her to get her name splashed all over the media! If she can play this incident right, she could see her name written in golden words in the history of humankind for saving a little girl from the clutches of a Witch! So, without losing another moment, with her head held high like some warrior, heads as fast as she can towards the Headmistress office to make an even bigger fuss! Once the Headmistress has her story straight, she at once sends the peon to get the teacher involved, Ms. Fox - The Great Villain of all times, to her office-room!

Principal looking angry: "You witch! Do you have a stone in place of your heart! Has your soul long died, leaving behind a body that is now only spreading foul smell for little children to inhale and thus die a slow death from your corpse?"

An absurd action can only find its justification in an equally absurd cause! Ms. Fox is very aware of all the mental ailments she suffers from! Afterall, it is all God's fault for giving her a body that can never let her live her life to its maximum potential! Secretly, she hates God for giving her such an ugly body that can never let her fulfill her real desire of becoming the top actor in the film Industry. All her pent-up hatred towards God's injustice towards her, she let it escape over ruining the future of these little children, whose mannerisms are close to how God must look and act! Afterall, if it not for God's evil manipulations she would be enjoying a future that she rightfully deserves! Every time that she opens her drawer the sight of all kinds of medications that she is taking for her various illnesses mock her, laugh at her putting her once again in doubt over God's love for her and His Creation! She wonders if it is her wrong choices that led to her poor state today or is it that God is some merciless tyrant waiting to crack his whip on anyone who tries to disobey Him, even slightly! All these negative thoughts and hatred in her wants her to hurt God's most beautiful creation - children! Every time she looks at this little girl Mayuri's confidence in herself, hears her care-free laughter that knows no fear of people's reaction, reminds her of her own laughter that she had lost long ago... Unless the jealousy in her consumes her victim, it will instead keep consuming her only! So, for satisfying this fire of revenge she had secretly begun playing and experimenting on this child's mind to show the child how much more superior she is to her and since she cannot do so by increasing her own skill set, she instead widens the contrast by lowering the child's abilities! Now to save her own neck, she produces some new form of absurd lies that will justify her absurd behavior!

Ms. Fox: "You fool! It is not me who is foolish, but the people like you with your secular ideologies who are! For all you secular fools give us non-believers that 'all creations are the same because they have been created by the same God,' while people like me with progressive scientific views know better! The truth is that there is no God, and we are the creators of our own life, 'Aham Brahmasmi' (I am Brahma, The Lord of Creation)! Religion is a great concept, not for finding truth but for finding our lineages! This way, we can make rules that will ensure that all our future generations become rulers while the rest our slaves! Using our advanced knowledge of human Psychology, we can use those tricks to our advantage. We can use these time-tested results from well-documented experiments on children in techniques that can dumb down any child while raise another who bring out the best in our lineages! Now let me tell you a well-kept secret found by research conducted by NASA, The National Aeronautics and Space Administration an independent agency of the U.S. Federal Government America, that ninety-eight percent of the children fall in the genius category! What that means for us is that there is a chance that our generation loses the number one spot! Thus, it will not just mean that our future generations will have to go through the mental trauma of tasting defeat but also is our duty to increase the contrast between us and them by creating conditions that can only lead these unfortunate ones towards darkness without them even suspecting the evil plot behind their current pitiable states, while we will just put our feet-up and eat cake all day! The goal of religion is to become a majority so we can sway the vote banks which can then pass laws that will help trample over the rights of the minorities!

Principal: Your talk is like some queen of hypocrisy yet, I who you accuse of being an ignorant one, will give you an important lesson: You think you are doing your future generations a favor by protecting them from wilderness but now think again by putting on glasses that can help you see into the future when different possibilities take shape! If our Generation were to become number one not because of their skills but trickery, then can you not see all the harm it will do to our future generations! Lack of challenges in their life will make them lazy. Once they become lazy their willingness to work for themselves to take care of their and their family's needs will go down. When that happens the whole family members minds get corrupted! Once that happens the whole society will get infected by the epidemic of greed! When this happens know that the end of life is near! Remember that both of us are friends because we share the same end-results, but my way of getting there is different than yours!

Ms. Fox: Quit arguing, you secular fool! Now listen to my way which will certainly ensure our victory! All we need to do is to use the strength of our numbers to drown the voices of any minority! Whether funny or not we all laugh together over cruel jokes that we will make over their culture and heritage, their appearances, things that they take pride in, everything that is truly their asset! This way, soon enough they will start doubting themselves and their ancestral beliefs! Now they will start to secretly curse God for having them to take birth in a misfit family and now their only desire would be to either become like the Majority or die! If we do not take any action now very soon the minority will become a majority! We must be especially careful with this minority Group - the Khalsa Religion! They have the blood of great Saints, who proved their survival abilities by transforming themselves into soldiers when the need of the environment was to fight to defend their freedom against these tyrant forces of radical Islam Mughals! If it were not for their sacrifices the whole world would have gotten painted with the same color of one same Religion! So, if once they know of all that they are capable of they can easily overtake us! They will take all our positions in the industry, while our little prince and little princesses will be sitting on the sidelines, twiddling their thumbs, without any of the cakes of which they are so fond! All this talk of bitter truth is making my heart palpitations so fast that now I need to rest! So, please leave now and let me strategize some more over my action plan!"

The Headmistress does not like the cruelty in her approach and yet because they share the same goals, even if against her ethics, gives her her implicit consent by not vocalizing any word of decent!...

Once, the witch gets the Headmistress's implicit approval, she clasps her hands, first runs left then right not knowing how to celebrate her recent victory! Without wasting another moment, the Witch's evil mind starts producing new ideas of torture right away! Now every day the sole source of entertainment in her boring life is to invent new ways to torture the little girl, just enough to not cause any rebellion from the fellow students!

Like in a story of the King whose life lived in a parrot by proxy by an evil sorcerer! Every time that she wanted to hurt the king, she would torture the parrot, similarly Ms. Fox too starts giving pain and discomfort to the daughter to hurt the father. So, by proxy, she gets her revenge from the father! However, unfortunately for her and fortunately for the child and her family the daughter can understand the real reason behind the teacher's evil intentions. So, now what does she do? Being smart she reasons. Since it is only the knowledge of the pain to the daughter that can be the cause of pain to the father, she will just not relay further any stories of her tortures back home! Simple! With this revelation she begins to do what a child does beautifully – Forget. She reasons, "The witch can only torture me till I am in this domain of school where she has power over me however once out of school, I am under the power of my caring family! So, let this witch teacher enjoy her deceptive small victory over me, while I enjoy my real victory of coming out of the fires of her tortures unscathed! No evil Witch can now ever have any evil effect on the happiness of my family!" With this thought, the little girl smiles as she says the new lesson of life that she just learnt, 'Day's baggage ends with the day'!

Nature too has its own ways of serving justice. As someone who rightly said, 'that His stick's sound is not heard but felt! Due to the witch Teacher's primary occupation of stressing over her new plans to destroy a child her own psyche begins to attack herself! No surprise when Mayuri learns about The Witch's high blood pressure and anxiety attack due to which she had to stay in the Hospital for over a month! And when the cat's away, the mice will play! For all we know, it turned out to be the best time of the little girl's school life. As the days progress, the little girl's nature matures. From a complete chatterbox at home to completely silent in school! The girl whose rank would be amongst top ten now slides down to bottom ten from a total of fifty students! This serves as a blessing in disguise as the illusion of their victory has made them complacent enough that she can now breath enough to survive these troubled times! She laughs and says to herself, "I have been desiring attention and recognition from these privileged people thinking that they are superior to me, but now I can see that they are plain arrogant! How are they any superior to me when the only different between us is that the families in which they had birth was some rich privileged family while mine in a middle-class minority! For that matter how is their families even superior to mine when these families are rich due to their ancestral wealth or corrupt practices while mine is still being able to send their children in a good school despite losing all their ancestral wealth during all the looting during the India-Pakistan Partition of 1947. All this revival of our family is based on the power of their brain and hard work! So, even if God gave a choice to choose our family, my choice will still favor a minority middle-class family as I be a minority with no pride than a majority privileged class that is just arrogant and hollow from the inside!"

Now with her new initiated eyes, she further edifies, 'The teacher's evil motive is to make my life a living hell, so much so, that I complain to my parents. Then once, I complain to my parents, my parents will get angry and hurt. When they get angry, they can take some rash decision of pulling me out of the school and put me in some other school! Since this school is the only one which offers swimming, it will be a big loss for me and a win of the witch's evil motive! Come to think of it, that old hag has nothing to lose in ruining my life, as her career has already peaked and the only path for that witch is downhill, while on the other hand, I am still a small child, for me these are my foundation years and as my father always says, the basic principle of architecture states that, if the foundation is not strong the building can never come out strong! Ethics may say I am a coward, an escapist for running away from my problems, but I say that instead it is your understanding that is wrong, as now with my new aware eyes I can see how brave and mature I just became, by staying in the battlefield and facing the problems! By learning to adapt and adjusting to alien environments, I feel smarter than before! Afterall, why bother with expensive suicidal kamikaze attempts, when the same issues can be resolved by becoming a nothing/ shunya(zero)!

Little Mayuri to her Mother Aditi: Whenever the question arises of exploring the cause behind our choices, we like to believe our choices reflect our true self. However, this statement is extremely easy to say, but for anyone to try to lead such a life is the hardest and most elusive, as the level of self-discipline needed to lead such a disciplined life is one of the most challenging to say the least! All of us are slaves to our basic survival needs at the minimum! A child's eyes are curious, inquisitive over discovering new things, learning without any pre-conceived notions. Meaning, it is an excellent opportunity for adults to see how an untrained, unbiased eye would see, instead what these wise adults do? They not just kill their opportunity to gain experience about how we became what we became today, but instead we punish them for their original thoughts and even worse also pass our faulty beliefs over to them, fearing that if they did not stop then their own children might become the torch bearer for another bloody revolution. This is risking their lives and since the value of a child's life is dearer to the adult parent than the child, the parent becomes an excellent instrument in destroying the child's individuality and perpetrating obsolete beliefs and lies! When the basis of a belief system becomes fear and not some healthy set of proven tautologies, it can never produce any healthy lions but instead can create mostly pale and coward individuals only! Our religion has astonishingly great real-life heroes who never hesitated in sacrificing their lives for protecting their freedom of living a lifestyle that is true to their belief system, but now the environment has changed, and our Religion has drift-ed too far from its essence – freedom, the very reason for which it was born! Now all the emphasis has shifted to mere outward phys-ical appearances, and this must be one of our religion's biggest fol-lies!"

Mother Aditi saying laughingly: My little girl, your chronical age is nine, and yet you talk like a woman who is ninety, so from now, just like Baba Buddha ji from the Khalsa History who too in his early years showed a wisdom that was beyond his years was hon-ored by this title, we too will from now on call you, amongst your many other names as **'Grandma Baby Mayuri'**!

"Jai Baba Buddha ji ki; Jai hamari beti Grandma Baby Mayuri ki" in Hindi. (We salute Baba Buddha ji; we salute our daughter Grandma Baby Mayuri).

Mayuri smiles, Mother Aditi too smiles but not over the same reason, as for the mother the cause is over the simplicity that is the most precious ornament for a child.

THE REVERED TEACHER /
MY SON! MY SON!

Rasri aawat jaat se sil par parat nisat
(When a rope keeps going repeatedly over the same spot then, even a
hard material like stone starts to show signs of wear)
- An ancient wisdom quotation in Sanskrit

Mr. Termite is a math teacher, bald headed, in his late fifties. Had a son after patiently waiting for over ten years! This son is the apple of his eye, someone through which his signature will live for generations to come!

His conduct outwardly is always ethically correct in front of all students so that they never suspect that his allegiance is only towards his son! The rest are his son's competitors, so it is his duty as a Father to use his knowledge of Kut-niti from Vedic Science, The Art of using Psychology for unfair gains, to ensure that his son is always ahead from the rest of the pack! All un-ethical tricks he is using to have his son always be at the top, he rationalizes them to be part of his Fatherly duties! Since his higher duty as a teacher of all directly conflicts with his fatherly duties, he ends this battle by choosing his allegiance to his son only finally!

The teacher now religiously follows his secret evil plot. His strategy is that when in school he will teach as a professional who imparts just enough knowledge so that his students can get average results but once home, he teaches his son advanced shortcut techniques! In this way, he ensures his son always gets top grades leaving everyone else with a wide margin.

As fortune would have it, Mr. Aakaash Singh's only son Chandrashekhar is also Mr. Termite's student, a batchmate to his son. One fine evening, cool breeze is blowing. Not wanting to miss such a beautiful weather, the teacher decides to bring his books outside and conduct his coaching session outside instead. Right then Chandrashekhar sees the teacher and his son Prince and his close friend sitting outside. Since a small race is all both the boys want in this weather, so Prince also leaves everything behind and comes to hold Chandrashekar's hand to go for a run around the block. As Chandrashekhar comes close to the table lying next to him, his glance accidentally falls on the contents on the table. There lay some intriguing cryptic geometric figures which make an impression on him. He wants to ask his friend more about them but knows not why he does not! So now both boys are giggling and racing around the block! At that the events of that evening seemed like any other evening until he sleeps the night and then wakes up the next morning! In the morning as he lay half-asleep all the events of the last evening along with the visuals of intriguing puzzles come back to him with a starling life-altering revelation: **This whole system is laid in such a way that there is one path which everyone is trained to follow and another one that is kept deliberately secret from the rest to preserve its sanctity from illiterate people who know not how to preserve the beauty of the new environment which must have stolen the blueprint from the heavens to bring another heaven on Earth. Thus, I can see now how all these educational materials, teachers and guides impart knowledge which written to target the people in public domain. So now a System that was meant to raise the qualities in a child to God-like levels has instead become a perfect ecosystem for transforming** them into mindless sheep! So, the right way is that we start looking at books/teachers only as an initiation vehicle and then after getting knowledge from them not limit ourselves too just them! In this discovery process, once again revisit those topics, this time exploring more on one's own, experimenting more to discover new secret shortcuts! This is the best way I can give my soul the pleasure it looks for in experiencing things. By doing things with full precautions one can experience both the pleasure in right way and the pleasure in the pain in wrong way is indeed the right way ...

Since the teacher cannot bear anyone other than his own son to come first, I need to protect myself from any unhealthy comparisons. So, the best way to protect is to hide my new mission from everybody, after all some wise man rightly said: "When living in the same pond as the crocodile, it is wise not to alienate it!"

With this awareness, I salute the absolute teacher – mathematics, science, knowledge, in other words the knowledge of the way God runs and thus is the right way for us to follow. It is only when I solve problems my-self, will it become my second nature. Now for me to make a prayer for studying and not for sports is not possible. So, I say my customized version of Guru Mantra given in the Skanda Purana: May the spirits of organization and intelligence of the knowledge of symmetry bless me as I try executing this cart-wheel that I have been trying for fifteen days now:

Gururbrahma gururvishnuh,
gururdevo maheshwarah |
Guruhsakshat parabrahma
tasmai shrigurave namah | |
(*Guru is Brahma, Guru is Vishnu, Guru is Lord Shiva. Guru is verily*
the supreme reality. Sublime prostrations to Him.

And lo-and-behold his joy finds no bounds as his feet automatically jump and execute a perfect cartwheel! On seeing her son Chandrashekhar execute a perfect Olympic-grade cartwheel, normally any soccer-ma would encourage her son to follow gymnastics as a career, but Mother Aditi is no soccer mom, so she immediately puts ice-water on all his budding inspirations, by scolding him; 'I had told you not to do this, you can hurt your head, and when you hurt, everyone in the family will feel hurt! Since I know, you do not listen to me, I will tie you to this pillar till you promise me, you will not do it again! As his mother is tying him, he smiles as he just experiences a Eureka moment in knowing the answer to the question which had been bothering him for so long:

Question: 'What is the difference between a Nazi Tyrant and a mother'?

Answer: 'None.'

PHASE TWO OF LIFE: WHEN THE BODY IS KING

She has vanished,
now I am all alone,
playing with my flute by myself...

CONSTRUCTIVE FOCUS / HOW A PERVERT KILLS HIS BOREDOM!

Chandrashekhar: Why do you not appear?

I am straining so hard and yet all that my efforts have yielded is this hemorrhoid! After wrestling after long, which seemed to me like some endless eternity, I try every trick from yoga to stay the course. However, I suspect that I must be a star in a class of attention deficit persons, as sitting alone on my throne is driving me to tears already! Now as I am complaining and cursing, serendipitously my eyes fall on a poster from some one-star rated movie in my daily newspaper with images that hit the spot! All my pain magically vanished! On seeing these nothing short of miraculous results then everything reverses. Now I eagerly wait for my bathroom breaks to happen. When sitting on my royal throne, boredom or idleness can never defeat me as I always go prepared before going for my fight. This should clear all confusion about why I am still in the bathroom even after the reason for me to be there is long over, as needless to say because my real topic has still not ...

DEGREES

Vidya dadati vinayam, Vinayam dadati paatrataam,
puratatva dhanamaapnoti, dhanam dharmam tatatsukham
(Knowledge gives Humility, Humility gives Character,
when the one gets both, the one now experiences a   joyful existence
forever)
- Sanskrit shloka from Hitopadesha 6

THE IDOL OF CLASSIFICATION SYSTEM BASED ON VALUE (THE VARAN-SYSTEM); MIS-TRANSLATED AS CASTE-SYSTEM RESTORED BACK TO ITS PEDESTAL!

Father Aakaash, with his heart of a poet is preparing himself of fulfilling his duty as a father of giving his illuminating lecture that will help his daughter chose a vocation where her passion lies and yet he is at a loss as to why every time he tries to his surprise, he cannot say anything! Then he realizes the real cause behind this conflict! It is mainly because ethics and materialism are opposing forces, and this is the age of Kalyug/ Age of Materialism. How can I mislead my own children when my own experience is contrary! Working without any expectations is ideal but the only place that I have seen it is in children's playground! In this competitive dog-eat-dog world, there must be a new hybrid approach to kill two birds with one stone that I am going to talk to with my children.

Father Aakash: Whenever I need answers, the first thing I do is to find my guru, an example of how The Architect of All implemented the solution for that problem. Then it is just reverse engineering from there. Even if Kriya Yoga has many beautiful teachings yet one of their secular view of giving equal importance to each of Creator of All's creations, directly opposes the teaching of The Varan system of grouping people based on value, so to put at rest all these conflicting views I will have to do my own investigation on the matter by using my strict scales of Critical Reasoning, in-order for me to do justice to my Dharam/duty as a father who is to guide his loving daughter. For finding the right answer I need not go far as the answer is right here, by exploring the way by which The Creator of all Creators has created our bodies. When we lose an arm, we still survive but when we lose our heart, the person cannot, meaning God has given every body part different importance then who are we to say that this way is not the right way? Now, regardless of whether or not you subscribe to dualistic or non-dualistic views, this statement is a fact regardless of whatever form of glasses you switch to, that is that this observation of mine, has already been leveraged by ancient Vedic Science of dividing our society into Varna(Categories)/ mis-translated as the dreaded Caste, which are based on the "value" that they bring to the table and not the lineages, even if when the Horses that are pure bred are crossed their products are of high quality! The reason that this beautiful system could not get its due respect, is because instead of being value based it quickly degenerated into inheritance based!"

Mayuri: "Keeping in mind all the advice from my family and well-wishers, weighing various possibilities coming from a lengthy battle of a divided mind, I have been able to narrow down to two choices: Either a college degree in the language English that can help me in communicating with most of the world population or a college degree in the language of computers – 0/1 or Either/Or in other words the Language of Truth!

It must have been one of the many divine mysteries that all this while my mother kept a library of books in English Literature due to her teaching needs, not realizing that like a monkey I copy her and try to out-do her! Result, I am already a graduate in English Literature. So, even if it means, I have the security of having a paycheck every month for the rest of my life as a schoolteacher and is in line with my teleology as a writer, I will still not pursue this stream! Why? Because the greatest asset of youth is in the high amount of fire that they have in their belly! If I do not invest them in quenching their hunger for new and unconquered lands, for challenging my mental and physical abilities to push through their limits, for exercising all areas of my body which have still not been engaged in order to reach my full potential then without a doubt I have defrauded myself, that I am have become old much before getting old and also never fulfill my secret dream of having The Lord Inder, The Controller of Natural Forces, bow in awe of my prowess!

Ma Aditi: I want to know the big secret behind how a young girl is being able to divert her body's natural urge for constant attention from people to some dead computer screen!?

Mayuri: What fascinates me about computers? It is how a computer is like that intelligent friend of human, who knows everything and yet in real is a dumb inanimate piece of metal that just regurgitates what us humans just fed it! This irony is precisely what attracts me towards it! Thus, it only makes sense to choose a field that is completely alien to me, which tempts me with its bits and bytes, a field where there is a lot of new things to learn, a stock that has a lot of room to grow!"

PURUSHARTH / TRANSFORMATION
OF A BOY TO A HE-MAN

Meaning to a man's existence

When evaluating the Risk involved in any action, more weight should be put towards the downside consequences versus the upside for any Man as it is only when he is able to shoulder his responsibilities towards his family's needs does he become qualified to be a Man! Which also means that this decision can make or break a Man, so Prince now actively takes counseling from all sources and then keeping all inputs from various sources in mind, he uses his own brain to come-up the answer which is right for him and him only! After many deliberations, his vision clears, just as when in encryption experts uncover the real message by cleaning the slate with chemicals, and bring the hidden message to the front, so emerges the message meant for him, and only him, with golden letters flashing in bold colors, which he announces aloud to the universe, "My way is not a walk in the park, but the way which goes up the mountain, down the river, through the ditches. I will burn mid-night oil to ace completive serious tests as this will instill in me the discipline needed to earn my wings, just like a caterpillar first digest itself, and then certain groups of cells survive, turning the soup into beautiful eyes, wings, antennae, and other adult structures to finally transform into a beautiful butterfly!

Thus. begins his journey in getting a master's degree in mathematical subjects. It did not take him much time to realize the importance of time, so whenever any invitations for fraternity parties from the college would come, he tossed them straight in fire without even opening them. Afterall when one's whole life is dependent on this one stroke, there is no choice left for any strong-willed Man but to inculcate self-discipline in one to the level of being able to make a sacrifice of all other desires just to fulfill this one burning desire of desires of making one's life oneself and one's own way! It is only then do we see the beautiful moment of the caterpillar transforming into a beautiful butterfly. All his sacrifices, long strenuous hours of burning mid-night oil finally pay off when after long suspenseful moments the results come confirming his strong mathematical abilities which help make him the youngest person to have scored the highest!

STUDENT LOANS

A shout from the voice of fear forces Father Aakaash to reconsider his decision of taking another financial burden of a student loan for his daughter to get a college degree!

Father Aakaash: And if at all I can accept another financial headache then does it not make more sense to invest this same amount towards buying more land. I am not young anymore and shame on me if I still have not seen through the deception of time! Question is not if but when the time will reverse, and it is not the strongest who we see survive but the ones who had saved for the rainy day! My either/or: invest in land or towards my daughter's education. Investing in land will secure my future and potentially many more to come while investing in my daughter's education is a thankless event as ultimately, she is like a collateral with me for her Husband. When she gets married, it is highly likely that I will also have to bear the entire burden of just another platitudinous lavish wedding! Compounded with all this added financial burden might just be the final limit! Even after breaking my back just to support her needs, she might never return these favors and even worse could fight with me to get her share from my property! I dread the day when I must depend on my children to take care of my survival needs! On the other hand, buying a house is like having an obedient son who will be with me when I need the aid of my children the most - old and having trouble in taking care of myself. The likelihood of house prices going up is highly likely, given that most people still rely on abstinence as their preferred method for birth-control in India! Meaning population is bound to grow and so investing in purchase of Land in India is a sure-fire recipe for success!

But then again, why am I feeling so uneasy with this decision. Must be the ethics in me that wants me to reconsider this decision which can only come from a stone and not a father who loves his daughter more than himself! If I were to invest the same money towards the education of my daughter, then I am not just investing in my dear young daughter's future but also my own, as the brightness of her future is directly proportional to the light in my efforts and me! If I am to let my daughter go to a college that costs less but does not offer the courses of interest to her, then I can see her grow up as a lady whose life's content is just a sad saga of could-haves and would-haves on the other hand If I give her monetary assistance to help her pursue the Arts in which she has passion I can see a lady of substance. When she is working on things that motivate her, her daily life will be full of joy because working for the sake of working is despair while working on things where one's passion lies is indeed where happiness lives! And when I see her come-up as a woman with substance then I feel content that all my efforts bore some nice juicy fruits! Burying my gold in a property my returns are finite, while diverting the same funds towards the growth of my children my returns become infinite as now, I win many more points in the eyes of the Eternal! I shout:

'Vote for Sacrifice!
Vote for True Love!
Vote for Giving!'

1991 WHEN I SHED MY OLD SKIN TO TRANSFORM INTO MY NEW SKIN OF ROSE QUEEN

THEN I LEARNT SUBJECT 'VASTRA-GOPANA SHASTRA FROM SANSKRIT LITERATURE' - THE ART OF USING CLOTHES FOR HIDING BODY PARTS

Dear Mayuri's Diary,

Aplam! Chaplam! I must do a headstand to see as everything around me has reversed! I can see the hidden chameleon in me changing colors to florescent and vibrant colors to match this new environment of freedom! Every time that some naughty draft of wind blows off my veil, exposing to the whole world all its hidden contents for them to see, I do not have to worry about it tarnishing my family's prestige anymore as much! The fellow students are mostly from my age-group, so I did not expect too many surprises there, but when I found how the youth from different cultures does not just look different but also follow different traditions, I got one of the most pleasant surprises of my life! What a beautiful way of learning new ways of doing the same things, after all beauty lies in diversity!

Now that I am far away from my only confidants - my family, I feel the need of one. Taking my mother's advice, I have now started writing a diary. Why a diary? Because this is one of the best ways of getting a glimpse in what one's heart is secretly wanting in a language she can understand! The words are like a useful detective which can help uncover many mysteries behind our own mysterious behavior. So, I too begin using this tool to critically analyze the situation to uncover the real reason behind my actions!

My childhood has taught me to the importance of flying under the radar and the strategy has paid off beautifully but now I surprise myself with this unknown lustful force in me that will not listen to me and has a head of its own! This lustful energy now wants to reveal itself! Like some snake that had to lay coiled in small dingy box for a long time, the snake of lust in me too can feel it popping up its hood with a force that throws the cover miles away! Like poison cuts poison, I too want a taste of that deadly venom called youth to cut all poison of youthful desires writhing in me! Now experiencing reality as a third person bores me, now I want to experience by living it!

Now for a plan to rule every man's heart! Being a student from City amongst these simpleton students from various Villages, my Stock is already high! So, I need not put much effort towards attracting attention from these Village simpletons and yet underestimating these Village Girls might prove for me a fatal mistake! This I do not say out of my own inferiority complexes but from my observations of how quickly that Village Girl stole the glances from myself when she walked-by wearing a beautiful Rose Flower in her hair, deceiving him into seeing herself as the Rose itself! These Village Girls look innocent but with their knowledge of 'Vastra-Gopana,' the Art of Concealment of Cloths, they are anything but! Armed with these tricks they are almost invincible by paralyzing the brain of the mass man, in these matters of entertainment there is no place for any thinking! Now what does this Smart City girl do to beat this mad rush for the number one spot in the popularity charts in the entire history of this College?! First things first, I stand in front of the mirror thinking of short-cuts that will get me up there! It becomes easy to see that simplicity does not sell well with vain youth, especially as saw many times that vanity runs with its clown bells and shiny motley colors which is enough to entertain any madding-crowd hungry for anything which catches their eye! The Venom of Youth running through my veins demands from me to get not just one but every man's attention, to rule every man's heart and then make them my slaves forever! So, to fulfill this vein desire of mine, I first start a fire. I am now taking off all my simple attire one by one, then throwing them in the fire. Next, I am taking off all the posters of warrior queens I had glued straight in the fire too. Now on the same wall I am putting pictures of the most popular sluts of the town instead! This next Revelation must come to me as some big gift straight from the heavens, as now unlike my competition, I do not have to bother sitting in front of the mirror for hours prettying my face, not even spending hours in some gym for sculpting every muscle in my body! Why bother about anything when the secret to my vein-man's heart is where his eyes go greedily and stay stuck there – these Legs that go miles and miles! This is where the money is! So, now I too jump in the same bandwagon as these Village Girls and am learning 'Vastra-Gopana' - The Art of Concealment of Cloths.

Is understood, who just won the coveted Title of **'The Rose Queen of every Rubberstamp College Man's Heart - 1991 - Miss Mayuri Ghai Birghi'**! ...

THE MERCY OF THE INFINITE IS INFINITE

Dear Mayuri's Diary,

The deception of love! When the ratio in a college is five girls in a class of forty-five students, one would think the law of averages would prevail and so every girl can expect around a set of eight prospective suitors or so, however in actual we find the opposite! Everyone is fighting with each other to reach the Rose Queen, in more precise words to reach the one girl who is unattainable! Now I realize you cannot have it all! You must sacrifice some to make the higher priority Goals a reality! Due to all the distractions that come from becoming a mini-celebrity I failed my first-year exam! Now I like all the attention but not at the cost of repeating an entire year and carry the resultant black spot on my degree which could have ill-effects on my bright future career! I feel ashamed to face all the students and teachers in the college, who were already making fun of me behind my back. I am now sitting in my room in the girls Hostel, not knowing where to hide when suddenly I hear some other fellow girl student's voice, who is also sailing in the same boat as her, shouting on the top of her lungs, 'The University Rules have changed! All students who failed with marks within a margin of five will not have to repeat another year! This exception is being made for this year only! Viva l' Board! Long live the Board! Hooray!' Hearing this announcement all the girls start peeping out from their rooms! Due to nervous excitement from the news a surprised me began peeping out of my window, only to lean too far that I fall right out of the window. I get up massaging my newly acquired bump on my forehead due to the fall, supplying some much-needed comic relief to all the observers! I am brave, rubbing my small brain injury as nothing I go closer to the source of the voice to hear again, as if it were some heavenly revelations so I could not hear, I open my ears to hear the announcement again. Yes indeed, my ears had heard it right the first time too! On seeing this heavenly intervention for me, I know not how to justify this joy that I am experiencing from this thought of being a recipient of His mercy! But the next moment my rational mind makes me dismiss it as some silly feeling backed superstition ...

DELIBERATIVE DEMOCRACY

Dear Mayuri's Diary,

How is this even possible? I, who has always taken pride in myself for always standing up for those things that are in line with my ethics, but now I have no explanation for my own impotence in not just being able to stop the wrong but also stand with the group which are brainless stones throwers!

So far, I am enjoying the jokes and laughter I share amongst the group members. Little did I know the secret sinister agenda behind Groupism is not silly merry making but to surrender one's own thinking abilities to the group leader! Even if I feel odd doing things for the group leader, I know not why I comply to her wishes without any voice of dissent! All these subconscious mind-control tactics of the Groupism finally surface into my awareness the day when the bully put me to my first test of assisting her in subduing our cook to give in to our unreasonably high demands by harassing him, exaggerating his mistakes on his face and then if he still does not surrender, we all together threaten him to have the authorities then come to remove him off his job! Now as per the plan I am sitting executing the plan faithfully! I feal an uneasiness and yet to my surprise like some puppet l am doing exactly as the bully wishes as if the wish were mine but really, it is not mine but the bully's! That night I sleep thinking nothing of the incident but the next morning at the early hours of three - four am, I find myself fully awake. My mind is active as if it had been processing the whole event from the day before and now, I began to put my own thoughts into order: Shame on me! I just became the kind to whom I can never relate! How? As now I can see that I just became an impotent who can do nothing even if she knows right from wrong! By surrendering my individuality, I became a mindless puppet in the hands of a tyrant who will use me for reaching a goal which is not even in line with my ethics!

This is what will happen when Yama, The Death Broker as mentioned in the Ved shastr/ Literature, will come to decide my fate after my death: Yama: Why I did something in which I did not believe?

I: I did it because my leader said so.

Yama picks me by the throat and throw me straight to Hell!

I: Why? Afterall, I obeyed all the orders diligently!

Yama: Because God gave everyone a brain to think. Simple. Case closed.

After this convincing hypothetical conversation, anytime I saw any group member recruit, I would simply vanish from the spot! As the most asset I must preserve is The Infinite in me!

THE DEADLIEST BITE OF FIRST LOVE

When a face becomes the face

Dear Mayuri's Diary,

People had alerted me about this this vicious snake called erotic love whose bite has poison so potent that once it mingles with the blood leaves its victim incapacitated, incapable to even beg for life and yet I know not how all my smartness stopped working when I faced my assess in the form of my new classmate! Looks like whenever the God of Erotic Love Kama goes on a mission of arousing two sleeping potential lovers then the probability of Him finding success is more in cases where the energies of Youth with hearts still not exposed to the powers of love but seeks to find the one who can arouse their feet to dance to the immortal song - love!

At this first stage of my erotic love, the one face that appears from other faces is of fellow student, Vishwamitra. Our senses are in-sync with each other and that is why magically we find our paths collide. Like when I am entering, he is leaving making us laugh every time this happens! I am so surprised seeing the transformation within that I ask myself shyly, "I feel I can relax with him and be as silly as I really am because a village simpleton's simple thinking is too simple to mind anything." The way we city-folk do things, the Village-folk do the same thing backwards! So, for me to not laugh is impossible! Now a fool will take my wild laughter as some attack on his Ego and so could prevent him from developing

143

any deep feelings for me, but since he is not one of those ego maniacs who think they can get the girl by changing her to their ways, he instead does the opposite by never stopping me from saying or doing silly things, to the extent that if ever he feels she is still very reserved with her responses, he takes it upon himself to ensure that she goes back to her true nature of just being silly! Like when He was joking, he told this funny incident: "When I invited for a lunch at the Ritz she refused. When I tempted her with tickets for a movie she refused, but when I invited her for some tangy golgappas at the street side shop, she gladly accepted my invitation!"

THE TRIGGER THAT
AWAKENS THE LOVERS

*Fear of losing to the competition acts like the trigger which forces what
out what lay in the unknown depths of the subconscious self to reveal
itself to the conscious self, trampling over all assumptions of superiority.*

Dear Mayuri's Diary,

It is just another day of bliss with no special omens alerting the
Hero and Heroine of this Rubberstamp College of the significance
of this day, when what was a rumor for people became a fact now.
It all starts when the Hero produces a new silly game on the fly.
The game as he explains is like a Quiz, where the contestant has to
say a word quickly that rhymes with the word given by the quiz
Leader. He lets the lady go first, since I am still unprepared, I say
whatever is in front of me - "tree." His response - "me." To which
I cannot resist doing some comedy of my own by mimicking him,
saying "me me me! All you can think of is your conceited self! He
gives me a dirty glance. Now it is his turn. The word he gives is
"glove." When I hear the word, for a moment this girl who has an
answer ready even before the question ends knows not why she is
unable to say the answer even if she knows it! I wonder in disbelief
if it were some trick of him to say the loaded word "love" from my
mouth meant for him, if it is some ingenious way of his to get a
hint of my feelings for me without bruising his ego?

The final trigger cause happens when with the threat of separation appears with the entry of the third wheel! My best friend named Cheena is drop-dead gorgeous, and she too begins to show signs of attraction towards the same man as me! Now every time when Cheena comes, I can sense insecurity and jealousy consuming me! So, one fateful day, I decide to put an end to my curiosity of knowing the truth: Is my love requited or just some figment of my imagination! But how can a woman go against her nature of inwardness and secrecy, so what I do is indirect form of interrogation, which comes naturally to all of us woman, especially when dealing with these chameleon-like men who are quick in changing colors with the changing environment! Then begins my dangerous psychological game, the outcome of which could end all happy times with him, but I do not care whether the outcome is in my favor or not just an end to my curiosity! What I secretly desire is to now jump to the next level to experience the pleasures, a pleasure for which she has the lock but cannot open herself as the key is with him!

So now, I am enacting my little unscripted drama which changes direction dynamically with the situation! I tell him seriously that I really think he will make a good pair with my best friend and because I am not selfish, I am even willing to assume the role of a broker to ease in sealing the deal. Now being proud from winning the Title of the Rose Queen, my assumption is that every boy in the college wants me and only me! Which means that the only image that has occupied his heart is hers and hers only! So, now when he learns of a proposal from some other girl, he is sure to refuse the Villain Cheena, he is a man of character and such a man does not make fake promises to anyone unless they have genuine feelings for them and since he has feelings just for me, he will immediately get down on his knees and confess his love for me instead!

However, this does not happen. The scoundrel has a little rebel hidden in him that reveals itself by answering with an answer that is completely opposite to all her expectations -a brief YES! Now my situation is akin to the monkey who is sawing off the very branch on which he is sitting! At this moment, like a ton of bricks a revelation dawn on me! That all this time I had a diamond and I never cared about it but now even worse is that I know his worth but will have to give it to someone else who might just take it without even showing any feelings of gratitude towards my invaluable sacrifice! I vomit a little in my hand! This new entry - my best friend Cheena certainly does not love him, and he too does not love her or her best friend. Why? Simply because none of us have any notion about what love is! Now when the situation is going out of control, something must be and that too quickly, else the next day the person who used to circle her only will be happily walking arm-arm with another woman who is her own best-friend! Double deception! As now I will not just lose my potential lover but also my best-friend, whose value will get doubled as now I need a friend who will help me cope with hellish days that lay ahead so!

Poor me! The whole intent for the drama has reversed! Until the whole drama is rolled-back to safety, I can see dire consequences coming my way! This giant stone is hurling down a mountain towards me! If I do not do anything to stop it now, all my desires of experiencing the joys of Youth, will get crushed, replacing it with a lonely life with a rosary in one hand praying to God for forgiveness over sins that I was meant to commit but never did! The even bigger problem is that I cannot even go fight with my competitor, drag her by her hair through the mud, knock her out senseless and then claim him as my trophy, but since my competitor is no enemy and is her bosom friend in who I see the image of my sister I know not what to do! Now if my sister-like-friend agrees to the proposal then no matter which way the wind blows, my days of loneliness are certain! If my friend says yes, then I lose him to my best friend. If I do not follow through my promise then also, I betray him and even more her, in some sense. So, my best bet or the only choice left for me is to steal a march on her sister-like-friend, by confessing my love to him! Thus, making him her lover instead of letting her "sister!"

Now that all my womanly curiosity has won over all my womanly inhibitions, I see no harm in taking a harmless peak into his heart. Slowly I can sense something magical is about to happen, the moment in which a girl leaves her veil of shame to become a bride who surrender herself herself completely! As both confess their love for each other, to the lovers the whole world seems to pause for a moment, the sea tides seem to have paused before resuming their efforts in trying to kiss the elusive moon... Once the brief pause is over, when the world resumes its untiring activities, the sea tides too busy with their renewed efforts in trying to kiss the moon, the new-born lovers too now wonder over the meaning of such a meaningless confession!?

A DESIRE FOR THE FORBIDDEN FRUIT

Life is a synchrony of a teardrop and a laugh. A teardrop, for that
one object you could never reach. A laughter, which follows, on seeing
one's own foolishness.
- Mast Mayuri, The Intoxicated Peafowl Dancing in the Rain

Dear Mayuri's Diary,
"When I see at him with the knowledge of him coming from a small village with a background of farming makes me see the simplicity in him, a divine property which wants me to surrender myself completely to him and yet I am unable, possibly because the cause behind my hesitation can see the hidden contradiction in this assumption! On amplifying that voice, I can see his dark side of him seeing me as his conquest, a mere trophy for showing-off to the world his superiority over the rest of his friends. Once the world sees the Rose Queen begging a village simpleton, I will become a laughingstock while he on the other hand will start getting the kind of respect worthy of worship! Now what does dear Mayuri do? Problemata: How do I quench my thirst for pleasures which only he can give without the risk of any bad situation of blackmail created by this very person who says he loves me today? I do nothing. I wait till the good time meant for me will come - my wedding night! This way if he is the one meant for me, I enjoy with him, else if it is not him, I will still get my pleasures.
  Once bitten twice as shy. Due to failing in the first year due to distractions that came from winning the coveted Title of Rose

149

Queen, I am now doubly aware of the importance of constructive single-minded focus! It is a good thing for me that the Great Almighty went out of his way to bail me out of that horrible situation, but the bad thing is that the probability of a second miracle in a row is next to nothing! Therefore, now I no choice left than tricking my heart into focusing on my highest priority - my Studies! Now what strategy can ever trick a mischievous heart? I tempt it! I program my heart to go into a deep sleep so I can use my mind towards achieving my career goals. And once that happens, I am very sure he will be so impressed by my smartness that he will leave everything else and agree to be my slave, ready to do whatever I ask him to do!

WORTHY?

Truly, the anxiety hidden in knowing the results of the final year results ends equally in both cases of pass and fail with the same result – joy and relief! The person who has passed is at peace over a feeling of a secure future ahead while the one who has failed is also at peace because now one's uncertainty has met its closure!

Mayuri and her hero too come to the same stage to get the results. The Hero had come with the expectation that both will fail but that did not happen! He has failed while the one he saw as his loyal companion for life has passed! Now when he sees this contrariety in the results, he is fuming as he sees it as betrayal of betrayals, while she finds the irony in the situation as humorous instead and bursts into one of her wild fits of laughter that she suspects runs in her blood from her mother! This laughter he perceives as some big kick in his chest to wake-up from this spell of attraction that this witch has cast on him! He is the superior one, when both are facing the same headwinds, it is him or them together who should have come out victorious and not how things turned out! While on the other hand, with all the adrenaline rush from her victory running straight to the brain, floods with it all her thinking abilities so much so that she fails to see the seriousness of the situation and instead puts salt to his wounds by childishly jeering at him saying, "O my illiterate simpleton from a small village in Bihar, the University Rules must be changed to allow a dictionary in the examination halls! Your intelligence at a genius level but because the question paper is in English you fail!

I beat you!

I beat you!

I beat you."

Followed with more laughter.

Once she is finally able to compose herself and then lift her head, she soon finds out that a fatal mistake has just occurred! Her hero had completely failed in seeing any humor in her witty remark and had already vanished from the spot! Now she can feel that her cheeks which were full like a red ripe mango from all the laughter a few moments before are now pale like one that has just been sucked out! She now realizes that indeed she beats him in the competition, but just dug a grave for all possibilities of a future with his budding love! Now needless to mention that her humor has completely backfired as her dearest of all's face is now reflecting a cocktail of anger and humiliation!

He vanishes, and she faints!

Now that all the euphoria has vanished, she can feel a wave of empathy run through her for him! She can now empathize with the pain that he will have to go through when he sits with his juniors. With this thought, she feels double pain one for him and other over the realization over her bitter situation! Now she stands there like a stone, shedding a silent tear over the grave of her first-aware-love, over these glory days of the youth will now never come back again.

WITCHES DANCE

O the vicious tortures of youth! O the tough battles that a girl just blossoming into a woman must go through can look the great battle of waterloo pale in comparison! The court room is live now! Today's jury will issue a final verdict on one of the most serious conundrums: he loves me or loves me not!

The devil's Advocate in a demanding tone: "He, says that he loves you and yet he doesn't come forward to ask your hand for marriage, then he has to be some just another cheap hypocrite."

The Angel's Advocate in her sweet voice coos: "No, no! That cannot be right, as someone whose voice is free from any malice or pride, a voice so powerful that when you hear in your ears, your whole body begins melting like chocolate!"

The false-ego's Advocate, taking center stage with a head held high: "Have you not forgotten how harsh and arrogant he is, he does not celebrate any festivals, a person who cannot dance and sing with other people when customs demand, then he must have a stone in the place of his heart."

The intellect's Advocate makes its entry and says in an equivalent tone: "Are you not ashamed to utter such derogatory words for someone you loved because you saw the image of your Father in him? Although you had put yourself in a compromising position with him, he did not take any advantage of you!"

The warrior Advocate comes interrupting any other voice: "This is the language of cowards, to not move forward is like a virtual suicide of your soul.

Forgiveness Advocate falling at her feet and begging her sobbingly:

"Have Mercy! If you are hurting, he must feel these tremors too! He is not in a good spot himself and the cause of his despair is you."

Fear's Advocate making its appearance from its hiding place: "It must be something that you did or say to offend him! That is why he must be taking his revenge on you by always keeping you in the dark by being evasive and never transparent with his actions. He hides secrets from you, it is because he already has another woman!"

Ethics Advocate's entry with a calm voice: "Maybe, it is all your limitations which must disappear somehow for him to welcome you in his life in order to make a new, clean start with you."

In-justice Advocate finally breaking its silence with shouting at her: "That scumbag showed you a taste of love but never the whole meal! He did not have the power to balance the fine scales of justice between his duty towards her versus his duty towards his near and dear ones!"

Justice Advocate in a forgiving voice: "By staying with you he taught you what laughter is and by not staying with you longer than his time was over, he taught you what love is..."

Since this block of code runs in a loop with no exit clause, we leave her happy in her infinite loop and wisely move on to the next topic.

HIDE AND SEEK

Dear Mayuri's Diary,

After several rounds of 'Guilty,' 'not Guilty,' begins the game of hide and look for. Only an innocent heart can fall in love because the moment thinking gets involved there is just no way that one can never play this high-risk game! Now the joy of my eyes only depends on seeing him, every resemblance of him makes me run towards that source, but all that joy turns into double sorrow when I find, my find is like a mirage that will disappear the very moment I found him! I must find the scoundrel from his hiding place to get back from him the most asset that he stole from me – this heart of mine! So now that this time is critical for my survival, forget these old friends which now only offer nuisance value of wasting precious time by chatting and now replace them with friends which will help me survive the demands of one of the most dangerous times of my lifetime so far! So, then it was of children who are toppers but now it is of boys with a notorious reputation! Once it so happens that by some stroke of good fortune, I happen to be sitting in earshot of this group of notorious boys who just happen to mention the precise name which I am looking for! Which also means that with this new reputation of hers getting a noble husband might not just become challenging but next to impossible! With such a strong deterrent any woman with self-respect would stop her mission cold turkey but since I am not just smart but also a woman had by the evil spirits of unfulfilled desires, in my mind is never a question of finding a way to get over him rather of how to find his hiding place!

I surprise myself with the smartness I show in keeping the covert mission discreet. After frustrating long hours of waiting for him to appear at all the places that he would frequent my patience finally pays of when I learn all about his cunning! All this while a silent observer in me would marvel at all these unplanned meetings only to now discover that he would cheat a little to make those meetings look accidental to make me surrender myself completely to him! I also find his real places of visit, not the tea shop but the local pub! How silly of me! All this time I was thinking I am the smarter one laughing and making jokes on him only to now realize that there is nothing in my hands! It was him who was the Master and I a puppet in his bigger game! How slowly and steadily he stole my heart from right under my nose and I did not even notice! Never knew that this clever me could ever get tricked and that too not by some smart city Alec but a village simpleton! Just how much I hate myself now for not being him!

THE CURSE ON ALL DELHI GIRLS!

She has vanished, now I am playing my flute all by myself.

Dear Mayuri's Diary,

I am double elated! First for the conquest over my impatience and second for my conquest over my sleep! How? As till this day I held the title of sleeping long hours only after Kumbhakarna, the character in Ramayana who would sleep continuously for six months but now I am surprised to see myself enduring long frustrating hour after hour of jabber from someone who must hold the title of the most boring man on the planet! Even when the only thing in my mind was my dear sweet sleep, I was able to control it for the greater good of getting some information of my long-lost deceiver, even if I would have been even happier if my ears would have gone deaf before hearing about my forgotten lover's dreadful curse to all Delhi Girls! Even-if this news has killed all happiness over my victory in executing my covert mission of extracting information and that too in such a way that his friend could never figure-out the real reason behind a Rose Queen patiently listening to all his nonsense sob stories and that too with my beautiful and precious smile!

Now I put the timeline of events based on this new piece of vital information: The very day when we revealed our love to each other he was flying high from his newly earned bragging rights over his conquest of the Rose Queen of the college. He had celebrated the happy news with all his drinking buds in the local pub with some cheap local alcohol to take himself even higher. All was good so far but once the euphoria ended depressive thoughts took over. After many nights with himself and alcohol, at the local pub he said his golden words as a curse to all the city Girls, especially Delhi: "One would think that once all the hardships of war are over, the winner will get to enjoy all his rewards but nothing like that happened! From all the lessons I have learnt in seducing a girl from these village girls is that indeed it takes a lot of time to get them to that point-of-no-return but when that moment finally does come, it is so beautiful that all the Investment of time and patience in enduring their constant insults on our male-egos finally pays off when the spark in us ignites a forest fire in them! Once that happens the woman becomes had with supernatural powers who is now capable of taking the man to seventh heaven, however when it comes to these city girls the only expression that comes to my mind is Aplam-Chaplam – everything around me is upside-down! Just like this case, how I assumed that getting my way with this city-girl from Delhi would be as easy as pie only to find these girls are only a big tease! I got the lesson of my life! These wretched Delhi girls dress provocatively, walk around with a big swagger, tempting the man into believing that they are ready for his advances, making all of us college boys jump over hoops to just get a chance to sit at the table next to her in the Tea shop while she does not even know anything about the dead bodies of the boys who just sacrificed their lives just to be near her! I always thought that her innocence is just an act, is for luring a stallion like me into her trap of charms and she well understands the real intent behind my advances. In short, I assumed that it is only a matter of time before she will melt in my arms! However, all my hopes get dashed when even after investing about a year of study hours in tolerating all her non-stop nonsense chatter, thinking the reward will justify all my sacrifices but that did not happen! When finally, the victorious moment came this genuinely nice lady did not even give me a peck on the cheek! Result: neither did I get heavenly sensual pleasures, nor an advancement into my career goals! Marriage with her is out of question as I am a Hindu and she a Khalsa. For any man to want sensual pleasures while still finishing studies is nothing but toxic! It is virtual suicide! All this talk of sensual pleasures at this stage is a big farce and can lead any person to one's destruction! Thanks to her for revealing to me her selfish side that I can now see the bitter truth, which is of now having to re-invest another whole year and go through the humiliation of sitting with my juniors! Now my open eyes can see that the insanity in pursuing her as my goal should really have been towards my education! Let people now call me cruel, but I will neither send nor receive any letters from her! And even if she tries to use my friends to send any messages, I will shoot that messenger with my own hands and if still her memories prove victorious in distracting me from my career goals, I will take comfort in alcohol! So now the only voice that comes out from my bleeding heart is a Curse to all these faithless Delhi girls with an ugly black scar in the middle of the forehead, so it serves as a warning to all us Men folk to never fall into the trap of their fake charms!

She is **dead** for me!"

THEN I TREMBLED – A BROKEN IMPLICIT PROMISE FROM MY VILLAGE SIMPLETON!

Dear Mayuri's Diary,

These hypocrite men sit all night talking about their woman, while really is only an excuse to go to their real love - my sworn rival - alcohol! If only I knew the scoundrel is just looking at me as some piece of entertainment for some nice evening, then I would have burnt my veil of womanly hesitations and transformed myself into a whore whose sole purpose of her life is to entertain you!

Every time I took off my armor of doubt and shield of critical reasoning this arrow of love showed no mercy on me as it pierces right through my heart right from under my nose! My curse now is that my soul must continue dragging this body which has already exhausted all its potential! **This silent teardrop is a sign of my impotence in my inability of saving my first erotic love from dying tells me that the occurrence of events is not solely dependent on the individual's strength but the likelihood of them happening is when the outside conditions are working in-sync with the individual to achieve the same goal!**

My life is a teardrop for that one object that I could never reach. Failure is not with the attempts, but the hidden delusion in me which sees an object where there is none!

OPTIMIZED THROUGHOUT

As soon as the final exam is over, it is pens down followed by a record-breaking sprint to the local railway station for the eager students to get back to the open arms of their dear Mommies open arms! True to the saying birds of the feather flock together, so too the students belonging to the same region including our Hero Vishwanath who along with other fellow-mates bond together by their birth-place allegiances. Us city-folks are often seeing marveling and envying the solidarity that these village folks show as if the clay in their land has some magical properties that unites them which makes them see one's success as something that is in some convoluted way their own! Since the rules are more relaxed for these local trains most of the youth prefer to stand near the exit which does not have any door, which for them means the freedom to stick once head out to experience the wild experience of high-speed winds touching their faces! Which also means that one wrong step and they lose their lives! No sane person would risk their lives like this but then who is not familiar with the careless decorousness of the youth, who only desires that thrill which has a close encounter with death! So, to make the moments more pleasurable one of this brotherhood decides to fetch some delicious food for himself and all the rest from the pantry compartment of the train. Little did he know his good deed was about to get rewarded, with an even tastier treat - a well-endowed mature woman, and that too alone and that too sleeping and that too with complete privacy of a first-class cabin! Now if that is not some green flag from the heavens what is! Now in this situation ethics has no place but the brain, to use all its cunning to produce some plan that will fulfill the hunger of not just him but all five of his dear friends from his brotherhood too! Now given that there is only one woman, but men are five and knowing that the modesty of a woman might prevent her from entertaining all five at the same time without completely falling in her own eyes, so the men huddle up close and whisper the strategy to each other so that the fallout is not so unpleasant in the end. So now that the first stage of strategy of Planning is complete, begins the next phase of execution! As per the strategy, the smartest in the pack goes in first. He first takes her in trust by pretending to be her well-wisher. Then he gives her a blindfold to put! She stares at him wide-eyed and asks, For what? He produces some lame excuse, like it will help block out all the light from coming in her eyes, just so she can sleep undisturbed! The laying single woman sees in him some angel in disguise, so does not see any foul intentions behind his help. She thanks him for his kind gesture. Puts on the puts on the blindfold. She sleeps. He finishes her initiation. Now once that the hardships of battle are over why delay the celebrations? Let the good times begin, as someone once wisely said that an oven takes much time to heat-up but once it reaches the required temperature baking more breads simultaneously proves to be more energy efficient and an enviable throughput.

IMPOSSIBLE / I-M-POSSIBLE?

Dear Mayuri's Diary,

This college has given me some most beautiful memorable moments of my life and yet prolonging my stay will not prolong my joy but be a hindrance to my next leap into more dangerous and challenging fields! Passing this exam is critical as without it she cannot say the final goodbye to college life, you are tempting but I cannot be bound, ahead of me are many more mountains to conquer that still beckon me... So, I too am furiously coding away, trying hard to nail down the test. Time is ticking away. For me to pass the test the program must process in the background and display 'Hence proved to be true' else display 'Hence proved to be false.' Now I am incredibly pleased with my performance. I push the button to execute the code my end to see the golden words on the screen but that does not happen! Dumb computer! Now I am floundering to make the program run before the examiner comes to her desk but to no avail! Every time I run the program the computer would display nothing, a blank screen as if I am so smart that in front of me even the intelligence of a computer is too dumbfounded to react! The examiner is coming close to my number, and I absolutely cannot afford to lose an entire year and that too for something that is not even her fault but some of the unexplainable absurd computer glitches! And when it is survival time, I can say with experience that my instincts now can outrun any computer! My mind now produces a genius idea and can fix the problem! How? Am I so intelligent that I could change the whole algorithm in a matter of few seconds to save my skin? No. I do not consider myself as some genius by any means but can confidently say that I am smart! I just added an inconspicuous statement that prevents the actual code from executing and instead prints out a static statement which will always print the same line of 'Hence proved to be true'!

The examiner comes who had been seeing her from long, seeing her struggling in trying to get her program to run, so now when he sees results that are against his expectations, he stands there stunned as if he just saw some miracle! These results that he is seeing are in direct conflict with his convictions and yet he cannot dispute it as the computer is like some Gospel. It cannot lie! He exclaims, "Miracle! I just saw a miracle happen in front of my eyes! Here I was thinking this task is impossible to be in a few minutes but now thanks to this young girl for showing me that the word impossible is really 'I am possible' in this dictionary of the brave and intelligent." I say a short thanks to him and as I walk quickly out of his presence, I let out a deep sigh of relief for dodging that bullet for sure! Ethics will not be pleased but at least I am not not dead! Seems, I am just another silly being always trying to do the right thing as best as I can. Saying this I wipe an imaginary sweat from my brow proving once again to myself that indeed I am not some genius but just another silly being just not from Planet Earth but Venus?!

THEN I BURNT ALL BRIDGES LEADING
TO PLACES OF WORSHIP

Mayuri is laying in a Yoga Cobra Position with a book laying in front of her, a ruse for tricking her mother into believing that she is busy in reading the content of the novel while her Mother being her Mother is double smart so she is trying hard to hold her tongue till her usually chirpy daughter breaks the uncomfortable silence herself, but to her surprise she has still not heard any word, not even the sound of a page being flipped reminding her of the words of a poet who once rightly said, "when the lips are silent, the heart is full!" Mother Aditi wonders to herself, "Is not then what appearing to the naked eye nothing but the exact opposite of reality! A naked picture of actuality hanging upside-down, just like when the world says sun rises in the east and then sets in the west, is false but in the given perspective true! Fact is that the sun which appears moving is static, while the Earth which appears static is really moving. Similarly, myself being a mother too can use my deeper motherly insights that can fail even the topmost detectives from Scotland Yard! These aging eyes can now quickly detect some turmoil beneath that calm exterior on my daughter's face."

These mothers need no advance degrees to learn these tricks to trick any criminal into a confession, as this advanced Science just come to them naturally after hosting and nourishing a parasite more than their own self. The daughter bears her secret in her heart, like an arrow that keeps getting driven deeper and deeper by the moment. In this scenario her Ethics demands from the mother to kill her own daughter, who she loves, by pulling the arrow out of her, thus rid her from all the pain finally!

Mother has some inkling, that she might hear something that she does not hear and yet now that she stands aware of the root of the problem, she begins her role as some hard-hearted tyrant! Being a deeply religious woman, who believes in defending religious beliefs over her own life and if necessary, the life of her daughter's too through who her blood still lives! She stoically tells her decision: "My duty to The SuperKundalini and my own religious beliefs are higher than my duty as a mother to you. So, if it comes to choosing between my family honor or you, I will not even flinch an eye in sacrificing your love, you, and the boy in question as my offering to The SuperKundalini! You do not agree to my decision, the consequences will not be severe. There will be no further debate on this topic. You cannot say anything that can change it."

There is no difference between a Nazi or a mother. Both are control freaks! Mother sees herself as a representative, whose duty is to protect the whole religion from collapsing, even if it means sacrificing her own blood for it! Since, the same blood is also running in the daughter's veins too, the daughter is ready to raise a storm that can put the entire world in a turmoil and yet when she stretches her hand to pick her sword, her hand trembles, the sword drops, as no explanation can ever justify going for a war whose cause is long dead! To cause all the bloodshed of one's own, just for the sake of fighting is absurd and even-if all the youthful energies have taken firm control over her head, is not enough to reach that point of a rebellion!

Now whenever the topics related to religion arise the daughter's young hot blood boils and she begins a Tongue War with any of these religious fanatics who happen to unfortunately cross paths with her! So vehemently she argues with them as if these were the very people who have murdered her first love and yet now that the only possibility left is talk which cannot alter any outcomes, she derives her joy out of this whole episode by some enlightening debates to shut her opponents' mouths! She starts the attempt to convert all the world's religious fanatics into aware individuals one person at a time starting from her mother.

Mayuri: "My dream is that now that the cause for which Khalsa Religion was created has been fulfilled, all of us now unite back with our Hindu origins, just like River Ganga and River Yamuna unite ... Why does our society discriminate over Religion when the eternal laws do not? Is not religion one of the biggest man-made deceptions, as on the one hand their manifestos claim that it can help us connect to God while really their main real secret agenda seems to be is to divide mankind over their bloodlines, their Gotra/ Lineages and so this way, it is not just their own future that is secure, but also of all their subsequent generations to come!?

If we see closely, we find uncanny similarities between the way that the solar-planetary system is and the smallest particle in any matter - an atom is! Can we now not see how enforcing human laws based on Religion contradicts God's Design Principles and therefore are bound to lead our lives into the ditch of unwanted chaos!?

The main reason that religions has become a huge burden on us, and the future generations is because now it is us who must carry the burden of the carcass of a dinosaur which has long lost its relevance, is neither modifiable nor extensible - both properties of a poor design! **The only relationship at Eternal Level is simply humanity!**

Ideally the main intent behind any place of worship is to offer a place where people from all levels of society can get together with the motive of discovering and connecting more with the Spiritual Aspect of our existence, however instead of meeting that goal, the goal which we ended up meeting is just the exact opposite! The devil in the form of money and power has made their home here. I can now see how religion has become the opposite of the intent of its creation!

If The Creator of All has designed us in a such a way that everyone have their own separate brain and not just the Leader of our Pack has, then does it not mean that the expectation is that we all use our own too?! Is to not use our brain the way God intended a form of insult to his Design that he intended for us?! Why listen to these Religious Preachers claiming to know God and His ways, when even the Authors who wrote about Him, say agreeing in unison, that God and His ways are simply incomprehensible! Then how can anyone stand on a pedestal and claim that he can help us understand God when on the other hand they are also saying that He and His ways are incomprehensible?!

When the very founder of my Khalsa Religion Guru Govind Singh has himself said He is not The SuperKundalini, he is His slave and if anyone says otherwise, may he go to hell! Then who are we, with much lesser awareness levels than Him to not obey His instructions for us? Undoubtedly, Guru Govind Singh ji is one of the Greatest of Greatest saint-warriors to have ever existed in world history! He is the one of the most fortunate one amongst us all as God chose him to destroy the evil tyrant forces of the Mughal Emperors who were out to convert every person into their own religion. These Mughals burnt millions of books, did irreparable damage to our Vedic Heritage and one of the few braves who fought with them valiantly were people from my Khalsa community! The sacrifices of people from Khalsa Religion are un-paralleled!

Some of them tortured by burning them alive, some from being sawed-off from the middle, along with many other evil forms of tortures that are impossible for a normal person to go through, which means for anyone to be able to go through such tortures must be someone who has developed Powers that are God-like! Shri Guru Arjun dev ji, the fifth Guru of Khalsa was made to sit on a hot, burning plate, with hot sand being poured on him and when any person can tolerate such immense pain and yet not surrender then must mean that that someone has to be someone who is blessed with Superpowers so much so that these blood-chilling stories can make anyone wonder if God himself has taken birth in his Avatar/form! Khalsa history is full of instances of Khalsa Saints showing unexceptional valor in staying strong while having to go through pain which was crossing all pain thresholds and yet not surrendering to the evil forces! The youngest sons of tenth Guru - Guru Govind Singh ji, one six and one nine, courage and strength level, no human can ever reach in the entire history of Mankind! By choosing death over living a life with compromises with the Ethical Self, they indeed reached the levels of God itself...

There choices were death or death before death, they chose life by choosing Death!

We come from the lineage of these great people and yet today's Khalsa is losing its character due to false interpretations over ages now! The Khalsa authorities are trying to distance themselves from the Hindu Religion to have a separate identity. This is the biggest mistake the Khalsa Religion is making as the Vedic Heritage is not the property of Hindu Religion or any other! Vedic Heritage is like a manual for a scientific approach to living, meant for teaching us about our relationship with the ecosystem that we live in, so that this beautiful creation can co-exist peacefully. Hindus are just another religion like Khalsa who inherit the same Vedic Heritage, then it is the biggest loss for Khalsa Religion if they label it as the property of the Hindu's and start distancing themselves from this ocean of wealth of knowledge, written by our ancestors, for the benefit of everyone! Why should Khalsa History lose all that knowledge from the Ved shastr/ Literature, when our history does not even begin from the day we were born! Khalsa Scriptures are an addition to the Vedic Heritage and not a Subtraction!"

Mother Aditi: "Our Religious Duty is to protect us and our lineages only. You are only saying this because your love for a man from different Religion failed! Your lustful desires cry over the loss of your object of desire and yet I give a deep sigh of relief! You say you want to get married to this man not realizing that if this love-story had not ended the way it did, you would have been miserable! Marriage would have been like investing all youthful energies in trying to put life in that one moment that is long dead, just like these golden years that you had the good fortune of knowing what 'falling' in love means!"

Mayuri fell silent, shed a silent tear over my impotence, made her heart a little Temple of The SuperKundalini and stopped going to any synthetic places-for-worship Businesses!

THE EXCLUDED MIDDLE

Dear Mayuri's Diary,

This pain over the loss of the one and only who could ever quench my thirst for experiencing the powers in love, is immeasurable! Even more is my Faith in love! For me to love again is impossible as it takes a Heart to love and that I do not have with me anymore! These tears teach me, that **life is a teardrop for that one object that I could never reach. Failure is not with the attempts, but the hidden delusion in me which sees an object where there is none!**

Even if the outcome of this love-story is of no consequence anymore still the warrior in me is still blood thirsty because the cause is still there, because this toxic environment that favors only cowardice and not the divine values of empathy and love is still alive and flourishing over the carcasses of failed love-affairs, because these artificial man-made conditions which will never let any prospects for any inter-religion marriage to flourish are still active!

This Epidemic has not only infected my Past but also my Future Prospects as now I am having to choose within a box of my Religion and that too with limited options! Now I must choose between the two following Scenarios: Either I marry outside my religion just out of spite for this whole religion-based society then it is not fair to the other partner as the fundamental Principle behind any marriage is Love while the basis of such a Marriage is the very Principle that is against my Ethics - Vendetta and Hatred! So, scratch-off this possibility for good!

Now when evaluating the other "or" Possibility of marrying

within my community with the consent of my Family and the groom's then all my and his near and dear family circle will be happy except me! Compromising with the Ethical Self in me means that I am a disgrace in the eyes of my Father of All Fathers! To spend the rest of my life as a spiritless coward who is no longer the self that it was meant to be, is a compromise that is also unacceptable. So now since both the choices mean death for me, I choose the possibility of the excluded middle to never marry!

Despite knowing that this became one of the main reasons of Bhisham Pitamah in Epic Mahabharat to lay on a bed of arrows still I too like him to stay firm on my resolve take this life-altering Pledge!

Using this burning fire on this candle as my witness, I burn all bridges that can ever lead me towards blissful domesticity by taking this pledge:

I WILL NEVER MARRY!
I WILL NEVER MARRY!
I WILL NEVER MARRY!

PHASE THREE OF LIFE:
WHEN THE BRAIN IS KING

THE PRIMAL DESIRE FOR
PRACTICAL EXPERIENCE /
TAUTOLOGIES IN EXECUTION

Degrees are like Philosophy - lot of relevance in idol gossip but nothing in Practical Applications...

A FACTORY PATTERN / WHEN I COULD NOT STOP LAUGHING

Dear Mayuri's Diary,

High on power and money, these multinationals take pride in their abilities of having the most talented people to work for them. Dressed in their best finery, smelling with expensive designer perfumes, and flashing their obscene money from their bulging designer purses which any queen of sass would envy, they will use all tricks in the world just to meet their Target numbers! Beg, borrow, or steal to get these fresh graduates in their beautiful web of handsome bonuses, filthy rich salaries, a dream of a secure future and not to mention the Honor and Prestige that comes with it, even if such high words are a dinosaur and are really words used for evoking some laughter!

My youthful energies are now burning on full cylinders, they want me to create new systems that can change the world, to satiate my thirst for learning by not just reading but by actual implementation! I begin to feel invincible! I jump two feet on the bandwagon feeling unstoppable only to find that the Role assigned to me is that of a cog-in-a-wheel which will enable me to do this same task effectively for sure but never grow out of that role! These tasks, must be a work of some crafty Fox of a manager, as is clear from tiny chunks she has made that will ensure that the bigger picture never appears! These assigned tasks do nothing towards enriching the skill set for learning the art have an opposite effect of dulling the thinking abilities. To hide their true intent, they have thrown in temptations of fancy cubicles, free phone and not to forget some free staplers thrown in for some comical relief, in this process stealing from us our asset of our youthful energies! As a Fresh Graduate I feel ashamed of myself for having sold myself short, ashamed of becoming just another hypocrite in this Hypocritical Society!

It is the Youth that make the Society and not vice-versa! When has becoming one with the 'dime a dozen' crowd ever paid, that it will now? Ancient wisdom says that every individual is powerful like The SuperKundalini, having exemplary powers that can move Mountains with just the tip of a finger, then why do we not see such miracles in this age? These people know not that they just threw away diamonds of their most valuable Years in exchange for these false comforts, which money can never buy back! When I saw this, I laughed! Picking up my bag and left never to return ...

WELCOME THE LEARNING-TREE INCORPORATED / WHEN I COULD NOT STOP CRYING

A BUILDER PATTERN

Dear Mayuri's Diary,

Leaving that high-paying primo-crap job cold-turkey should have left me anxious over my future but this did not happen and instead I am experiencing a strange calm and gratitude from the soul in me for not subjecting me with the torture of sitting all day and doing nothing challenging! Not choosing a job that is offering high pay along with the security of a stable job over a job that is paying less but is giving me valuable experience in my trade might seem foolish as ultimately to survive in this highly competitive dog-eat-dog world we all need money, but this is being short-sighted! The priority for an amateur should be learning and gaining experience. The more skillful the person the more the money one can expect to follow automatically. So, now the next company that I choose is one that offers me a steep growth curve by giving me the experience that will sharpen my saw never the one which cheats me of my real thrills by deceiving me with some fancy rewards like a personal cube with a personal stapler thrown in for some comic relief!

It is as if it were just a matter of me praying with conviction that now my eyes could now see what I did not before - a small and simple worded advertisement looking for new graduates. I saw it as a good sign as it suggests that there is no Human Resources Department which means there is no intermediaries creating confusions just so they can push their personal agendas of getting their nephews and nieces over real talent! My eyes popped in disbelief on seeing such a rare learning opportunity which will give me an opportunity of getting my hands dirty with the core components in a complex system! Now getting this job means everything to me! Once such an experience is under my belt, my foundation will become so strong that even if the technologies change, I can go with the flow! But all my hopes get dashed when I read the next sentence. I meet all the requirements for the job but the one that is also mandatory! My resume has every skill that a newcomer can have except that mandatory prerequisite that is necessary for me to fulfill all my high ambitions! Damn fate! If only I had the required project in assembly language and not the C language the job would have been mine! Now what do I do? The thought of consequences would deter any wise person, but since I am not at that level of these intellectuals, I do the unthinkable. With trembling hands, I lie a little in my resume! Even if it is something that the court of ethics might let me get away with a wink but not the courts of any country! To not lose this excellent opportunity of a lifetime, without giving any more thought I risk it all by making a small modification. I justify to the ethics in me by this reasoning: Since the implementation is the same and it is just the language that is different is like a small technical difficulty, erasing which is necessary to fool any radical manager who might jeopardize all my goals otherwise! I smile when I learn the results from the tricky round of interview ‒ Pass and that too with flying colors!

Now for the next round, I am putting all my efforts in the choice of attire. I learn from the news readers how they dress, so that attention stays more on the content on my Computer-Software Engineer, than my dynamic personality. So, I choose some simple yet presentable clothes, well-oiled hair, and a charming smile as the only ornament for my angelic Face! I am good at impressing people with my communication skills and yet I save them for much later. I do not start any unnecessary conversations, speak only when spoken to. My gaze is steady looking directly ahead or the floor to avoid any eye contacts. This I do because this way no one can make any certain impressions of me and then everyone around me is busy trying to decode the mystery that I am!

Turns out that the hiring manager is also the project manager, in short, he is the most important person for me currently as in his hands lie my entire future. He sounds deeply knowledgeable and must have good intellect how else do you think he is running a whole business, for me it is a sign that he must be some cunning negotiator! Being a small company, he tells me that because there are no complex hierarchy in the company he will not have to go through several layers of approval, so he can make his offer on the spot. Saying in a very matter-of-fact way: "We are a small company. These big multi-national companies can offer kinds of monetary benefits which the small companies can never even dream of, yet I am confident of what I am offering and confident that being smart know that this offer has as much benefit for me as you! Is not face an index of the inside? And when it does reveal the secret to the outside, it only betrays the inside! That is why a poker face makes the best gambler! He offers me a salary much less than the industry standards. Still, I accept the offer with a smile. Sign on the spot to become the latest proud employee of the company THE-LEARN-ING-TREE Inc. On walking out of the office, I cannot help but laugh over out-smarting the most cunning of the cunning Businessman as I say to myself, "Mr. Manager, you who may be the best negotiator ever born on the planet but still not better than me as you just got deceived by my poker face as in reality it was me who was getting ready to pay you for gaining the experience but instead now you are paying me for the experience I am gaining! Please accept my gratitude once again!

On the first day of my starting my new job, I have the pleasure of meeting the other employee Siddharth, who just started with me is looking miserable; The small size of the Office is an insult to his prestige! He is constantly comparing the amenities that people working in big offices get! Due to his quibbling nature, he cannot find any rest till finally he decides to leave! All the colleagues, including me come to see him to wish him farewell. I smilingly say to him, "I wish you well my dear colleague, my rival, may you find your peace and happiness in doing whatever pleases you." And then waving him goodbye, I whisper to myself, "I will not envy your pleasures as my intelligence abhors the things that you find thrilling!"

VIRTUAL SERVANT

Just conquered a mountain, even it was of my clothes only hehehe...

Dear Mayuri's Diary,

I have seen that if I am doing just one task single-mindedly, I can conduct many complex tasks but the moment a worrying thought of other pending tasks enters, I fail!

However, to create such a disturbance-free environment in this modern world is virtually next to impossible, especially with this monster-size house that I live in, which needs my constant attention, along with the many other tasks that I must do just to support my basic Lifestyle! So, what did I do to enable myself to do tasks sure footed? First, I looked for my answers in how our ancestors dealt with this problem. Well, they hired Servants! Great idea but damn these high paying Politicians for not doing a good enough job in keeping the poor, poor enough! So now what was dirt cheap then, now it costs a lot more and then also, even if you still chose to hire the outcome is still a compromise as managing of these workers is a whole another headache to deal with!

So now what I am doing? I am setting up an automated Virtual Servant for myself! I spend a generous amount of time up-front in the first set-up of all the available options customized to serve my needs, my way!

Now on too other tasks that also need my full attention! ...

CHAIN OF RESPONSIBILITY

Dear Mayuri's Diary,

First let me set the context by narrating a story that my grandmother told me when I was still a child. 'This is a story about four people named Everybody, Somebody, Anybody and Nobody. There was an important job to be, and Everybody was sure that Somebody would do it. Anybody could have it, but Nobody did it. Somebody got angry about that because it was Everybody's job. Everybody thought Anybody could do it, but Nobody realized that Everybody would not do it. It ended up that Everybody blamed Somebody when Nobody did what Anybody could have!' Now that I am working in the Corporate World, I can appreciate it better. So, I refused to accept the offer for a managerial position even if the monetary benefits far outstripped what my current position as a developer was getting! The title is associated with a lot of power over the rest of the team and more prestige and money and yet if I choose this possibility, I rob myself from all the joy that can only come in seeing one's contribution into the creative process come to life! Also, giving guarantee over the quality of my own work is one thing but when it comes to being accountable for someone else's work nightmare begins right then. I am barking but no one listens! Therefore, for the sake of my sanity, I politely dodge all promotions!

MUTE THAT TONGUE
MISS CHATTERBOX

Once the life-changing product on which I had been working on, putting in over fourteen-hours in a day, not to forget the hours put over the weekends with my team in Learning-Tree Inc. is finally ready, we all in unison were ready to sue the scientist who told us that time is a constant while what we just saw was that the time shrinks when people are enjoying their work!

Mayuri: We all fellow developers are rejoicing on seeing our effort take shape, little did we know that we just celebrated our own funeral instead! While us geeks are excited over the thought of nice rewards coming our way as a token of appreciation for our work, the Management has already made it is list ready for axing the fat cats amongst the already thin cats as now the need is not for developers but of marketing teams inclusive of beautiful Ladies and slick talking Salespeople who can now sell the Product! Deception Alert right there! A Person with integrity would at least give some notice in advance but these businesspeople are like prostitutes, the only thing that matters to them is the balance sheets showing higher Profit Margins!

It does not take much time for the Manager in finding his scapegoat! With true feminine nature, I too have trouble keeping secrets. My tongue is itching to brag about my success in a place where I did not even meet the criteria for admission! How I not let some silly hiccup, come in the way of what I wanted! And who can be better to brag to than the Person who had foolishly walked away from the opportunity of a lifetime - Siddharth putting my career in the high gear! In my euphoric mood, I call him to tell him the secret which enabled me to get this job.

Now I am laughing and telling him all about how I fooled the Manager into believing that I am a pro in Computer Language - Assembly, while really, she knew nothing about this one but instead knew another Computer Language - C! The truth is that I learnt that language as I was using! I laugh even harder as I make him more aware of his losses in comparison to my gains! For the same bet where your carrier sunk miserably mine took off at escape velocity!

What mostly catches a thief is not the smartest police officer, but its own Tongue, as the tongue is competing with the mind and because she has no mind to process her response, is quicker and can end-up putting the person in greater trouble!

We still live in a hypocritical society, full of quick to judge people are the ones who will never be able to see the genius behind my accomplishment I could never bring myself to share it with you but now I do not know why I am going against my own Values! The next moment what do you think I am doing!? I am calling the very phone who will get kill himself when he learns about how much he lost in the same transaction in which my gains were simply infinite! Once I am letting my tongue slip-out all the dirty tricks I employed to win, I trembled! Now I feel as exposed as a naked man standing in front of a defeated person who just learnt the cause of all his misery is me and is a good chance that the first chance, he gets he will not hesitate in firing a bullet right through the middle of my forehead! Now the situation for this clever person is more like of the mad man who kept cutting the very branch on which he was sitting!"

Now that the cat is out of the bag, there is no telling how much damage the cat will do! Siddharth first looks around at his huge cube, then his dear stapler and finds some comfort for some time. The next moment he is cursing his tasks which are minor, monotonous and brain-numbing. After weighing diverse options, this disgruntled employee comes-up with a plan to take his revenge! With a cunning smile on Siddharth's face, he loses no time in calling the Manager on the phone to tells him everything. All about how she had made a fool of the company and more importantly, the manager, himself! He begins by describing the deviousness of this arrogant woman who lied to climb the corporate ladder, trampling his Image as the smartest businessperson in the whole corporate world by some new-comer and the humiliation does not just end there because this person is a woman in our male-dominated Industry and who is half his age!

Hearing all this and the upcoming budget cuts gives him a good excuse in wielding the ax on me in the cruelest manner he could think of. The drama does not just end with firing me on the spot but also ruin all my prospects of ever appearing as a competition to him by spoiling my history which companies refer to for making their silly background-checks!

Now I know not how to punish my silly tongue for ruining everything for I had been working hard for years, all destroyed in a matter of few seconds! The only consolation that I have is that I got what I wanted and that no cruel boss can ever snatch it from me - Knowledge!

When I get home, my mother already knew everything about the firing from my job, conveyed by my generous manager himself conveyed by a personal phone call.

Mother Aditi: It is in our own interest to learn to keep our secrets and not even share it with these silent trees! Let me tell you a story which will help you grasp the point better: Once upon a time there was a barber who shared a top-secret about the king not having any ears to a tree! Days went by and nothing happened. One fine day some tree-cutter cuts that tree and then makes a drum out of it. When the drum gets in the hands of a drumbeater and then as he went around the whole town beating the Drum, the Drum would start revealing the king's secret to everybody: 'The king has no ears! The king has no ears! The king has no ears! The King felt so angry that he had the drumbeater executed!

Moral of the Story: My Dear little Chatterbox Daughter, your face should not reveal anything that is happening inside to anyone including me! Just, lock all your secrets in your heart and then throw that key in the depths of River Yamuna!

THE WHITE SWAN CARRIER PATH

After much deliberations, with keeping all inputs from various sources, his vision cleared, just as when in encryption experts uncover the real message by cleaning the slate with chemicals, and bring the hidden message to the front, so emerged the message meant for him, and only him, with golden letters flashing in bold colors, which he declared aloud to himself, "My way is not a walk in the park, but the way which goes up the mountain, down the river, through the ditches. I am that swan, whose wings are still weak, eyes still hazy, and yet has the wings, powered with a willpower that can help me fly across the oceans... Just like a swan, as mentioned in the scriptures is a bird who is equally at home when on land or when in water; Similarly, I feel that whether I become a geeky Math Professorial in India or a Hedge Fund Manager in The New York Stock Exchange, NYSE, does not really matter, what matters is, that I have the fire in me, burn bright every day on the thought of working on my job. Then I can put my soul into my creation. Once a product carries my signature is bound to be beautiful. Then, when I see my creation, my soul will swell with real pride that can only come by doing a decent job. This thought puts my body in immense peace, otherwise a life without the challenge of solving new puzzles every time I start my work, my body will sink in despair ... With that concluding thought all my doubts have gone, I know my choice. It is where my passion lies.

Once he gets his direction, he smiles with peace spread all over his face...

A GIANT LEAP TO FREEDOM

Fly bird, fly!
Make your nest oceans away,
where you cannot hear any distracting cries from the loved ones,
breaking away all bondages of Native Culture and Religion biases,
so, you can listen to the silence beating in your heart,
To discover that you are an enigma in yourself,
solving this labyrinth in me is indeed time well spent...

1998 – THE DOT COM BOOM / DEMAND AND SUPPLY RULE!

Fire flowers are blooming, creating a beautiful view as if there is fire everywhere, in perfect harmony with the dawn of the dot-com era, in the early 1990's. It is a war time! Like in a War, even if a person has committed the worst of crimes, he still gets pardoned, recruited as a Soldier, similarly now all my faults too get pardoned, recruited as a Computer Engineer!

Being in the right industry, at the right time, is the magic pill for success! The internet is just taking off at the speed of light! If the same amount of investment of efforts here, give returns many folds, then it is not cowardly, but foolish not to jump onto this Boat to Heaven!

Mayuri, heaved a sigh of relief when she saw, when demand is outstripping the supply, background checks are being only for some comical relief and this crack in the system came as good fortune for Mayuri to slip through! Her gamble of working for a company for experience over money pays-off, that too with Infinite gains! She now has upper hand when negotiating with the strong companies in the US, who were willingly throwing filthy amount of compensation to get her to choose them! Their only concern? They do not lose her! How the tables have turned!

Holding her ticket to the US, she does not forget to call Siddharth for thanking him to become the cause of her losing her career in India, as if it were not for this hard kick, she would never have tried looking for a new opportunity, due to being stuck with her old company where her growth had already stagnated and would not have started looking elsewhere due to her feelings of loyalty for the company which is instrumental in giving her career a strong rock-like foundation.

MOTHER - A SILENT
MELANCHOLIC BEAUTY

Dear Mayuri's Diary,

Every time people give credit to me for this monumental achievement of mine, I begin to feel uneasy. I begin to question myself to find the cause behind all this uneasiness Then as my eyes are darting back-and-forth all the anxiety ends as my eyes rest when they see the picture of my Parents Wedding Picture. I smile as now I know I have the answer to my question! The reason behind my uneasiness is that when I am accepting the credit as my sole achievement, I am really being a thief who is stealing the credit from the real architect behind making this moment happen! Someone whose wrinkles are hiding many untold stories of a love that gives without expecting anything in return! Someone who makes silent sacrifices of one's own desires to make her children's desires a reality! I never had to worry about hunger as mother did an excellent job in managing the heavy meal requirements for growing children so well that we did not even know what hunger means! This helped me immensely, as this freed up a lot of time for me to focus on my demanding career goals! She sacrificed her desires of going for parties and social gatherings just so we children could!

With this thought, I have tears in my eyes. I am now running toward my parent's room, singing out loudly for everyone to hear,

'Hail Mother for her unparalleled Sacrifices!
Hail Mother for bearing pain to give us life!

Hail Mother for painting her breast black, so we can fly away from her to conquer new frontiers!'

Then when I see my parents sitting side by side, first I touch my mother and father's beautiful lotus feet as a gesture of my gratitude towards them. I thank them for showing me the meaning of true love not just by words but by their actions, a debt that will take for me many lifetimes to repay! You were like the wind beneath my wings, enabling me to sour even higher and thus be successful in completing this daring and life-altering Voyage across the oceans all by myself!

C(D)REEM BOY!

Mother says parting advice to her dreamy-eyed daughter, "I always shielded you from the evil eyes of the deluded souls that exist in the real world. The sheltered life that I created for you has its relevance in a sheltered environment of a loving family. When the Designer of all Designers created beautiful Rose Flower, also created a thorn for its protection. Which teaches us that not everyone is a friend! Your sheltered eyes still only see goodness in everyone, while outside is a jungle out there; and since the rules of the jungle are vastly different learn to adapt with the demands of the unfamiliar environment."

One would think that after listening to this little philosophical dissertation, the daughter will never get in trouble, but problem is that how could she even hear a word when her body and soul are already in America having engaging rendezvous with the best of the bread at the one stop shop for the whole big imperfect world - America! ...

THEN I LEARNT THE
SCIENCE OF SOCIOLOGY

DAY AND NIGHT DIFFERENCES

Dear Mayuri's Diary,

As I open the golden door to freedom of living my life the way I want, I feel vindicated for all my actions which made ethics frown. If I were to calculate the size of changes and preparation needed, I could never had been able to make the leap to Infinity, so I tricked my brain into looking at this life-changing at it some non-event, a nothing, so this way the whole anxiety which comes from grand expectations vanished!

When people see me, they mistake me to be some inexperienced, frail, vulnerable foreigner, who they can trick easily, but what they do not know is that I am well-armed, wearing my armor of my smartness, my vocational skillset, which makes me invincible. Wearing this armor, no evil monsters can now prevent me from getting situated in a country with differences as wide as night and day!

SHE THINKS SHE IS SOME GODDESS!

Never could have thought that I who always saw herself as the fire in a speech, will ever get to see a day when I discover that the stutter in a speech is also me...

Dear Mayuri's Diary,

After my unpleasant experience with my first aware love, I was sure I will never be able to love again. What do you think happens next? I am in love! There is no catalyst potent than love, I feel possessed with demonic powers strong enough to die in my pursuit for my target. I, who has slain India in one step, will have this Cowboy from Georgia on his knees in no time! How pure he must be, after all white is the only color that reflects everything, keeps nothing for itself... He must already know all about my prowess as just being here and working in the same prestigious company as him. Is proof enough, so I need not tell him all about it, and so instead to impress him will use some other techniques under my belt!

Using some pretext, I go to his cube in-order to impress him with my intelligent philosophical insights on the more interesting topics in the world. However, that did not happen. Instead, much to my horror all words coming out of my mouth were nothing but an unintelligible garble! If my dear Boss Atlas were someone who is a fellow colleague, he would have burst out laughing on my face, but since he did not, he proved his superiority by managing this embarrassing situation very elegantly by just looking away helping me recover enough to make a hasty exit from the spot! Shocked from looking like a complete bungling idiot and that too in front of the very man I wanted to cut this tongue of mine for betraying me at the most crucial moment of my life when I needed it the most! But because of her past stellar performances in clearing all sorts of misunderstandings I need her to perform once more, when I have my next 'accidental meeting' with him, dressed in my brand-new stellar Avatar! Since I am no bungler but a fighter, without wasting any more time, the same day, I hit the local mall to buy myself a whole new wardrobe! I buy make-up that matches white people, this way he will see me as one of his own and then embrace me into his strong arms! as if I am competing with my white boss to show him who is really the superior one, I will transform my skin into white too! I check my wallet, no new money yet, which means ideally, I should be waiting for the next paycheck, but these are exceptional times, means exceptional steps too! So, I use every cent from my meagre savings from my earlier job in India to wipe my Indian identity and transform into my new white American version!

I forget my original accent and instead try talking in American accent but only succeed in speaking with an accent which can nei-ther be called "American English", nor my native tongue Hindi, but a cocktail of the two which can best describe as 'Hinglish'!

Now I first have a little bon-fire of all my clothing which remote-ly would clue people about my origins! After the burning ceremo-ny is over, I buy new chic high-heeled sandals, buy men's clothing to look more powerful, clothes that were bolder, almost clashing colors, put on fake rouge! Now I know not why, I the picture of the red butt of a monkey just flashed in front of my eyes! Dismiss-ing that negative evil thought, I go on to smear my face with white Talcum- Powder. Again, I have no idea why I am looking like some brown-woman, wearing a borrowed face from some white-woman! Even after all the massive changes I have a strong feeling that something somewhere is lacking, something which is showing her true origins and so, lo and behold out go my long black hair, cutting of which is like cutting sacred ties with my religion and my nationality!

As I cut my long hair, I laugh with Guru Govind Singh ji, the founder of our religion, and say what he would have said today on seeing the Khalsa of today, 'If only I knew making a new religion will make my future generations stop using their brains and not adapt to the current times, then I would never would have founded another religion in the first place!' Now by breaking the Khalsa rule of never cutting your hair to adapt to the new environment, it is me who is being true to my Khalsa Spirit, by freeing myself from the false notion of Khalsa! Now I even suspect a conspiracy behind it by the enemy who is tricking us by using our love for our ancestors against us, so we stay in the dark and never progress! It is only now by choosing for self myself what is best for my survival in the new conditions am I being true to the essence of my religion, while earlier I was just a coward!

This new make-over will have my boss ogling at me only, for sure! Now I feel pleased with my new transformed version. My looks make me look like a native, but I know not from where to get the matching attitude as without it I have a bad feeling that I am looking like a monkey from my native land!

THE START OF THE GREAT LEVELING BETWEEN THE FILTHY RICH WEST AND THE INSANELY POOR EAST

My Boss Atlas is still unaware of my new transformation into Chhandi, The Warrior Princess! After my stunning make-over I want to run straight to his Cubicle for him to see me, but damn these womanly hesitations embedded deep in us women's Nature, now I will have to wait till the coffee break! After painful hours of waiting, I head towards the kitchen. My plan is to just take my coffee cup and then quickly leave giving my Boss just enough time to see my new stunning Avatar! Unfortunately for me he was not alone but with Ann, the human resources manager. Now I have not just succeeded in winning his attention but also the attention of the evil eye of Ann.

I am leaving but curiosity in me makes me invade all privacy rules preventing us from eves-dropping on private conversations:

"This foreigner thinks she is some Goddess! Once we know we can import monkeys from India for doing our high-skill jobs too, that too at the cost of a banana then in no time we shall see everything inverted! They will be enjoying our lavish lifestyles while we will be sitting on the sidelines eating bananas! I can foresee the great leveling of economies happing in the extremely near future!"

He picks two bananas lying in front of them.

"Will you like a banana?"

"I hate bananas!"

"These foreigners from poor countries are not just content in taking our jobs as now they have started eying our menfolk too! It is our duty as the pure breed to pounce on the first opportunity of firing her from her job and then the strict Work Visa Rules will ensure that she gets sent back to where she came from!"

I am now giving a virtual pat on the back of past-Mayuri for not falling in the trap of privacy laws that only protect these sinners who made these laws! If it were not for this feedback, I would have only become a laughingstock in the eyes of the man I want, never his Heroin! I am feeling sick to my stomach as what I just heard was my death-sentence for a life that did not even get a chance to perform! What makes me feel even worse is that my assumption of seeing in someone as my life-long confidante turnout to be dangerous! He has absolute power being one of the most influential people in the company, the moment I end up doing something silly that upsets him that will be end of my life in this Promised Land for sure!

DEVIL'S NOTICE - THE H1B VISA

Dear Mayuri's Diary,

How I envy these people who can eat about anything without any trouble! Since me ALSO being one of those unfortunate ones who cannot, the key to our kind's survival is to avoid any unintentional hurt of bloated egos who might take it as an insult if you find their food unpalatable! Therefore, to cut any possibility of any such fatal occurrence making a meal out of me instead of the cow, I decide on not going to the party after work and make my secret plan to sneak out of the back door and then head anywhere but the party!

"Na bajega baans, na bajegi bansuri"(Without a Bamboo, a flute cannot play!) Convincing myself, I jump from my chair to leave unnoticed, but damn the Law of Attraction, the very person who I am trying to avoid is the very person who is about to enter from the same door from which I am about to exit! Now him knowing my driving skills, his best possibility is to be off the Road when I am on that Road, so acting like a good Samaritan he offers me a ride. Seeing I just hit a brick-wall, I too accept this invitation to my funeral with a smile!

All colleagues including myself are in the big Garden, enjoying a free flow of appetizers and drinks. We both have now arrived at the event together. In front of us are a sea of dishes for everyone along with our dear Human Resources Manager Ann. We both sit together as Ann immediately begins doing the honor of fixing them with a plate of a nice looking, juicy burger. I try to be positive about this incidence and try to use this opportunity for diffusing all the tension between us. I strike a little casual conversation and then with my mouth-full of food I ask him more about this object in my mouth that has an alien taste like never met ever before! Cutting him short, Manager Ann starts answering for him, "A beef patty that I have made myself just for this occasion!". Now I will do anything to impress my boss and fit in with the high-class people, so despite knowing that it is against our religious teachings of not eat this animal I begin swallowing this bitter pill! Now the cause behind my inability in eating this animal has nothing to do with ethics but once again, yes you guessed it right, my dear Mother! How? As she must have done a wonderful job of teaching me of never eating cow, as without my knowledge, the rebel insanity in me, conspiring against my will behind my back, shows me who is the boss by completely overriding my rational attempt of going with the flow! Like a reflux all contents in my stomach make their way out with full force from my mouth and then like a fountain of gross motley of various beautiful colors, settles comfortably on dear Ann's elegant designer shirt with 'Pretentious People' embroidered on it! This shirt happens to be particularly special, partly because her dear father had so lovingly gifted it to her on her birthday! Manager Ann now knows she is looking like marshmallow dipped in chocolate and so no one can blame the rest of the crowd formed of fellow Immigrants from bursting out laughing!

Now Ann in a tyrannical fit of anger shouts, "To prevent such a travesty from repeating again, we should give her such a punishment that will serve as an example for all the future newcomers!"

I am full of dread as I can see this event as the icing on the cake, which has all the potential of sealing all my future-prospects not just with him but also with the company and not just that it also has the potential of completely uprooting her from even before her roots can attach themselves with this Promised Land!

Ann's face is now fuming red like the setting sun on my whole career life, as with a tyrannical surge of vengeance, she shows no mercy as then, with one blow hammers the final nail in my coffin! She dismisses me on the spot. The Visa on which is like sitting on a keg of bombs ready to explode in a second's notice! Now this special visa which is meant for professional immigrants is something that the Devil itself must have crafted. He called a meeting and invited the best brains straight from hades to come-up with best ways to torture the vulnerable immigrants and then the devil was incredibly pleased when he saw this product and then lovingly called it the "All-will-work-following-American-standards-but-will-get-wages-same-as-their-poor-countries".

What gives this Visa its bite is this clause which when exercised by the Employer at once changes the status of the immigrant worker to illegal!

Due to the knowledge of my new status of illegal I am now full of dread! I soon find out from other fellow immigrants that fortunately for us immigrants even the employer cannot do such an open injustice openly because of their fear of revolt from other fellow immigrants on this unpopular decision, so I am relieved when I learn about their favor to me of giving me a grace period of a good ten days!

The Manager Ann is at her sarcasm's best as she says in her sing-song voice 'Thinkyaaow,' trying her best to hide the effect of sarcasm on showing over her face. But her wide fake smile evaporates as soon as I kill her sarcasm with my sarcasm, by shooting her acid tongue by my parting arrow laced with sugar from my sharp tongue.

"No, no, thank you for firing me!"

Now she cannot control her poker-face anymore and burst out laughing loud over this remark that was coming straight from the mouth of someone who had just won the title of the biggest loser! Laughingly she continues, "Now I have heard every cloud has a silver lining, but even if I were to put on my most optimistic rose-tinted glasses my eyes would still fail to see any visible or hidden positivity in this event for you!" Now a laughter that was still in control, transforms into a hysterical one!

"You are mistaken, yes there is a lot of good hidden in this apparently unpleasant event," as I answer back with a confidence that puts Ann back into doubt over her own statement!

I continue: **"This bullet that you shot at me, is at the bubble of arrogance that I was floating in.** When I first landed on the American Soil, I thought I was invincible! My pride had put false notions in me, which made me function as if I am the lotus in flowers, the fire in a speech, but now what my new initiated eyes I can clearly see that the stutter in a speech is also me and that the cactus in flowers is also me, that the Infinity is me and zero is also me! What I assumed to be the ceiling in my jump from America to India, is just a steppingstone on the American soil! By ending my employment, you have showed me that the reality is much crueler, that I am a mere slave who is at the mercy of her master and that a slave cannot afford to forget their limits..."

The next instant Manager Ann goes silent.

The next instant Mayuri turns her back to leave from the door she is closing forever, while seeing from the eyes at the back of her head Manager Ann's enormous eyes, melancholically watching her go ...

HE THINKS HE IS SOME GOD!

Burn all these DNA theories that have only divided us from each oth-
er,
have diverted us from seeing us as we all really are - not just a mere
combination of the five elements in nature, referred to as Panchboot in
Vedic Science,
Fire, Air, The Infinite, Clay, Water
but are a Kundalini/ Soul that is under the supervision of Super-
Kundalini...

Dear Mayuri's Diary,

I am burning inside from the humiliation caused by my pure-bred American boss by rejecting me! Even if everything he does looks perfect as if God himself came to Earth to do His work through him, it does not mean my abilities can never reach his level! I want to take my revenge, but not by running with a dagger after him but with my secret form of revenge! I will sharpen my saw and will rest only once my worth is so high that it is me who will ignore him, and the cause will not be spite or vengeance but simply that he is just not worthy of my attention anymore! ...

SHARPEN THE SAW

In the Tree Ecosystem, when the leaves begin to wither the trunk does not divert its energies towards saving them, but instead just lets them go, as their true value now is in their ashes, while the value of the Young now, is in their energies in using those ashes to function as manure which will then support new life! Learning from this system, when the dot-com bubble bursts, so do the stock prices, so do the insanely rich salaries of the Information Technology (IT), so does my life as I am also a computer programmer!

All of us computer programmers are no fools who cannot see that our demand is high mainly because we are at the beginning of this new demand Curve. The moment our supply starts outstripping the demand our value will crash! So, our fault does not lie in not being able to see the risk that we are in, but we damn this never-ending optimism in us as even when we are planning for our worst days, we can see is us sacrificing our Friday night Pizza from the Local Shop! Thus, surprised by our own poor forecasts, especially from a brain that can forecast wild weather data with uncanny accuracies, failed in forecasting their own fall, is indeed a travesty! We sit there scratching our heads wondering 'how could my intelligence not see this coming, me, a brain that is powerful as God himself?'!

Mother Aditi counseling her daughter on the phone: "Sharpen your saw! Time is of the essence, either you can waste it all by agonizing over your misfortune, or else you can reverse it by investing it towards enhancing your skill set! The fact that you are still safe, is because your skill set is still in demand, however tomorrow when new innovative technology comes of which you have no knowledge whatsoever but since the demand is for the other one, then, chances are high that, you will become the dinosaur of the industry! Often, it takes a hard kick in the chest for triggering that electrifying insecurity that is needed to trigger one to push oneself to conquer higher levels!"

THEN I STOPPED SOCIALIZING WITH MY OWN COUNTRY PEOPLE!

Dear Mayuri's Diary,

Whenever I see the people from my own country or even people having resemblance with them my heart rejoices and yet I do not make any attempts to send them any friendly overtures, rather I deliberately avoid all eye-contact, not because I have inherited anti-social tendencies from my mother but because if I do not respect my time limitations and begin entertaining both disjoint sets I am sure to lose my sanity! To come oceans away only to experience life the same way as before is absurd! Also, I am too shy to admit to even myself but because of my secret wish of knowing The Creator of Creators various creations way of living so I too can be more like him - beautiful, both inside and outside!

With this thought in my mind, contrary to animal nature of flocking with the like, I stop all my interactions with my kind!

THEN I LEARNT THE ART OF HAIR STYLING
AND COSMETIC PRESENTATION SKILLS

Out of tender feelings of love, most people, often than not, begin
neglecting their own body-care needs for their loved one,
mistaking it as Sacrifice for their them,
not realizing that by doing so, they just jeopardized their own mission
of supporting,
as you need this body in a good condition to be of help to others ...

Dear Mayuri's Diary,

The rejection from the Bachelor of America has killed all possibilities of any union with him, neither in the Present nor Future, still before his killing, he has redeemed himself by gifting me, with an image of the Future-me! A me who is more like him, afterall he is one of His most Beautiful Creation of Creations!

With this edification I am now planning on never skipping on my bathing routines!

INSPIRATION FROM THE
SHOCK-JOCK HOWARD STERN -
THE KING OF ALL TEACHERS

Dear Mayuri's Diary,

How when time becomes favorable, the

all-powerful Destiny serendipitously brings all the required Actors together to the same stage, still amazes me no end! Here I was just thinking I am going for meeting a friend only to find I was going to meet a friend who will become a major part of my daily life!

My friend is listening to the Howard Stern Show when I walk in. As I am hearing the wild show, I jump with joy as what I am just listening, is precisely what I am looking for! A Heaven-sent answer to my current requirement for survival! What better way to get a ducking in the American Culture, than listening to Howard Stern's four-hour talk-show in the car radio, while driving to work, thereby perfecting the daily commute times by listening to a show that is as American as Apple Pie! Not a single moment of boredom, and you are laughing all the way! Now, my message to all those women from the Howard Hater's Club who have already started with plotting on how to censure this book too, to not stereotype me also as I am only doing it for learning purposes only!

A special shout-out to dear Howie! If you are reading this, then accept my gratitude as I bow to your genius repeatedly, just like any of your true die-hard fans! There on the air, you are the undisputed

King, you can say anything, similarly, here in my book I am the undisputed Queen, I can also write anything! And if you ever invite me on your show, then I tell you in advance that no matter what you say or do, *'I WILL NOT TAKE MY TOP OFF!'*... No, not even for a million dollars!

WHEN I LEARNT SUBJECT 'KUT-NITI SHASTRA FROM VEDIC LITERATURE' - THE ART OF USING THE KNOWLEDGE OF MANIPULATING PSYCHOLOGY FOR UNJUST GAINS

A GOOD DEBT IS NOT A BAD THING

Just like a person who has had a terrible experience before while sipping on hot boiling milk, becomes double cautious so much so that even while sipping on water he begins to blow over it to first! Father Aakaash advice to his daughter is to follow a conservative and simple lifestyle. As every Dollar saved is like a Dollar earned, plugging the leak by minimizing one's expenses and then using those savings towards paying off the house mortgage as fast as one can! his strategy appeals to my intelligence but since I have not just inherited his style of thinking, but also have the energies of youth with me, which want to go one step even further! Thus, here is my thought process behind this improvised strategy of mine: Being a Foreigner, I do not have any advantage of some robust ancestral tree backing all my causes like these Natives do, so to offset that drawback, I go the extra mile by researching for that same inside information that they have access to, so this way, I too can enjoy the same fruits of labor that these "preferred ones" do! Now that the Bank is already contributing its share in making my castle, I should be happy and content now but that does not happen as now I begin to look for ways to not just live free but have someone else pay for my castle! Now If I were to live like a miser in my mad-rush to pay-off the loan faster then, in a way I am robbing money from the budget-share that was originally meant for the purposes of merriment! With this sacrifice the only thing happy will be my Wallet, never my Heart and so no-deal! So now what do I do to avoid sacrificing my standard of living, I produce a good strategy to conquer this problem: Either buy two properties from the loan amount. One in which the I live and the other on rent or else I treat my own property as two, where the owner and tenant are living in the same property! The beauty of this system does not just end here, as now this asset is immune to the market fluctuations as now even if the property value goes down should not be a cause of much concern as this asset is like a cow whose milk will keep nourishing its owners for generation to generations ahead! Now if this cash-cow starts appreciating in value in earnest, I will take it as a bonus check from the Heavens Above! This way, I will always be swimming in safe zone!

And with it begins the odyssey of this Robin Crusoe over uncharted waters, the biggest financial life decision, as not just an owner but also a property owner! In 2005, a new star is born in the horizon with the purchase of a two-bedroom condominium in Quincy, MA, where I start living as a Property Owner with another Roommate from Hell, called by the name of The Negative Energy Person. As the name of the roommate suggests, we are looking forward for some fireworks and we are not disappointed! Now that the stage is set, let the battles begin!

CREDIT HISTORY

The even-eye helps. Doubt over-friendly overtures, mis-trust hostile overtures!

Dear Mayuri's Diary,

I have the great fortune of dealing with a blood-sucking leech in the form of my Roommate who I like to call as 'The Negative Energy Person.' Due to us sharing the same social status in the Society I find myself getting engaged in constant un-healthy comparisons!

Every time she opens her wallet to pay, her greed and blood-sucking nature tries to find the loopholes in every situation so she can suck as much as she from my rightful share! Her genius thought process working over-time: 'The owner might just be my twin for the sake of easy comparison. I am the smartest of the two and yet by this one move of hers of buying a house and then using me as a renter to help lift most of the financial burden makes me feel used for her evil designs! The jealousy in me gets more fuel when I must pay to someone who is not even half my brain prowess! The reason I cannot do what she is doing is that the Bank will never give me a loan due to my negligence of letting the record of all my past evil find its way on my credit report! Still despite it all, it is me who is the smarter one as with my fantastic knowledge of the law no one can ever outsmart me!'

Trusting her on her word is a mistake, as for her words are a form of Weapon in her hands, which she can twist and then present it in a way that fits her agenda of never paying for her meals! Like this one instance when this leech comes to me to borrow my favorite fancy hair clip. I do not ask other people for their things so when other People do so, I have a hard time relating with them. When someone is asking in Person it becomes difficult to refuse the request. I too am yet to learn the art of saying no, so I agree to give but as I am climbing the stairs, I am feeling so generous that I am now thinking of giving the matching bracelet too! When I open my jewelry box, my eyes accidentally fall on the gold earrings which she had borrowed from me last year for a party. That sight triggers in me the memory of the whole incident that had left a bad taste in my mouth. She had borrowed them from me for attending a wedding. I trustingly gave them without much thought. Now what do you think happened next! She says she cannot return them as she lost them and does not have any money to buy an equivalent replacement. I remember how after that day; all my peace had vanished! The only thing I could think of, was of ways of getting my valuables back again! Then my stress levels doubled, as now I was not just doing one job but two! As once my real job ends, right after begins this new job of mine of going to her house, then sit all evening with her, requesting her to find the earnings! This Drama finally ended when she finally gave them back to me! It is not just this experience is the cause but also that this woman is not poor who cannot fulfill her needs but is a woman who has never learned to live within her means! Judgement: Guilty.!

A smile now adorns my face as now I have the answer I need. Now on to the hard part - conveying the bitter verdict to the Guilty!

I decide to deal with the matter with smartness. Had this friend been honest with me the last time I would have given her much more than she had even asked for. This generous Mayuri would have even given the matching necklace-set that goes along well with what she had originally asked for. But now due to her poor image in front of me that possibility became an impossibility! But what I can still do is attack it with a balanced approach. I do lend her one, but with something that I can afford to lose...

THEN I BURNT MY INNOCENT BABY PICTURE / THEN I LEARNED KUT-NITI SHASTRA, THE ART OF USING THE KNOWLEDGE OF MANIPULATING HUMAN PSYCHOLOGY FOR UN-JUST GAINS

The child in me must die to make room for the
mature woman to arrive...

Dear Mayuri's Diary,

At this Time, when I am floating on the wave of overconfidence, thinking, nothing can go wrong now, not realizing that in my haste of winning the prestigious Title of "The Next Millionaire of This Greatest Nation in the Country - America", I just jumped into Hell's Fire by bringing in the first willing Woman as my Room-mate, without any real checks whatsoever! Little that I know what a Pandora's box I just opened! My pure expectations see in her a mere disposable source of income per month. While her impure intentions take seed the moment, she sees in me a regular person with no apparent immediate Family support with their strong Bank balances needed for fighting costly eviction battles and so, she begins her dangerous War Games! Armed with her superior Knowledge of the Law, which she had learnt, not for defending the weak or anything like that, but for manipulating the System, so that it always works in her favor, In addition to her credit is the Title of Scholar in Psychology, that entitles her to use some of her tricks for getting away, from not just not paying for the basic Services that she is using, but also take as much as possible from the host's share of the meal too! Now what the current status is, that she already knows the War has started, while I am just somewhat waking-up as I too catch her observing all my actions minutely, but still a fear of fights and un-pleasant confrontations make me close my eyes like a Pigeon does on seeing the enemy approach, a reaction which pleases the manipulator as it is completely in line with her intent of having me live in fear of the yet invisible enemy! Now that she has her confirmation that she is dealing with a person with the knowledge in trickery of a Kindergarten kid, she starts all her psychology tricks on me! Having an upbringing in a family with strong moral values, with great emphasizes on honest dealings, I start feeling very confused by her controlling, cruel, and vindictive mannerisms. Still noble in my dealings with everyone, I knew not of all the harmful effects daily battles over petty things can cause to a body! I kept ignoring all the subtle warning signals from my body for this negative person every time I would receive any of her frequent texts, not just at regular but odd hours right before my sleep time! Slowly my behavior is changing in ways that I cannot even relate with my own reactions anymore! Every time the payment gets delayed or missed, I begin feeling anxious over the whole drama that will now follow just to get the share which is rightfully mine! By now, I am feeling completely out of control of my actions. Now my situation is comical to say the least as despite owning a house, due to fear of the roommate starting a fight the moment I enter my house, my situation is like some homeless person for who the only secure place for sleeping is under the office toilet sink while the Roommate sleeps on my Hypoallergenic Queen Bed!

For some reason, I needed to enter in my own house to get something and then leave as quick as I can, but that did not happen. She has caught me by her sharp eyes! She at once pounces on this opportunity and starts a yelling match on the top of her lungs, now I get furious too and now I am also yelling back at the top of my lungs! The whole neighborhood is now watching the show! To avoid further embarrassment in front of a peace-loving community I leave as fast as I can!

Fear and trembling grips my core when I see the very person who I let-in my house as a friend is now conniving behind my back of finding ways of occupying the whole house for herself and her blood relatives to live there for generations to come while making the conditions for my survival in my own house so hard that now I am sleeping on my office Toilet Floor!

Now that I am an Adult, facing real life challenges discover that sadly the Backbone of our Society is not Ethics but Materialism! Now my aware eye can see how in this age of Materialism all these Divine Properties like honesty, faith, character, and other Divine Virtues are terms that best describe a dying breed of 'Purush' in Sanskrit/ Gentlemen in English is facing extinction, while the terms of money and success are associated with people who have already sold their souls to the devil! So, in this upside-down environment what are my options for survival?

As I begin asking the right questions and simultaneously reliving the nightmarish incident as if serendipitously, I hear my wit saying to me a saying which carried the seeds of answer to this problem! When a dog barks, barking back is absurd. So, the toolkit of trickery which they are using to destroy me, I too, can learn it and then use the same methods back to destroy them instead!

With this thought I can now see myself smiling. Now the first thing I do is to burn this baby-picture of mine as a symbol of the death of Innocence in me and as a punishment for indiscriminately trusting everybody and thereby putting the adult in uncalled for trouble! Then I pick the book on 'Kut-niti Shastra, The Art of using the Knowledge of Manipulating Psychology for un-Just Gains'!

AN EFFECTIVE SWORD

What are Negotiations and Resolutions?
~ The Art of saying a lot, without saying anything...

Dear Mayuri's Diary,

At the first moment, when I held that extra-Income Rent-Money in my fist, I could then see, the great potential in this seed which, when blossoms, will yield returns that will help lift this curse of Poverty, of having just enough that keeps me from rebelling against "The Tyranny in the System"; not realizing that all these high-expectations of mine, are busy in ganging-up behind my back for jinxing me instead! Surely but steadily, the tear in the veil of Diplomatic Protocols begins to reveal alarming thuggish misdemeanors, seeing which, makes me bang my head against the wall, cursing that moment when I dug my grave myself by letting my greed overpower my thinking, thus making me welcome my own Death, myself! Now my assessment cannot be dismissed as some blown-up fear-based problem, when I say that, if not checked now, has the potential of bankrupting me to the last penny! This Devil-in-disguise can take advantage of my simplicity, drug me with mind-altering drugs and then instead of her paying her dues, I will not just be bearing the load of my sustenance but hers too! It is in the inherent nature of a Leach to suck blood off the very Host in which it lives, so it is not the fault of the Leach when it attacks but of the host, who let it in in the first place! With this thought I first lower all my expectations to expect only the worse from this Enemy

Camp. Why? Because when I set my expectations low, I set myself
for success as now they can be easily shattered, while on the other
hand when I set them high, I set myself for disappointment as then
you are also relying on goodness in a Person and that is foolishness
as most of us have already sold our Souls to the Devil, what is left
is a decaying Body which breaths, just to slavishly fulfill its body's
addictions which money can buy!

Which also means, I must find a way to co-exist with a Devil!
Now how do I sleep peacefully in my room with the snake hissing
in the other room!?

Since the fear of the whip from bad Karma is virtually non-existent in these thugs, these people are dangerous! This situation reminds me of the teachings of our Tenth Guru of Khalsa Religion -
Shri Guru Gobind Singh, who instructed us to always keep a
sword with us for self-protection and so, in this also lies the answer
to this problemata, of how to live under the same roof with snakes
in the other!? The status of communal harmony between us now,
is that I suspect physical violence and harm can occur anytime! I
inferred this, from my Observation of her Face every time she in
my physical proximity and is parting from her dear money straight
into my hands! All the strong streak of Jealousy and Hatred seems
to be baked-in in the money from which she is parting! I will not
be surprised if in some random fit of Jealousy and Hatred she
picks her axe and then beheads me! The urgency for the need of a
Security Guard both inside the house, and outside my Room, is
not an understatement!

So, respecting and listening to my Guru's advice, I decide on
always having my form of sword next to me all the time! Carrying a
sword by an amateur like me is substantial risk, not so much to the
opponent, but myself! As what is meant for my protection also has
the potential to attack me instead! So, this weapon that I have decided on, is immune to these issues and so, without any further

delay I reveal it to you Friend: my Wireless Cellphone! Having a Cellphone is like a powerful Weapon which can deter many violent crimes!

If my thought is going towards involving Police for solving inside home fights, is a sign that the situation is so volatile that one small mistake, can blow-up into an all-out war anytime!

Now I plan my every move and countermove now, by first putting the thinking cap of the Devil itself, reminding myself once again, that the enemy's smile is like a poisonous vixen, waiting for the right time, to snatch the prize of victory, from right under the nose!

Now I discover that battles are won not as much by swords, but by the power of the Tongue! When you look at the Enemy as an Object of Pity, means you are underestimating their Intelligence and when you are looking at them as an Object of Envy means you are overestimating their Intelligence. Still-Face/ Silence is a proven Method of being able to get rid of the Negative Person. While the Negative Person is wasting its energies in destroying you, you be the stronger one, stay busy in Building your Nest just the way you want! Being the Smart One, all your efforts go towards Creative activities, which will help cultivate the Divine quality of Self-Discipline and where there is self-discipline, there is Victory! Recognize, be very aware that, the Negative Person's favorite tool is Sarcasm, which they use mercilessly on their Victims, so they can break their willpower of which they are jealous of, because they themselves are sick and this is their sick way of dealing with their own inferiority complexes! ...

AN EARNEST EFFORT TO RESOLVE THROUGH A VERBAL DUEL, BEFORE ANY BLOODSHED BEGINS

OM Aing hreem kleem Chamundaye Viche
- Vedic Literature
Meaning of the Mantra:
OM: The symbolic sound of the Cosmic Being
Aing: The SuperKundalinidess of Conception
Hreem: The SuperKundalinidess of Life Kleem: The SuperKun-
dalinidess of Destruction.
Vichche: Victory.
These three forces, referred to as Chhamundaye, when work in coop-
eration can produce the violent force that can kill troubled times and
fear!

Dear Mayuri's Diary,

Things are now so bad, that I cannot ignore the fine tear appearing through the Fabric of Social Protocols! My now awakening Third Eye, has already been able to detect the true reason behind this Roommate-from-Hell's rebellious ways, especially at the Time when she is parting ways with her True Love - Money, which what that really means, is that under the surface, an Implicit War has already been started!

All these conflicts, which I thought were spontaneous, till I started realizing the true intent behind all this Drama! These fights really, were just another platitudinous, carefully planned move of this Devil, designed to put fear in me, so that I start obediently doing whatever she wills! This open injustice, if not addressed now, is sure to become so toxic, that it has the potential of taking the whole Body with it! Since rocking a Boat with a Person in it, is not an everyday Event and bears serious consequences, I am agreeing with voice of Goodness in me and what most Best Business Practices Advice, I too decide on giving a duel of War-of-Words a fair chance, before any blood-shedding begins!

Most People think that a War-of-Words, must not require as much extensive preparations and that it is safe from any bodily harm than sword fights! However, this view is True only for those illiterates, who still are un-aware of the effect, of the Energies that are governing our bodies. Just as we ground Electricity, for protecting us from getting electrocuted, we too need something similar! So then, how do I Ground myself? First, I throw my Heart somewhere deep in the Attic, as there is no bigger enemy of the Thinking Brain than an Emotional Heart! Next, I self-hypnotize my Mind to be fair in my dealing, as I might be able to avoid the wrath of these Man-made Courts but never from the the wrath of Karma!

I remind myself once again that no one is doing anyone any favors. Knowing from experience and some earlier observations, that whenever the stakes are high, the Heart tries to take over the job of the mind and since the Heart does not have a mind it is easy to see that the outcome of all these superhuman efforts are bound to Fail! Once I have reminded myself of the need of my mind to perform at its best, as Mind is that one tool in every person's hand which when relaxed has the potential of taking one out of any Hell's fire and then somersaulting my body straight into Heaven's Pleasure Garden while conversely when its tired, has the potential of becoming the cause of my destruction. So, now how to Relax the Brain? I am feeling Fortunate as this question just triggered a memory of this ancient age-old secret trick which I had learnt from Vedic Literature! Thank you Mayuri for listening to this voice of reason over the din of all other silly voices! Method: Lay down with eyes closed and just let a free-fall of all thoughts run without any Resistance for the next twenty minutes. Now open your eyes and now you are fresh to face the battle that lays ahead!

Now I am sitting here at the negotiation table face to face with that Roommate-from-Hell. My mind is now alert and is viewing every Move as one in a chess game. As the opponent is laughing outside at you over his victory in killing your pawn, I am laughing on the inside on seeing how this fool just fell into my trap, clearing my way straight to his King's jugular!

My first instinct is to reform my opponent, by my well-intentioned advice, only to find that, I am just preaching to the choir! If they were not morally bankrupt, this stressful moment would never have happened, in the first place! Once this awareness dawns on me, I rein in the Horses of my Tongue tight, leaving it all to that Almighty's Wheel of Justice Karma to reform the Guilty! ...

GET OUT.

"A foot forward with Faith and then failing,
is not a betrayal of Faith, the lack of it,
carelessness most of the times is the culprit we are looking for! ... "

Dear Chhandi, The Smart Warrior Princess's Diary,

Every time that the Yama, The Death Executioner cracks his whip over my faults, He gets a bad reaction out of me, however when I see with my new vision, now enriched with these new Avtar's that the Devil transforms into, I bow down with Gratitude to Him, as now I just avoided a costly mistake of building the House over something that has a fault in its Foundation itself, afterall, if ever there were a Vote on The- One-Building-Principle-that-is-a-must-have, then it would have to be, a strong Foundation!

Squatters are like rotten food. You just must vomit out the toxic food out of your system as then only can your body give-out its much-needed sigh of relief, afterall, is not the relationship between a Service Provider and a Service Consumer, same as the one that exists between a Snake and a Snake-Charmer, where both the sides are infected by the same disease - Greed, and when Greed over-powers thinking, no side is willing to take even a cent of a loss!

Thus, I conclude by taking a firm resolve of not letting any pity weaken my resolve or for that matter even let the false appearances of these leech-like roommates furiously packing their Bags, fool me into giving them yet another chance! I will now rest only once I have complete Legal Possession of my Land and take all the legal steps needed that will ensure that they stay so far that even their shadows cannot cast their darkness over the sanctity of my pristine abode anymore!

Next, I feel glad on seeing the loud rebel Taurus bull in me, who always takes pride in having its way, is now sitting in a corner, cold and ashamed, with her tail between her legs, ashamed over its selfish nature, which has caused me major embarrassment amongst the most respected People from my close-knit Community!

I now have more respect towards the Rules and Regulations of the Community and understand their value better! I now realize even more, my fault in introducing misfits into my friendly Community, thereby dis-respecting their security violation!

My selfish desires for more and more profits, had made me look at the Law Enforcement as a big nuisance in Individual's growth plans but now after walking through   Hells Fire, I do not need a team of Scientists to confirm the validity of this edification, that People tend to walk the straight line better only when there is some kind of Fear, such as long costly Legal battles versus just Fear of the punishment that awaits them, from The Karmic Laws of every action having an equal and opposite reaction!

After going at war with a Guru of Kut-niti - The Science of Unfair Gains, my own gains in Psychology have now quadrupled due to a halving of my Innocence Component while simultaneously a doubling of the knowledge part about the techniques needed in spotting, Traitor Judas amongst the loyal followers of Jesus! Still, despite this complete theoretical gain and loss analysis Sheet, I must caution you that, there are much more safer options, in gaining experience than jumping in the fire without any prior knowledge of the nature of the beast that you are about to tackle!

THEN I LEARNED ARCHITECTURE

Dear Mayuri's Diary,

Just when I thought this battle of possession of the Golden Key is now over, I quickly realized that by saying that to myself, I just jinxed myself, as in front of me lay a greater Battle than before!

Since due to the strict privacy laws, I have never had the honor of inspecting these forbidden premises, but now that I do, the hidden value of these laws, start revealing! They were acting like a shield for my mental nervous breakdown on seeing the extent of the extensive damage that had been done to my property!

Now, my first instinct is to just take the loss, sell it and then, run as fast as I can to Country Banana Republic! Next what happened, must be a clue, into how the Merciful of All, functions when it comes to rewarding the deserving! I was trying to lift a heavy Desk for moving. Now, my goal is to lift it slightly higher than the height of my sleek moving-tool, so I can slip moving-tool in through that foothold and then it is all smooth sailing from here, as now this tool is enabled to be able to do its magic! Now, I was able to lift it but due to it being heavier than my arm strength, it could not be raised enough for me to sneak in the moving-tool! Now, the heavy Desk, which was supposed to fall back, under these situations, ruining all my efforts, did not... Instead, the desk fell on a nail which was protruding out of the wall, thereby enabling me to finish my Task successfully! Now I am standing in wonderment, not for being able to do something which I thought I could never do, but because of an unknown feeling that an invisible force from the universe was also collaborating with me! With that knowledge suddenly from an ordinary girl I become someone else, someone with more superior powers! Suddenly impossible has now started looking as I-am-possible to me!

Now cleaning-up for myself I have done several times now, but the rebel in me abhors the idea of cleaning-up someone else's mess! So, for inspiring myself for that, I first trick myself into believing that The SuperKundalini will serve his Justice by having the squatters mistakenly leave their bags with cash which might help recover the money they swindled from me. This thought at once puts a spring in my feet as I leap out of my bed and clean-up the whole place efficiently. Cash I did not find, but in the process got what I wanted - clean premises!

I soon discover that it is not the curse of my wallet that I should have worried about, but from the ghost of the roommate which is still haunting the place with silly Mementos of memory of events now imbedded in every particle in that place!

Mayuri: I feel overwhelmed by the Mountain of Modifications which I will now have to make due to the unbelievable filth these cunning pigs were living in!

Father Aakaash: If one is expecting to see a sparkling house and not a filthy pigpen after bringing in pigs, then it is not the fault of pigs but with the expectation of the Person blinded by greed, who let them in in the first place! Just change your expectation, then you will not be disappointed with the outcome!

Mayuri: If I do not make these changes, I will be in the hospital and my investment in this house down this now filthy toilet drains! My neighbors might feel threatened thinking I am trying to out-do their Houses, while really for me, either pay for these upgrades or pay the Doctors for having me just take my next breath...

Now I know I have no choice but to hire a person who has good knowledge of building science but still do not know how I will pay?!

Father Aakaash: I understand this is a particularly challenging time for you, but do not ever underestimate the strength of your own strong arms. Wherever there is a great learning opportunity one should jump over it! If you do not know anything of a skill, then it becomes more important that you do not let this opportunity slip! I want you to start finding resources which will teach you all about building science!

You need to think with a calm mind as only a calm mind can make right decisions. You, being a daughter of a Man who has proven his strength after surviving many challenging times, can tell you from my experience on how I deal with such situations which can un-nerve anyone. When I must conquer any mountain of problems, I first lay on my bed in a comfortable position. I close my eyes, then rest my eyeballs in the center of the eyebrows, which is the place where the Perineal Gland is found. You will be surprised to see how much focused, and clear your mind is functioning. I then clairvoyantly execute all the steps in my mind itself and in this way my Plan becomes more fault-proof as it has already been done, once before!

Mayuri smiling: Thank you, father for showing me the right Path and thank you The SuperKundalini for choosing Shri Aakaash Singh Birghi to be my father...

I am now borrowing time from all the vocation-related studies to meet my immediate goals. I start reading books, watching videos on building science.

I never thought this time will end but it did and rewarded me with a handsome appreciation in my Property's Value!

And I smile humbly, every time when any of my neighbors also make their updates in same style as mine ...

ANOTHER PLATATUDINOUS PLEDGE - LIVE EXCLUSIVELY WITH MY BEST COMPANION ONLY - MYSELF!

"No way in hell! A Marriage must be the Serpent that ensures,
its bit victim gets completely incapacitated,
never to recover again!
By the time the victim realizes its mistake,
it is already facing financial ruin,
costly custody battles for children,
not to mention all the pain that all the near and dear must have to
go through,
not as much over the natural empathy embedded in the situation,
but over their own impotence in not being able to do anything,
other than just be a witness to the beauty which lies in watching any
platitudinous shipwreck ...
- Chhandi The Smart Warrior Kaur

Dear Mayuri's Diary,

The temptation of living a life just the way I want, demands from me a sacrifice, a sacrifice of burning all my desires for a future that involves the pleasures of a blissful domestic life!

After staying true to my word by staying single long enough, soon enough, I realize that all this sacrifice is a waste! As the first thought assumed that chains come from domesticity, while really, they can come from the silliest things we buy, not realizing that all these little chachka's/ Objects-of-our-Desire, come with a cost of maintenance in the form of Time! Now I realize that whether buying a big house brings you prestige in the Society or not, it certainly turned out to be a big Beast whose other name is home which needs constant supervision and maintenance! So, news for all you quick to judge people, that there is nothing to envy here, just pity...

Come to think of it, who needs anybody anymore when dependencies on one another are virtually non-existent?!

In this Microwave Generation, where one is certain that the next meal is coming, one is guaranteed that one will have a roof over one's head, there's little reason for anyone to risk breaking their chains of slavery, especially when their only options are Devil or Satan!

For some reason, I feel more comfortable in the company of Women who have drifted away from their Culture than these pretentious Women who are taking part in some invisible holier-than-thou Competition of looking more domesticated than the other! So, if I cannot relate with this Class of People in which I am destined to be, then what was the need for me to fly oceans away just to lead a life which does not take advantage of this opportunity!

Why not fly?! Who will be a greater fool than me for not taking any advantage of this excellent opportunity of being away from a strict Family and yet even if I have all this freedom to do anything that I want, what good is it, when the real pleasure comes from eating the fruits that are just forbidden in nature! Initially there was a lot of excitement when meeting new people only to find all people are the same everywhere - boring! Just despair everywhere! 'Life has become as meaningless and empty as it can be! If I try to find entertainment in Marriage, it sounds even more scary, as I feel as if it was framed by some cunning sociopath who wrote a biased Manual with only one side till the three days of Honeymoon and very conveniently forgot to add any exit clause for those unfavorable situations!'

Is marriage then not just another form of market where bride-grooms are a mere commodity to bid, with expensive gifts and valuable dowry from the bride's family and the one whose bids outbid the other wins the hand of the bride, the inside beauty of the bride despite? The more the contrast in bride and the bride-groom, the higher the dowry, then Is not higher the dowry a form of disrespect to the bride?

The word "Husband" has lost all meaning in the traditional sense. Where are real men who would honor their sacred vows over their dead bodies? Now we have this new-age modern breed of Men who conveniently marry in great haste, then divorce in an even greater haste! Even after getting married over ten times, their complain is the same, 'dear friend, I could never find true love!'

In my profane eyes, a husband is like a dog without a collar and yet to compare him with a dog is not an insult to a dog but a hus-band, because the dog is at least a faithful and reliable loyal friend, while a husband is not; a comparison sounds fair to me only when the word husband is compared with a pig as a pig is only happy when he poops on himself and then rolls in his own poop! So, now you judgmental people, tell me if it is indeed my fault when I can-not respect this Institution of marriage and look at a Husband as just another feather on my cap, just to show-off in party circles and nothing else?!

After extensive socializing with the locals, meeting people from different occupations, I ended-up completely burning myself down to the levels of boredom! Finally, I am relieved when I took pity on myself when I realized that the source of entertainment lies inside, in exploring my own labyrinth than any of other entertainment ever found outside!

Now my goal is for a simple life, where we are not doing things just to please another but things that fit our lifestyle while respecting our bodily limitations. This must be a beautiful sample for a beautiful existence!

So, with this edification, I put my hand over a burning candle to take my new pledge: I will live with my best companion – myself, but damn the evil eye as the moment I said it, little did I know, I just jinxed myself, as this pledge was not just heard by me but also our Dear Lady Destiny, who immediately got busy in making a joke out of my firm resolve! ...

WHEN PARALYSING SNAKE-BITE: DESIRING A MI-RAGE / 2010 – WHEN I SHED MY OLD SKIN OF A FREE BIRD TO TRANS-FORM INTO MY NEW SKIN OF A DUTYFUL WIFE MAYURI

When we are happy, we cry,
when we are sad, then also we cry,
Then is not fair to say,
that the summary in one word for every life,
is 'a Teardrop' ...
Mast Mayuri, The Intoxicated Peafowl dancing in the Rain

FIRST THE HUSBAND DOES NOT GIVE A DAMN!

Husband Chanakya to his Wife Mayuri: When we try to mix oil with water we cannot, as it is against their inherent nature! Both of this material have proven benefits but when cooking if someone were to put water over heated oil for mixing it, it will not do what we intended it to do, but could prove harmful as it splashes instead, causing harmful skin burns to the one standing near-by. Such is my bond with my wife too. Our natures cannot mix, and yet we must meet our marriage goals!

Whenever I enter our bedroom, she enters under the blanket pretending that she is sleeping! Even if I were to have scorpions crawl over her and bite her, she will still lie like a cold fish does not say anything, the only sign of life in her is the faint voices of deep sighs!

So, to save this marriage from a complete shipwreck, we meet only for our procreation needs!

Frankly my darling, I do not give a damn!

THEN THE WIFE FAINTS!

lays senseless like some eighteen-wheeler of justice ran over her.

Dear Mayuri's Diary,

The moment I hear his footsteps coming towards my bedroom, I can feel a surge of fear and anxiety hormones flood through my entire body. No, it is not the thought of having to wrestle with a two-hundred-pound ogre but because of one more of the many favors that his mother has for him! She has such an excellent job in making him believe that he is a Hercules Avatar that now that suggestion has gotten hammered in so deep that he now actually believes it to be true! This delusion has become the source of difficulty for me as he is no Greek from any angle whatsoever, and even if he is all that, the problem remains, as I am no Greek Goddess!

Whenever he knocks my door, his expectation is that like some Pavlov's dogs I will start salivating just by looking at him, while it is the exact opposite which is the truth! My bodily fluids dry up, as if my body is in a state of rebellion and dread over the thought of subjecting myself to another session of spiritual rape! This is how the session goes: The more he tries to come near, the more I go further away, seeing my coldness towards him, he takes it as an insult to him, when I sense the disgruntlement in him, I go even more in the state of dread and despair! This cycle keeps repeating itself all through this long and un-ending nightmarish session! Thank you, Mother Nature, for reducing the Window for this act to two minutes for those two right days only! As the Philosopher Sarthi Kierkegaard once rightly said, 'Pleasure disappoints, possibility never' and agreeing him I say that forget pleasure disappointing as there was never even a possibility of pleasure there, in the first place!

When we look at Honeybees, they have separate bees for the purpose of gathering honey while for the purpose of procreation needs, they have a separate Bee. Now it is all making sense to me. I am really the worker bee who works all day to meet the financial needs of the house, problem here is that for procreation needs too it is me, like some labor shortage! So really, I am working double shift - all day in the office and at night with my husband! No wonder then I am neither able to be a good worker nor a good wife!

Frankly my darling, I do not give a damn either!

HAUNTING BAD DREAMS

Restless serpents of thoughts keep rising from some unknown source, haunting Mayuri's dreams!

After waking from one of her recent bad dreams, she goes to work. She is opening her file to read but can read nothing, how she can when her eyes are busy watching a re-run of the last-night's horrible dream clairvoyantly! She is experiencing it vividly, seeing once more an army of fat, black mice, entering her house that started running uncontrolled, ready to take over the whole house, seeing which her whole body is trembling! Leaving everything, she lunges to get her phone to make an urgent call to the Management. Once on the phone, her voice falters, fumbling for words she is telling them to fix this problem right away, no matter what the cost! It is either these mice or me who will live in this house! They sense her desperation but there is nothing that they can say to drive away all her fears! Then in a very grim voice they say, we know your ability of throwing infinite money to fix this problem, but we cannot even take your case if the situation is out of control! With these nightmarish words she comes out of her trance, composed from the outside but inside is a different story!

More Despair!

PEEKABOO IN THE TIME WARP

*Unlike the wise man who on hearing the loud lead-boot footsteps of
the enemy at his doorstep froze out of fear,
a child on the other hand stays blissful,
afterall there is no enemy strong enough to defeat his clever karate
chops ...*

With every repeated failed attempt at meeting her duty as a Wife,
Mayuri is now inside secretly to people and herself is sinking increasingly into the vice like grip of an unknown fear, dragging her
down increasingly with every passing day into dreadful despair!
From the seed of desperation sprouts a quest for Oracles/ Priests
who can take a small peek in the crystal ball, so that she can finally
get her laugh back when she gets to see just how silly and imaginary her assumptions can get, how much she just made a mountain
out of a molehill!

After knowing about the large amount of fraud cases in this
breed of fortune-tellers, Mother Aditi is strongly against going for
such a choice!

Mother Aditi: "Be patient! Especially when we do not know if
everything is pre-destined, or we are making our future every step
of the way? From my knowledge of the Ved shastr/ Literature, this
human form is precious as we do not just respond chemically to
situations like plants and many other animals but by the powers of
discretion too! As we have an ethical part to us, we are fully responsible and accountable for our every action!"

Mayuri fell silent. She very well understands the meaning behind the words and yet it is only a matter of time before the suffocating anxiety and restlessness will win and so before we know she has succumbed to the temptation. Disregarding all her mother's pearls of wisdom, she lunges forward to get her phone to get for herself the first available appointment with the forecast telling priest for having a harmless peekaboo into the future's cauldron!

THE PRIEST - A FORECAST
STRAIGHT FROM HELL

FACE TO FACE

An Eternal truth is that the opposite of reality is also a reality!

Mayuri is sitting in the waiting room of the priest who like God holds the key to getting all her desires fulfilled! Tall order indeed! Expectations are sky high; her toes are constantly moving up and down in her tiny shoes, revealing her unrest, hopefully it is still a secret from the quick to judge public!

Her clenched sweaty palms are telling the story of anxiety that must be running through her body. A plain-clothed woman is noticing her closely, but Mayuri is not noticing anything as she is too engrossed in coming up for solutions to get out of this mess that she is in. The stranger approaches her with a tissue box. Addressing in a courteous manner, she makes her chuckle with her wit by offering her a tissue which was an urgent need of the time, as if the drop from the runny nose that was hanging at the tip of her nose if not stopped in time, was sure to ruin her dress! Mayuri acknowledges it, as she had not been able to do an excellent job at hiding her silent sobbing. At first, Mayuri is in no mood of engaging any long-drawn conversations with a stranger, but then fearing that she might be hurting a good-natured, elderly woman's feelings and indeed her runny nose could use some help, she smiles and accepts her help.

Then to arouse the feeling of pity on herself and with the intention of making Mayuri feel superior to herself, so that Mayuri begins to show more information about her private life. To start an open dialogue, she starts to talk about her own personal life so that Mayuri also reciprocates in kind, thereby falling straight into the stranger's trap! The stranger begins by introducing herself as a single woman, who goes by the name of Diana, who had never given birth herself but still had aided many women in giving birth.

Diana: "The SuperKundalini should bless the most deserving couples with the most babies but what we really see around us is that most of these Intellectuals barely have any, while the rascals and witches of the world, who are too selfish to even take care of themselves have more than a handful! This scale of nature's justice does not hang properly and yet why do all teachers tell us to believe that the actions of Nature are just? In one scenario triplets are born to unwed mothers who try to find ways to get rid of their babies by using the most cruel and spiteful ways, while on the other hand desiring couples who even after going through advanced medical science procedures still get nothing!

Once Diana's words hit the right spot, in no time they are talking like old friends. Mayuri divulges all about her fertility problems along with some other intimate details to her new friend. Once the new friend has all the information she needed, she did not stay even a moment longer! As she is briskly picking up her belongings to leave, she uses the same time to say her speedy goodbyes. "Since time is precious, O my precious, one should not waste time in jibber-jabber and since I have already wasted over FIF-TEEEEENNNNN MINUTES of our time, I got to run!". The very next moment, she has already vanished! Noticing her magical vanishing trick Mayuri could not help but make a comment on her strange behavior: **"People are strange! Just a moment ago, she was like the loving mother from heaven, that one often finds in most Tearjerker dramas and the next moment she is like the stepmother from hell that we often find in most Horror dramas..."**

Regardless, after talking to the stranger, Mayuri feels incredibly pleased with herself, sees it as a good Omen to talk to an elderly woman who appeared just for her like some proxy Mother. Little did Mayuri know about the invisible spider on the wall who was seeing her very closely - The Priest, who is getting a live feed of the whole conversation straight to his monitor screen!

THE TRANS-MEDITATION SESSION

With high-expectations Mayuri enters the priest's semi-dark room, lit only with an earthen lamp. When she sees his silhouette in front of her, she feels as if she is like a little child in presence of her father who will protect her from the upcoming storm, strong enough to create a havoc in her just started Marital Life! Nervous to not offend him in any way, she first bows to him and then stands there waiting for his next instruction, obediently and with full faith and devotion. He enjoys her nervousness which makes him feel more confident in his Power, not in giving her what she needs but in his convincing powers. As if first training her to obey his every command he begins his practice session by first instructing her to sit on the mat across him just like a protective Father instructing his little girl. He himself is sitting on it in a Sukhasana (Cross legged) on a firm seat, covered with fake deerskin. His waist, spine, chest, neck, and head are in one line. He starts a small fire in a small earthen lamp that is situated at the eye-level in front of him. Looking steadily in the eye of the fire, he starts chanting Mantras which sounded enchanting enough she did not know the meaning of them. Hearing them she wanted to just leave everything and become his follower but once the chanting stopped, all the worries surrounding her came back to life. Now that the chanted has stopped, her mouth opens to tell her all the answers to her concerns and woes, but that did not happen. He interrupts her mid-sentence and instructs are to only speak when asked to. Being desperate she even manages to conduct this challenging task of not saying anything when one is screaming inside!

He begins, "I'm a trikaal-darshi, the one whose vision spans across the time matrix. You do not need to tell me anything, because I already know the reason that brings you here".

Priest: "Truth is bitter, do you still want to hear it?"

She almost forgets to breath!

Mayuri: "Just hit me with the truth! Nothing could be worse than the anxiety of uncertainty which has me in a vice like grip!" ...

Priest: "I see that your great name will be all over the media! Without going further on that aspect, let us bring our focus to the cause and remedy of your despair! There is no way to sugarcoat this one, so I tell it as painlessly as possible: 'I do not see you delivering any child from your own womb... "

Saying that, he comes out of his Trance like state.

Mayuri's heart skips a beat, her worst fears had come true! She puts her hands to her ears exclaiming in dismay!

Mayuri: "they say that ears go deaf for self-protection in an event of danger, then why is it that my eardrums did not burst now? These words which just like spears pierced right through my heart?! What a blow under the belt from Destiny! Whatever I fear, I take that some evil spirit casts a spell on me and then that very outcome takes its ugly shape in real!"

With trembling hands, she wipes her tears and gets-up to leave, when she hears a commanding voice from the Priest.

He asks her to keep sitting, afterall her job has started now, as far as he is concerned!

"Do you want a baby or not?

Yeeeessss...

Then I will give you a baby...

Bubububut... I never ask you for one...?

QUIT ARGUING!!! You know what your problem is?

Umm...umm... I do not know...

Your problem woman is that YOU TALK TOO MUCHHH! Golly, woman! When I say I will, damn well I will! For that to happen, I will need you to do everything exactly as I ask you to do!" ...

Priest: "Since I does not have the expertise needed for chanting specific mantras and performing certain rites, I will have to direct you to the ones who have expertise in your concern. Those specialists can help you in making your desire a reality but as these resorts are heavy on the wallet, I suggest you take another added Loan just for paying this new expense. I even offer easy financing with a zero down, zero interest but I can do this favor only for the first year!

On listening to the heavy expense that way overshot the budget for her medical expenses, she begins to take out her cellphone from her bag to consult with her husband before making such a huge financial commitment, when the Priest sees this, with one bold and sudden movement, he snatches the phone from her hand! From that moment forward, the Husband who makes her financial decisions is him.

Priest: "You look very educated and wise, but actions are still like a child! Do not you know his answer! Men do not think from their hearts like women do. Most men do not even believe in The SuperKundalini. He will only laugh at you, call you superstitious and unscientific! Do not ask him, ask me!"

Mayuri: "But you are also a man...," she says doubtfully.

He interrupts her thought at once and takes over again. Priest (Commandingly): "I am a man and that is why I how we think! You argue way too much, Woman! Golly! DO YOU WANT A CHILD, OR YOU ARE WASTING MY PRECIOUS TIME!!!"

Drowning what will she do! Therefore, no surprise there when she signs the contract on the spot!

Once out of the door, she is running headlong toward the exit. Her countenance is pale, eyes bloodshot, body hair erect, winds howling angrily around her, scattering her locks helping in hiding her face from the world. That is when the sky tore apart, pouring acid rain on her body, exposing her shame and disgrace... With the voice of the priest echoing in her mind, she knew not how to brace the impending doom, so she gets in her car and drives to the forest to hide herself there, away from civilization, away from all her fears, alone with the one best companion who will never deceive her - her solitude.

A CONSPIRACY THEORY -
BABY-MAKING SHOPS

If the horse befriends the grass, what will the horse eat then?
A Victim of some Secret Population Control Agenda!

Dear Mayuri's Diary,

Tormented by the knowledge of dark times ahead, the only options that I can see, is that either I surrender to my fate, letting the poison of a meaningless marriage poison consume me, leaving me in a state which is neither dead nor alive, or else I fight like a true Taurus woman, do everything in my power to prevent this rolling ball of Fire coming down at me with a furious pace, but when I see my enemy is no huge one-eyed Monster but a frightening 'nothing', I went silent.

Like a child in its ignorance is blissful imagining no enemy is strong enough to defeat their clever karate chops, I too, like a child, am trying different things to tackle these evil forces out to dethrone my little kingdom! Still not knowing what the showstopper really is, I waste no time in finding not just finding the best of fertility clinics but quacks too! Now I am on a mission, will rest only after I have fulfilled my desire!

I am now officially the favorite of all fertility clinics, quacks as I would give them any money they wanted. My closets are already overflowing with fertility products! I am so overwhelmed with information from this multi-billion fertility Industry that whatever the testimonials say I latch on to their every word as gospel and ensure that I have that Product too; I have now begun to enjoy the pain which comes from sticking needles all over my body as part of one of the many therapies, at least there is as if this is the only way to my goal then literally enjoying lying on my bed of needles after all with my level of anxiety, everything is fair Game! Miracle diets, even enemas which created severe gas in me which nearly killed me! In short, I am like a mad woman for who nothing is too crazy to try!

Afterall these exhausting exercises, you would think I succeeded but what does really happen? Dear Aunt Flo visits again.

After all these failures, I have now begun thinking out-of-the-box. Who is the culprit? Who else than these doctors themselves! Simple logic if a horse befriends the grass, then what will the horse eat? They can fool these overage Grandma's but not me! I am smart enough to see this big gap between what they claim and what their real intent is! So, from now on I will become my own doctor! I will change the doses in proportions that I feel will work or come to think of it, is this thought an intentional sabotage by the spirit of freedom in me, plotting against my married life goals as getting chained even more by the strong ties of blood and cries of one's own infant will make it impossible for me to see the glaciers in Alaska? ...

ANOTHER PLATITUDINOUS VICTIM OF POLLUTION FROM INDISCRIMINATE INDUSTRIALIZATION

'Does my toxic womb do what I do not have the courage of doing my-self, kills my babies even before they can open their eyes, thus saving them from coming to this planet Earth which has already stolen cen-turies worth of resources from the future generations?"

Dear Mayuri's Diary,

How quick are these doctors in writing a prescription without even finding the root cause! They know but I know not why they like keeping me in the dark. Damn these doctors! How can they prescribe me the right medication without even knowing why my body reacts the way it does? Since the disease in me, if I think hard enough, I can also find the hidden cause behind my sickness!

Since, Present is dependent on the seeds we sow in the Past, it only makes sense to look in the Past to find that serpent sitting in my womb which is devouring all my babies, who could only expe-rience the darkness of my womb, never a single ray of light ...

There is a strong possibility I became a victim of the toxic fumes coming from the monstrous sugar factory that was few miles from the college. I can vividly recall, how every time the factory would start its production the fires from its pit would push toxic smog fumes, engulfing the whole village with a dirty acrid haze that would slash visibility and the hazardous pollutant levels were disastrous for people with weak Lungs like mine! The last time when I went to a doctor to get my lungs evaluated, his report did confirm my worst suspicion - that my lungs are like of a person who must have been smoking over seventy tobacco cigarettes a day, this is after me not even touching any tobacco cigarette! So, the culprit is all the polluted air around me!

The biggest loss of my living away from my mother during the college days must be not getting good home cooked food made by my nourishing hands of my mother!

Yes! Now that my beautiful mind has helped me discover the problem, I do not need to waste any time on chasing Priests or even begging The SuperKundalini to fulfil my desires! Even if my Husband does not see in me any qualities of a mother, I will now prove him wrong!

Subhasham Shighram! Now my dear magician, just play your magic flute and make my milkers full of milk... hee-hee-hee.

Aunt Flo comes again.

WRETCHED AUNT FLO!

Wretched Aunt Flo! In vain you flood my panties with your never-ending Rivers of my blood! You always mark the start of my cycle with hope which always ends with despair! You always visit me at the same time, always bring the same results with you, an idem per idem, how about you surprise me the next time by not showing-up, show-up only when you have delivered all your broken promises.

All these three days, the emotions in me reach insane levels, like the tides in the ocean on a stormy night, jumping high to finally fulfill their desire of kissing the moon. One would expect that after failing many times they would tire and give-up. Wrong. They are insane! As now their efforts raise exponentially to satiate their insatiable Urges. Such is the pent-up energy in me at this time, my feet cannot resist from putting on my Ghoongru (A wrap-around belt with small Bells, tied around the ankles, generally by the Classical Dancers in India) to dance to the Indian classical Dance-form, Shiv-Tandav, which washes away all my stress with my tears, betraying all the mixed emotions of helplessness and anger deep inside me to the outside!

ENTANGLED TELEPATHIC SIGNALS

Is an ideal family not like the pair of one's eyes?
They never see each other and yet,
they must see each other,
As how else do we explain the magnificence
that lies in the Product
which, can only come,
when all separate entities,
sacrifice their individual Goals,
to combine as one Autonomous Unit,
that is in-sync with each other,
uniting to
ensure the success of meeting their common goal
of a beautiful Future ...
-    *Mast Mayuri, The Intoxicated Peafowl Dancing in the Rain*

Dear Mayuri's Diary,

What just happened?! Before I even begin my day, with all these necessary time-consuming Tasks, that are a must for the smooth running of this high-maintenance lifestyle of today, failing which, has the potential of causing severe headaches for me down the line and yet I don't do any of them, instead pick-up my Diary to keep a Record of this Feeling of mine, before the Mundane takes over and erases everything that this inside Feeling is trying to convey to me!

Right after I wake-up from a Dream with a start, I am now wondering if this word that I just heard, is not just "a" word but "the" word, or in other words a message, or in other words a Discovery of a Link between other Dimensions/ some other Parallel Universe!

This word that was uttered was from my father: 'Help'... Now, my Father rarely calls me on Weekdays, as he is cognizant of the time-pressures of a Working Woman, and having been a Working Man himself, is well-aware of the high workloads on Mondays, due to no work done on the previous day and so, when I see his name on the Phone's caller-ID, I am know doubly confused by the co-incidence! I pick up the Phone quickly, curious to know the reason behind his phone-call and when he told me that the reason for his call was to check-up on me to see if I need any 'help.'!

I fall! My tongue fumbles for words, I stand there, too taken aback to respond from this too-much-of-a-co-incidence, wondering how her dear father, even-if sitting Oceans away, already knows about her well-kept secret of being in a situation which now needs an intervention from her loved ones?!
Knowing that the reason behind her keeping her secret a secret, persist, I say nothing... Even if my father learns about my despair and wants to help, he cannot, instead the awareness of my pitiable condition, will become the cause of his despair instead! With this thought, I act nonchalant and give him false comfort by promising him to come back soon to see him and the whole family as soon as I am done tying some loose ends ...

TEARS OF BLOOD!

Dear Mayuri's Diary,

Anytime an invitation for a birthday party of any child of their close friends comes it instantly triggers my anxiety to jump through the roof as if it were some invitations for my own funeral! Like that one time when I ran out of excuses and so had to go! Worst mistake! There is an arrogant Mother of three sprawled wide on the sofa. Who better to flaunt her superiority on than the only barren woman in the pack! Thereafter, I know not what evil spirit has her that one after another she is directing all her cruel sarcastic remarks at me! Now a good sarcastic remark is often hard to say. Most often than not, it comes out as cruel, which amuses the author and his likes. I wanted to punch her face, but my fingers trembled and for some unknown reason to me could not make a fist! Then I tried to compromise with the situation with a more impotent than myself justification, "Her lifestyle is a direct contrast of mine. So, for her to appreciate mine is either hypocrisy or a disdain for her own life and if she does out of hypocrisy then she is a jealous woman and where there is jealousy, there is hatred, and where there is hatred there is no beauty, meaning that person is ugly! She is ugly! Now with this revelation, I can say, jealous people's view is a hidden perspective of themselves than others! Then I smile, but the very next moment I am repenting! "Shame on me! All this while I have been cursing people for not being empathetic to my situation but really the fault is not in them but in my impotence in delivering my promises!" Now I remember that fertility book did mention that that woman who did a fast for thirty days got pregnant right after! Nothing can stop me now, not even God! I will start mine right away!

INTERFACE / ESSENTIALISM
FOR EROTIC LOVE

Dear Mayuri's Diary,

The cause of my despair is not just the Knowledge of the sickness that is consuming my soul, but is over my impotence, my inability in making a choice that will enable me to move forward out of this current 'either/or' / 'Dharamsankat' in Sanskrit, which I am currently facing!

I hear the screams from my Heart, begging me to break away from this Relationship which must be a disgrace to this Institution of Marriage, whose foundation which should be be Love, but instead is mere slavery and desperation to achieve my high-expectation desires!

Now my aware eyes can also see, I am in a boat which is bound to collapse, still I am unable to make that leap to the shore, simply because I am too far ...

PARALYSING SNAKE-BITE:
DAY TRADING / DARK SHADOWS OF
FINANCIAL DESTRUCTION PLAYING
HIDE AND SEEK ON THE WALL

When the Mr. Cool-as-a-cucumber-Husband Chanakya, gets to know about how all the Credit Cards were smashing Budget Credit Limits, all funneling Various Quacks under the same umbrella of Infertility Treatments, he loses all his cool, gripped with a fright of his life, abandons all work that he had to finish, to come confront his darling wife!

Husband Chanakya: "Stop this wild roller coaster ride! This insanity in you which pulls you towards your destruction, this time however fatally towards financially! And if you ever wish to see what consequences of unrestrained passion can be, then try to learn from the dead bodies of the moths lying around the flame who could never learn from their friends and met the same fate as the rest of their friends - death and dissimulation!

O my dear foolish wife, stop spending money like water on something which is a gift from The SuperKundalini! Your God is smart, He only gives the amount that an individual's body is capable of handling, if you still try to overload your body, it is bound to snap!

Try to learn from your colleague, whatever her Godforsaken name is... Yes Sunita, I know not how I always forget the name of such a talented woman, still coming back to the point, just look at how beautifully she stands as a multi-hand Super Woman, juggling career in one, Husband in another and then on top all the Household chores too are done to perfection!

The list does not end just here. Her kind, even worship their husband as their Deity! While you, on the other hand get so exhausted, that by the end of the day all you manage to do is crawl into your bed, then put your heavy comforter, covering the whole of your head! For you to serve your body hunger needs, it is like going an extra mile to conduct your goal, with whatever little energy left in you! I admire you for being able to go that extra mile, but what good is it when this process is not sustainable and so, is bound to snap your back! Just Relax! I am your Husband now; As part of my duty towards you, I will always be with you, even if you are a failure as a wife!"

On hearing these words of comfort, now her body gets gripped with dread even more, as she had never been able to relate herself with couples who had accepted a lifestyle of a marriage without any children.

Mayuri: "Silly People! Why sacrifice one's freedom, just to become someone's travel companion?"

Then now when she starts seeing the glimpses of her future self, as one of the very Object of the Class of People who negate her essence, makes her sink even more in Despair ...

INITIATED INTO THE DARK SIDE
OF GAMBLING - THE MONSTER
OF DAY TRADING

The Power of Faith,
we learn from that person who stood naked in ice-cold water all night
and still came out alive,
as the Individual never lost Faith in the Lord of the Outside Powers -
Indr,
who will ensure his Worshipper Victory,
by changing the bad environment to the right one,
which will give the one a new Life ...

Dear Mayuri's Diary,

The first and only strict instruction from my dear Husband Chanakya to me as his obedient Wife, is to never investigate the contents in his laptop computer! So, dutifully, I too hang on to his every word as Gospel, until this fateful day, when he has been absent from my eyesight for more than usual, fault is not mine if I yield to the temptation of having a little harmless peak in the contents and so then, with true feminine curiosity use this opportunity behind his back, to do exactly what he had instructed me to not do! It is not as if the Ethics in me is long dead, but because Curiosity in me easily overpowers my Voice-of-Reason, so even before it can even utter its word of caution, I have already satisfied Curiosity's desire!

All signs from the universe seem favorable for me as contrary to his customary behavior, he himself has left his laptop computer open, so even if I did not want to pry too much, there is just no way that I not stumble upon his deception of mine! I throw-up a little in my mouth on seeing the secret that he had been carefully hiding from me! What if my high nausea levels would make me faint this moment with the screen open and he were to walk-in at the same moment...

Silly me! I should have already known that my rival is no attractive nymph from the Wild, but his actual true Love - Money! He is Gambling in the World's largest Stock Market!

I continue exploring some more! I see here and there, there are some losses but then there are some gains to recover some of the losses, net-net it is showing a loss, a substantial loss! Now is the time to follow the great teachings, which guide us women to correct our men if they are on the wrong path, putting them back on the path of righteousness!

I too stand-up to execute these commands of wisdom ingrained in me by my mother, however I know not why my knees buckle and automatically make me sit back down and think again! My own faith and conviction on the topic are now in danger of a reversal! Now instead of trying to reform my Husband I too become a victim to the same venom as him! Blinded by the possibility of having a new source of Income which can contribute towards reducing my mountain of debt which knew only one direction - upward and that too exponentially up! No, none of this debt money is for spoiling myself silly with Luxury items, far from it! It is all going towards fulfilling a desire, which most people get for free!

Yes! Indeed, what I just stumbled upon does carry solution to all my problems! Still, I wonder how is it that my Genius Husband's stock portfolio is showing hugely profound serious losses?! I think, it must be because he overthinks everything! Here is the secret, 'buy low, then sell high'! Even a monkey can do this! Hand over fist, people! Hand over Fist! I am all in! Now if I get that kind of infinite money then I will become the Messiah of Wall Street - The biggest casino of the world, then when that happens, my picture will be in the tabloids everywhere, then I will not even need to put up with this sick life of domesticity and for that matter why not just kick this husband out of my life for good! With this last thought, I become aware of The Devil's presence is now center-stage, so wisely I at once break this train of thoughts by slapping myself hard as punishment for straying to the wilder side!

What happens next? I too have now been initiated into the Royal Casino - The NYSE, New York Stock Exchange! ...

PARALYSING SNAKE-BITE: I-M-PURE LUST

"I am the fragrance in flowers, the heat in ambers,
the disturbance in storms, the eye of the winds,
What I need is that prick like Lord Shiva's,
that penetrates me and floods me with the nectar of life,
that can revive my dying soul,
What I need is a cup of poison from my teardrop,
to cut the poison that is my present body ...
Mast Mayuri, The Enchanting Serpent

-

THE SEDUCTION

After long deliberations and inputs from reading the "The Swindler's Diary," Chanakya is now able to narrow down, on a strategy, which will ensure him with maximum return on invest-ment (ROI), for swindling one's partner from their fair amount, by investing all the partner's income towards the house upgrades!

How quicky that a Rascal's plans get approved by Karmic Forces, is another Mystery that needs deep study indeed! Due to The Financial Crisis of 2007–2008 effecting the Architects hard-est, Husband Chanakya sees in it a fantastic opportunity to now start all upgrades, by hiring some high-quality talented Architects, for some great bargain prices! Since the birthday of His Wife Mayuri is also around the corner and since he must gift her some-thing for their Marriage Anniversary, especially because it is the first and so hard to sneak out of a gift without major fights! So, using this co-incidence as an excuse to kill two birds with one stone, he approaches his Wife with a proposal for a Water pool! Wife Mayuri choses to ignore all doubts, over his intentions behind this magnanimous gesture, afterall, the outcome is exactly what her need is! He adds, that since she is more enthusiastic about this project and his time-constraints do not allow any more, she now takes the responsibility of coordinating with this new architect named Faust instead! She accepts the offer, with a gracious smile. When Mayuri sees Faust, his strong built body like a stallion, re-minds her of her first love in America, even if it was un-requited, all wounds from losing that man seem to take new life in her, when her eyes first meet this Architect...

Who is this Beautiful Lady, Hiding under those Grandma Clothes!

Faust to himself: "Brave girl! No make-up! Not even a lipstick! Not even a Wedding ring! All the women I know, spend hours in the vanity room, wear clothes that let it all hang out, but here she is, dressing in a manner, no man will even bother to give her a glance even! What a display of appalling opposites!

Hiding behind those grandma clothes is a beautiful woman, who often weeps in solitude on that little girl in her who she could not save from her death! Have some patience my damsel-in-distress, the time of your nightmares are ending soon! I will be that knight in shining armor, who you have been waiting for to rescue you from the clutches of this savage who crawls on top of you every night and then enjoys what is my meal!" ...

WIFEY DOUBT

The enemy is fast approaching,
Yet she cannot understand her no-response as a response in this sce-
nario,
afterall, why would there be any,
when the pleasure is in dying, not living ...

As any dutiful wife's sharp intuitions, Wife Mayuri too, begins to sense some un-explained un-easiness every time when Faust enters in her domain, triggering in her warning bells, as if this man will have more impact on her life than her own Husband, and since such un-healthy comparison's with the Husband, even if harmless, has the potential of severe headaches in the future, she decides to avoid him and also disclose all about this feeling to her Husband!

That hidden seed of turmoil inside, finally finds its outlet at a friend's Wedding Gathering, where in front of everybody, the snake of confusions shows the darkness in the Future ahead! After listening to, stories after stories of wife's trying to out-do each other in some invisible holier-than-thou competition, Mayuri too does not want to get let behind and so in the process out-does herself, by wagging her finger as a warning signal towards her Husband, who is within earshot of the sister-in-law, "are you so blinded by your goal of saving money that you are willing to put your wife's security at risk by giving entry to some here-today-gone- tomorrow vagabond! Every time when I try to enquire him about his Personal life, he simply waives them aside! However, because he is also human, prone to error and since even the smartest ones have been found to slip in the matters of the Tongue, he also did, when in some casual conversation he started boasting about how much he has gained in terms of knowledge by experimenting with Human psychology! Made me at once wonder, if he also treats us too as his guinea pigs in his Psychology lab, where he can play with our emotions any way that he likes, just to get an answer to his absurd questions?! He has nothing at stake, if any of his experiments back-fire, while at the other end, what is at stake is my whole new Married Life, which if disturbed will enrich his knowledge base on my funeral pyre!

To diffuse the situation, Husband Chanakya making light of her warning, begins giving his answer in a nonchalant tone: "Faust made an offer that I could not resist! A twenty percent discount if I were to pay him up-front and if I do not take it now this offer will expire! So, without even consulting my dear sister I made the payment on the spot! Now my hands are tied and will have to move forward with him only as an Employee!". Now on seeing her Husband give more importance to his sister over her, Mayuri feels as someone who is still an outsider, is still not assimilated in the Family fold! Now her thoughts make an easy shift, towards the other man in her horizon whose thoughts bring a strange sense of security in her - Faust. She now begins to think about all the powerful coincidences that have occurred in bringing these two players under the same roof! How Faust too had to leave everything behind to come to Georgia while on the other hand her life too was also taking such a somersault that she too had to leave her blissful life to move to the same state as him! What a strange co-incidence! Also, this man sure cannot be ordinary, to have talked my genius brain husband into paying the full amount in advance! I cannot help but admire his genius in pulling off a feat that sure requires extraordinary brilliance!". Now when she sees herself admiring someone other than her husband, she at once dismisses the thought and punishes herself with a tight slap on her face, punishing her enough to never repeat such a mistake, as per the Culture, the moment a woman appreciates another man over her husband, right that instant, she loses her chance of winning the Title for 'The most dutiful wife," even if it were unintentional! To undo everything, she secretly repents by saying a short prayer in her head. Then it is as if her Husband is a mind reader, interrupts her prayer says, "Next time!" ...

HUNGRY!

Dear Mayuri's Diary,

I fear the voicemails the most, because now it means that someone has something meaningful to say! I am tired. Tired of dragging my body through endless insults just to feed this disconnected-from-soul-body's vain, mortal needs! Then does it not suggest that the most content people must also be the rudest, while the most hungry-for-more the humblest? I am sleepy again and need to go back to sleep again! What will do the trick of bringing this stone back to life? The thought of a good, cooked meal! I leap from my couch, off to the kitchen with a faith that can move mountains that I still have some desires left in me even if it is for my temporary body needs for some nice, hot delicious meal! Therefore, I bow to the genius of you Mother Nature and thank you for attaching this tiny stomach with a big appetite to my body, so now I do not go back to doing, what I love the most - sleep, sleep and some more!

...

SYSTEM GC ()

(System gc () - A function in Java Computer Language called to invoke garbage collector to clean the memory of the computer)

Lying in a comfortable Cobra Mudra/pose, gaze fixed at the computer screen, her mind is busy trying to solve the mystery of why, one day her day-trade worked for her, while the next day the same exact one failed! She is relieved when the chain of her futile thoughts going round and round in circles, finally find a break, by a soft knock on her already open door. She looks in the direction of the sound and if the observer were someone who did not know them before, would not have understood the cause of the smile is triggered by the presence of the face of the rare and always welcome - surprise visitor Faust! Assuming her smile as an invitation he sees no need for asking any permission to enter her private bedroom, he enters as someone would if someone knew the other person intimately from long ago.

Faust: "I have been keenly seeing, how your life revolves around talking with an inert computer screen only! This makes me feel sad! Why sad is because I have begun to care for my new "boss," and so I want to surprise you by sharing with you my secret hideout. This place is magical as whenever the stresses of work begin to overwhelm me, I take a break to go there and then I feel magically recovered and rejuvenated! Being four years older than me, I truly respect you and so I want to show you my respect towards you, by taking you far away from this Plastic world to a new world which breathes!"

She gets excited on learning about the age difference between them, as it is the same as her Younger Brother - Lucky Four! This mental association of Faust with her Little Brother Chandrashekhar instantly makes her trust him enough to accept his offer and then also there is her curiosity in seeing, if he is a genuine person or someone who is some secret recruit for some Pyramid Scheme which make fake promises of making millionaires out of zero! Not that these fake recruits are lying, as they do make millionaires but, just not out of us but themselves. When he does not turn out to be one of those, what a pleasant surprise it would be! Now, this new enthusiasm is enough to get her out of her Bed, but not enough to make her change from her house-wear pajamas into something more appealing and so she starts walking out in those pajamas itself! Now it is his turn to get surprised. He first looks at her from top to bottom in disbelief! Then he asks her politely to take a quick shower, change her clothes, comb her hair, and then come! If some third person were there, would have been one's wits end, trying to figure out the mystery behind her behavior, of not just complying to his simple wish that will make this poor Man happy? Because she is a Taurus woman, stubborn like it is symbol - Bull!

Mayuri: "It's mmarrrrwish!"
Faust: "What's marwish?"
Mayuri: "I said, it is my wish! Maarrrwish!
Faust: "When you talk like this, you sound like a Monkey, then is it my fault if I cannot follow a word, you just said?!"

Mayuri realizes she was being prudish. She blushes.

Mayuri: My allegiance is for my Husband only! It is only for him will I dress-up and no outsider, like you. I am going as is. Take it or leave it!"

Now his male ego gets aroused.

Faust: "Golly! When dealing with a stubborn mule, force is the only option left! If you will not yourself, I will pick you up and then put you in under the shower myself!"
Surprised by the thought of him executing his threat, she giggles shyly.

Mayuri: "Give me an hour to get ready"
Faust: "half"
Mayuri: "forty-five"
Faust: "Fifteen. Final"
Showing him a fist showing mock anger, she heads to the shower.

In the shower, she thinks, "What am I worth for? Nothing. Zero! Yet he does not think so. He sees me worthy of investing his most valuable investment in me - his Time! My worth in front of my own eyes is less than a drop in the ocean and yet he does not think so, as the way he treats me, is that asif my worth is in millions! If I do not give him a chance to show me what he wants, then it is a big loss for me, about his gains should not affect me either way!"

While she is finishing her gain and loss calculations, He is sitting outside, enjoying the sound of Water directly touching the sun-kissed brown skin of her body ...
After this small piece of Revelation dawning on her and him, their behavior towards each other takes a complete somersault! The mood must have changed significantly as her hands automatically

301

go towards clothes which flatter her slim Figure and some simple jewelry which put an unmistakable glow to her over-all appearance!

He walks surprised on finding just how the little victory over her has given him immense happiness while she walks surprised on finding that her true happiness is not in winning but in her defeat ...

TREE HUGGING HIPPIE

Now that Mayuri has left all comforts of her monster bed, her mood switches to flying high with Faust in his flaming red convertible! He rolls down his Windowpanes, she as if looking at him for instructions on what and how to do next, in this new type of car, mirrors his actions to the T! The weather enhances the mood by blowing a naughty gust of wind! How lovely she looks to him when those thick and long locks of hair fall over her Face by the wind, how handsome he looks to her when his red muffler on a yellow top is flying in the air by the wind!

When the weather is good, company fantastic, there is little reason for the mood to not turn up its volume from good to jovial!

This becomes clear, when she cannot help but let her humor sense entertain them some more with some of her good old humor sense and laughter. She laughs as she says, "Is this some trick of yours, of kidnapping me and then use me for getting some huge ransom from my filthy rich husband?! Then let me burst your bubble right now, as your plan is sure to fail as even if my husband is a fantastic figure, yet when put in a situation where he must choose between money or his wife, I have little doubt it would be the former and never the later!".

He smiles. She smiles. ...

CHATTAHOOCHEE NATIONAL PARK

Mayuri: "How is this even possible?! All this time I had a diamond under my eyes and yet could never see it! I drive past this area every day and yet it reveals its value to me only now?!

Who can be a bigger fool than me, counting all the Luxuries that I have been greedily accumulating as my Fortunes, were really they were my mis-fortunes due to their chain-like binding nature, while now when I am in the lap of Mother Nature, I can realize what I have lost and what I should salvage! Now with my awakened eyes, I can see, how the Merciful of All, has given to us in abundance, where we fail is in giving back with double force, so we can stay lightweight enough to fly across the oceans!

I can call myself fortunate to get a chance to see a Forest as back in my home-country, forests are just another abstract idea, which sprung from the wild imagination of the Rishis after smoking some of their favorite plant! Shame on us Indians, for plundering all the rich forest land we have! What we do not realize is that this is a crime against humanity! Being blessed with superior skills, we as Humans should be protecting the weak instead of just our bellies!"

Faust: "Do not beat your home country India for it, as it will not be too farfetched, when I say that the Indian Civilization is as old as Time itself and so has had a much longer exposure to Man's mindless exploitation of this Ecology than this Country on the West of the Globe! Since America is a Young Country, we should be using from the experiences of our neighbor India, otherwise we too will become it and not just it but this epidemic of materialism which has already devoured India, will now destroy us too, along with the Whole Planet!

So, then where do we go from here? Planet Mars?! No that is not the right answer! A Sacrifice of our Mother Earth just because we could not change our ways is not acceptable! Even if we find another planet, we will destroy it too, as simply because, in the process we have still not destroyed the cause!

So, what do we need now? A big revolution! With harmful pollutants in the air, there is just no way that we can continue viewing environmental problems with a dualistic viewpoint of seeing the land as separate countries, Oceans as separate for each country, Air separate for India and separate for America. We now need to see with a non-dualistic view where we stop looking at Land as Countries but as Land only, stop looking at Oceans as regional but Water only, Air pollution as not tied to a country Region but as Air only!

This is the main reason that, I have stopped seeing people by their nationality but as Citizens of the same World. As when one part of the world experiences hardships, the tremors originating from it, are felt by the entire world!

For Global Issues, we need to have uniform laws at a Global Level. Separate Religions trying to govern on top, becomes a superfluous and meaningless exercise. Uniform laws for all Nations, based on eternal laws, should be followed to ensure Global Peace and Harmony.

I want to shout my message to the entire world, to not get distracted from the real issues that are threatening this beautiful creation of ours as ultimately, we all have been created by the same parents when viewed at an Eternal Level."

Mayuri in a grim tone: "Who are you trying to save? Each one of us has already sold their souls to the Devil, from a long time now!"
...

IS HE AN ANGEL IN DISGUISE?

Wise Like a tree because, they stay silent ...

ANIMALS

Faust: "I am reminded of my diabetic cat who got neutered just as recent as yesterday, this should help lessen all the aggression I have to face every day."

A *stunned Mayuri*: "I want to know how it is even possible, that the same person can see injustice being done trees but not animals?! How is it even possible that these people who call themselves animal lovers are the very ones who take their pets to the vets for getting castrated, robbing them of their basic rights of procreation, being stuffed in tiny cages to be consumed at a commercial scale, amongst many other injustices, which I rather not begin now as it will require a lot more time than we have!

Yes, as humans we have proved to be the most fit for survival, but this does not mean that we should get the most share of everything. No, that is being selfish! Us being ethical creatures, means that we have an even greater responsibility towards the whole Eco-System. Due to commercialization reaching unprecedented heights, some people who are more aware want to just stop consuming all animal products and adopt a Vegan lifestyle! The effort is appreciable but since most successful and popular relationships found in Nature are symbiotic, this sacrifice seems an overkill! What we need to do here, is have a System that regulates the balance between give-and-take, but unfortunately due to the introduction of hi-tech machines, we are easily crossing all limits exponentially!

The city planners have indeed done a fantastic job in careful land assessments, putting price tag on every square foot of land,

and yet conveniently given the whole land to humans who can pay, while leaving nothing for the animals! I oftentimes laugh with this thought that, if ever we let monkeys also bid for houses, then we might just end-up trading using bananas as our currency! My heart bleeds when I see animals getting diseases that come from a sedentary lifestyle like obesity and depression! When you bring them home as pets, you kill them along with their role in the whole ecosystem! So, you either bring the whole outside ecology inside your house or else just let them go!"

Faust stands there amazed at how he just had such a fruitful conversation with a woman without focusing on the gender of the source ...

CONSUMER-PRODUCER
PATTERN - A PIG SOCIETY

Faust: Just like the complex organization of highly evolved insects like the Honeybees, who engage in a variety of complex tasks not practiced by the multitude of solitary insects, are divided into groups based on division of labor, we as Humans too are divided into groups. Since, the Business Transactions are the core component of this machinery which makes our Human World work, to understand the bigger picture, I have simplified it further by diving this fat class further into two classes - not over superficial attributes like color, ethnicity, and many other similar distinctions, viewing them as a society forming of two main classes: Consumer or Producer and unfortunately both sided are remarkably busy! While the producer is busy like a machine clearing whole forest after forest, to use that land for making bigger and bigger malls to not just meet but exceed the demand, while on the other hand is the Consumer who too is busy like a machine to not just meet his needs, but act as storage for all the future generations in one day itself!

The shrewd producer does not just rest easy, relying on human psychology of never being satisfied with what one has, he then comes with clever schemes to tempt the consumer to buy not just for his present need, but also for the rest of his life and the generations to come all in one shot! That is why, now we have a society who has long forgotten the principle, 'that we eat to live and not the other way around'!

My fear as a Citizen of the World is that the culture of consumerism has completely broken the backbone of the Ethical being! The moment he gets bit from this serpent of greed for more and more profits, from a free king of his own domain, he has now just become a slave, to his now high-profile lifestyle! This Materialistic Society has now successfully replaced Ethical behaviors with parasitic attitudes of take, take, and then some more, while not giving back anything!

Mayuri(laughingly): This tummy that I am rubbing, is growing but for all the wrong reasons!

When I first came to America from India, I blinked twice on seeing at the marvelous job that the Americans have done in building this Country! Initially, I thought that the beauty of America lies in its tall, beautifully architected Buildings but now I discover that the real gold is in its National Parks and the American People, who go all out to ensure that their environment stays clean! This Indian got a massive surprise of her life when she first tasted the water from a Spring here in America and I do not exaggerate when I say that the water tasted like sweet nectar, while in India, I cannot even dream of bathing in the rivers in their current state, even if it is our most revered river - Ma Ganga! Once as a teenager, when I could pick-up some courage to take a dip in holy River Ganga to cleanse myself from all my sins, turns out, whether my Karmic sins got erased or not, I sure needed a new shower for now!

Now that we are talking about water pollution, I see not why I should not mention anything about air pollution! The air is so polluted that when people wake up, they are unable to see too far due to a depressing haze covering the whole of my city of New Delhi! My happiness over my escape from there, gets eclipsed by my sorrow over my impotence in not being able to leverage my good state towards bringing the same happiness that can come only from living in a healthy environment!

Faust: "All this knowledge pouring out of you is not just you but because in you, you still carry with you the fragrance of the clay of a land where the Rishi's made their Home, their Honest values are ingrained in every pore of your body which is nourished by their blood which has become yours now, is finding its expression through your tongue! Like a fool, Human sits hunched up in front of his high-tech computer screens looking for ways to own more gold, not realizing that in the process they just lost valuable time in getting the real gold – Light from the golden ball of fire in the sky!

Mayuri: Also, that reminds me about Streetlights! I understand, it is hard for us living in good houses with nice curtains to shield us from those strong artificial lights to empathize with these trees, who unlike Humans do not have a tongue to voice their grievances! The benefits they give to us are just too many to even try listing them in a few words, still what they get back in return from us is unjustifiable abject cruelty! Why not repay their debt on us with more generosity and kindness? If it is a problem that the Modern Man has created, it should be him who should have to pay and not these helpless poor Trees! I am very sure that these very authorities who make rules of getting rid of trees to grab more land for their mansions are the very ones who will be passing amendments to change these anti-tree rules once they too cannot breathe due to lack of oxygen! I am sure that these same greedy hypocrites, will be scoring like mad men for planting them back! If all these authorities of the world were to listen to my view, I am sure the trees will double return their favor and bless them back in many ways that is beyond our comprehension!

Faust: "Most of the immigrants think that America is great due to its spectacular downtown night life, while really, America's true pride lies in the way we make earnest efforts towards preserving our Natural Resources, and yet, what you just called a forest is no forest, but a sterile gigantic size park to be more precise! A forest is where wild animals run free, do you by any chance see any at all here? No. The only place left for us to see them is either a Zoo or a Circus..."

Mayuri cannot help but feel immense respect towards her from him! Her life so far, especially after marriage had just been the same more-or-less idem per idem, till this redneck from Mississippi came along in her life! He laughed at her and with his his sapphire diamond eyes, looking in her brown eyes says silently, wake up! There is a new life outside your bedroom window, that Sunshine is for everyone but only the one who can open their eyes can see new frontiers! ...

Mayuri: You have opened my eyes to a whole new world! How can I ever repay you for this life-changing awareness? Here, please take this gold bracelet as a small token of my gratitude!"

He looks surprised and hesitant. She ties the bracelet herself from her arm to his. He accepts her token of appreciation with his charming smile. Mayuri wonders, 'if he is the angel who the fairy tales always talk about?'

Mayuri could have sworn they would have solved all the problems of the World this very day, if only it was not for the keen Architect sense of Faust, sounding an alert on seeing their shadows that had now started to look much longer than expected! Mayuri checks her phone. Damn Time! Time had indeed deceived them, un-noticed by them flew but not by the silent shadow – her husband. Proof? She sees around seventeen missed calls from him.

Faust(laughingly): "It is getting late. Let us go now, rumor is that the moon is an alien observatory that is meant to keep an eye on us. This stays a secret between us."

She knows all about the warnings of wise people of not sharing secrets with other men and yet she has little choice. She bends her head and says nothing!

As soon as she enters her home, an agitated Husband Chanakya asks her where she was and why even after about seventeen phone calls she never responded?

As much as Mayuri tries to tell him the truth she is unable. She at once distracts his anger with talk of giving him the money she owes him. Now he gets pleased in getting what he loves most, she gets pleased when he leaves all inquiry. End of fight.

She heads to the bathroom, the only place she has real privacy in her huge mansion of a House! Once sitting on her Throne, she first heaves a sigh of relief for dodging another bullet from her Husband but the next moment she becomes anxious over her own conduct!

Mayuri: "It was just a harmless outing with my newfound friend, yet why did I have to hide the meeting from my Husband who is all I want! Still why did God have to introduce this Man in my life at a time when the possibility of our future paths to intersect is impossible! Now when this other man's desire for me becomes un-bearable, he will kill my husband! Once my husband is gone, there will be little reason left for me to not marry him, even if he is the killer of my husband. We might stay happily together ever after, but we as a couple will never find respect in the society. As if, my life was not tragic enough, the thought of this new man's entry is mak-ing my life doubly tragic! To avoid more misfortunes, I must avoid him."

More despair!

IS SHE AN ANGEL IN DISGUISE?

She cries more for the husband's friend than her own husband.

The monster of the 2,008 fiscal crisis is advancing at a fierce pace, with its mouth wide open, devouring jobs, mainly in the housing industry! Since Faust is also in the way of the storm, he too becomes one of the collateral damages!

Mayuri is sitting next to her Husband and casually mocks about the ugly hole in Faust's running shoes! Then, she hangs her head in shame when her Husband tells her the reason behind it! It is not because, he is someone who is incapable of taking care of themselves, but because he has had no job from the past three months, and that is not so because he is not putting any efforts but simply because of external factors on which he has no power! Right then her head turns towards her own closet, the sight of it bursting with multiple shelves of shoes, makes her see, the injustice in the contrast of too much and too little for someone worthy, makes her wonder if she has been introduced in his life to reverse that injustice! She now begins to feel his pain just as any Wife does when she sees her Husband in distress!

Realizing that his Male pride might prevent him for accepting any monetary help from her, she begins creating small chores for him to do just so he can get extra money, so that he can stay afloat, till this tide of unfavorable times subsides! Before starting on her covert mission, she sees no point in asking dear Husband's permission, as doing so will only arouse more fights and misunderstandings for all the actors involved here.

When she is successful in filling his pockets by proxy, she feels proud of herself for being introduced in his life as an Angel, while on the other hand he too feels proud of himself for having such magnificent arms that can do anything! Faust's life is now taking a U turn as if he has just married a rich woman.

'Is she the Angel that fairy tales talks about,' Faust wonders as he is finally throwing those worn-out running shoes in the recycle bin! ...

THE ONE-EYED SERPENT

Faust likes a good challenge! What better than seeing if he can be successful in tunneling his thoughts into this kind of married woman's heart, who takes great pride in her belief that 'purity of love is to will only one thing' and for this dutiful Wife, her husband that 'one thing' is her husband only and then stealing her heart from her from right under her nose, then if that does not pull the farce of Institution of Marriage then what else will ever?!

Luck favors the brave, and he too gets his chance to show his muscle! It is early morning when he arrives in Mayuri's residence. Since he likes to hear some lively music playing in the background while working, he puts on some Music with words which could arouse feelings of love in the listener and a sound which will give an illusion that it is as if him singing those words for the Lady of the House, in the house at that moment! His voice, echoing through the whole house like some surround speaker reaches straight into the ears of the Woman he had intended for! The Music is doing its magic, as he has started to whistle and as he hears her footsteps dancing in her own room, he knew she also is listening to the same thing. Suddenly the footsteps change. The earlier rhythmic footsteps of back and forth and then back, had changed to steady footsteps approaching towards the bathroom. Without much of a thought, he jumps into the same bathroom, where she is heading, then intentionally leaves the door unlocked then and as quickly as he can, he pulls out his one-eyed monster out of his captivity all out in the open as his belief is that once anyone sees it, can never forget that once-in-a -lifetime view!

Ms. Mayuri unsuspectingly opens the door. Then whatever she saw makes her shut her eyes and lets out a scream which fortunately for her, no one hears, however unfortunately again for her, in that moment of a blink, is enough to send the image of the Thor's Hammer directly to her memory's permanent memory hard disk!

Her run ends as she lands squat in the middle of her husband's feet! Husband kicks her off as if she is some little puppy! Without aiding her in getting up, he asks her with an authoritative tone 'why do you look so flustered?' She stammers. She bites her lip as no matter how hard she tries, her tongue refuses to reveal itself the truth at this moment to this listener! Her story-telling qualities come to her rescue as she runs back as quickly as she can once over!

Now with her solitude, Mayuri sits and wonders, "How low will I feel when two mighty swords would clash, and the cause of their Fight is none other but me! Both care for me, just in different ways − one's love for me is like of an old man, for who I am like a habit, while on the other hand is of a Young Stud who makes efforts to see a smile on my face, is thirsty for the wine which only I serve..." Surprised over such a corrupting thought, that is insulting her husband, while praising another Man be presented to her by her heart, she at once punishes herself with a hard slap on her face so never can such a devilish thought can ever corrupt her allegiance towards her husband even if the Husband is really the monster in my fairy tale!" ...

HELL, HATH NO FURY LIKE
A WOMAN SCORNED!

THE SCOUNDREL OF SCOUNDRELS AND THE
PERVERT OF PERVERTS

This is her day to shine, so leaving all work obligations, she heads to a beauty parlor, to look the best-fit for the new Avtar she must now play! Indeed, she is looking juicy in her black party dress, revealing her bare skin under her shapely shoulders with spaghetti straps. Her earrings adorning her ears with a double-helix shaped twisted danglers, which match with her twisted desires, her Neck with a fiery Ruby necklace which goes well with the fire in her belly, her Arms with sparkling bangles that are reflecting all colors just like any peafowl would when it gets excited by the rain droplets falling on its skin and so begins to dance! Synchronous with her inviting looks is also her mood that is lively from all the blood reaching the furthest extremities in her body from all the dancing and singing she just did to the lively music in some club nearby. Her cheeks are now showing a healthy red, a sign of the bubbling life in her! Her Desire is even more fueled on seeing how her Friends look at her as some Object of Pity while themselves as the Superior one, as why not should they, when they own, what she does not and God willing the barren land may never get any rain....! This day carries in it the power of reversing her curse of infertility, which if not reversed in time has the potential to destroy

323

through all her body and mental stress thresholds! In short, her life depends on it!

When darling husband opens the door, she jumps on him, she thinks her recently learned trick from reading the Kamasutra Manual diligently is paying off, while he is relieved on finding his back could hold her weight without snapping! Instead of any welcoming signs, he rebuffs her advances. Now she gets angry over his coldness towards her.

Mayuri: "If you do not find me desirable, then why did you fly across states to marry me?!"

Chanakya (getting more restless): "It's impossible today! Even if you were to come to me in the only outfit that I like to see women in, I would still not touch you today! I am working under a tight deadline which I have already missed twice. Missing this deadline, a third time will mean I will have to face the wrath of my Immediate boss, who is already looking for excuses to fire me from my job! I am a mere slave to my job, loosing which will mean a career suicide!"

Blinded by her own fears, she sees his explanation as just another lame excuse!

Mayuri: "Cheat! Now all my doubts over your true intentions of not having another child are taking firm root in my mind, why would you, when once your tongue had accidentally slipped and reveled your true feelings over the matter: 'Having a child is a thankless job! One sacrifices one's entire youth, bends backward to raise them-up with the best of their abilities only to find that at the time of old-age when we need help the most, they are unable due to their own limitations!' I should have acted right then and then, but I know not why I did not! My whole Telos as a Woman is at stake! The difference between my energies and yours, is that I am insane for my wish to materialize, while for you it is just a nice to have!"

Chanakya: "You do not understand the wrath of my boss!"

On seeing that she is not getting things her way, she becomes even more aggressive, so this time she becomes more violent as she shuts off his computer!

Mayuri: "Leave everything NOW! All these subterfuges might work well with your seven-year-old daughter but not with a mature woman like me! You must be scoundrel of scoundrels to shower the feelings meant for your wife to shower them towards your lovely daughter instead!"

Chanakya, re-composing himself, just like a thief who gets caught with his hand in the cookie jar: "You jealous, barren woman! Whether or not I am a scoundrel of scoundrels you sure are a pervert of perverts for doubting the most-sacred relationship that ever existed since eternity!"

By this time, she has lost all patience! With a tone that is reflecting all the anger and anxiety she is feeling, she speaks.

Mayuri: "I am too busy myself to put up with your shenanigans!"

He goes silent.

His silence aggravates her even more!

She threatens him with fingers pointing like needles, "if you are not going to stop working then..."

"Then what? then you will spend your night with your dear friend Faust instead, right?! His response is dripping with sarcasm reflecting his hidden jealousy from his wife's closeness to their dear friend.

Now she goes silent.

Her silence now aggravates him even more!

He angrily retorts, "I feel used, manipulated to be used as an instrument in your hands to implement your evil designs! You do not love me as much as you love your dear friend Faust! Your reason for a baby is not because you want a baby with me only, but because you too want the status in Society that every vain woman wants which only comes from becoming a mother! As Shri Krishna in Bhagwad Gita once rightly said that 'a body of a woman is like a piece of Land. If the land is fertile, seed will certainly take root, if not then the seed cannot be blamed!' You are too silly to see the reason I stay so late in office! Infertility is your curse but by Marrying you it has become my misfortune too!" ...

A BAD OMEN

The more Mayuri thinks of her situation, the more fear and anxiety tighten their grip on her! Her mind is hyperactive to make this moment happen as if her whole future depends on the success of this one night alone! The Taurus Bull in her is angry, feels cheated and it is her duty to correct this injustice! But what is this? As she stands-up to fight for something that is rightfully hers she cannot! She has a lead foot, her body frigid. Is it because of the lingering disturbing effect of the last night's horrible dream that with a blink of an eye take away with it the Will in me to not give-up! The flashes of the Dream come in front of her eyes once more as follows: 'when she begins to embrace her husband as she puts her arms around him, he appears to morph into some mutilated weird looking diseased creature which is covered with warts all over! The moment she sees this transformation she gets so frightened that it appeared to her that she had intentionally ended the dream by forcefully opening her eyes! She interprets the meaning behind the imagery as a message to her awareness that the one she sees as her Husband is not meant for you! Now that she can see the dream take actual shape, she gets more desperate to get to her goal even if all the signs are not favorable! Her desperation now takes a dangerous turn by transforming into a burning rage, drowning all the screams of reason that are in unison begging her to let him go! Now anger has taken firm control over her, her acid tongue is now spitting fire. This worsens the situation even more as the flames of anger engulf the Husband too and so he too loses all his control! From here on bewilderment and delusion are in firm control over all her later actions! So, like some evil witch that will destroy anything and everything that comes her way, she too let all her anger find its outlet through her long and sharp nails, which she uses as mini knives for making deep wounds all over his body! The wounds are so deep that Blood begins to ooze out of them. Some outsider seeing might think, that the cause of the husband's bewilderment is his bleeding wounds on the chest, but that is not the case as the cause is the sight of blood stains all over the freshly installed carpets, which will now need a significant amount of Money for cleaning-up the whole mess! Before he ends -up killing her, he chooses to punish her by not letting her win, so he picks his bag and begins to walk hastily out the door. Seeing him leaving, her anxiety now grips her firmly. She uses a parallel karate move to lunge forward so she can grab him by his thighs, preventing him to leave. But that did not happen. Due to poor execution of her karate move, instead of him stopping in his tracks, she trips and falls with her body flat, face down on the floor!

Now she is lying on the floor with a broken leg, he is now in a position where him losing his job is certain. Fortunately, the Sun comes out to give a pause to this dance of death that had just started and seemed will stop only once it has turned everything to ash! ...

ACT 0 - IS SHE THE DEVIL IN DISGUISE?

Chanakya to himself: "The importance of this hard kick in my stomach by being fired from my job, cannot be emphasized enough! My wife is sleeping comfortably thinking that this event only affects my reputation in front of my peers, while not realizing that, she will also have to pay, if not double than my losses! Let the sleeping dog's sleep a little longer just enough for me to pull the rug from under her feet before she does mine instead!

Being the smarter one of the two, to be successful, I will first trick my ethical self itself, into believing that the wrong, I am about to do is the right thing. This way I am protected from any pangs of guilt or pity, which can potentially harm harm my own sanity instead! So dear Heart of mine, always remember, everything about her is fake and pretentious. She professes that the basis of her allegiance towards me is eternal love, while it is easy to see that, her claims can never be true, as the basis of this Marriage tie, is just weak bonds of desperation for un-fulfilled desires and fear of a lonely future! Her real allegiance is to her goal and since the path to get to that point goes through me only, she acts like a servant to me! Since she is not so smart to be that conniving, she does things in innocence as is clear when in her own innocent way, she rationalizes that whatever she does is out of love for me, while really, if I were impotent, then it is she who would be looking for ways of getting rid of me, no matter how painful or evil! For sure! Her love for me cannot be pure, as how can it be so, when really her heart and mind is completely full of a picture of a baby, even if it is mine! Her sinister desire has transformed her from some Angel to a wretched Witch! I cannot even recognize this person from the person that I first met. It is a symbiotic relation, where I have what she needs and that what makes her dependent on me, as the path to her victory passes through me. So, in a way, she is making a fool of me, and since she is at fault, then it is only fair game if I outsmart her before she makes a fool out of me instead.'

Ok then, now that I am fully convinced, I will stage a drama that the whole World will see and remember for ages to come.

Saying it, he bursts into his signature uncontrolled laughter,

"A Hahahahaha MuhahahahahA MuhahahahahA ahahaha." Once his uncontrolled laughter is back in control, he at once dials his best friend Faust number, after all what are friends for but to bail a friend in demanding times!?

Chanakya to Faust: "She must not know me! Now I will create such a drama that will expose her devil's mask of selfishness and deceit, not just for her own deluded self, but also for the entire world to see and rejoice with me!

Since, I no longer have faith in my own senses, as they have betrayed me far too many times now, to not acknowledge, the fact that there is some kink in me which always pushes me away from the path of righteousness towards the path of self-destruction instead! Therefore, I want to hire you, my dear friend, my only confidante, as a hitman to go and behead my wife!

Faust begins to laugh first. Then becoming serious, lectures his dear friend like a good friend would to any other good friend in distress. He counsels Chanakya to calm down as there is no situation so complex that cannot be fixed by some Good-Old-Counseling-Advice! So, he volunteers that he himself will go as his broker to counsel her. He can help her by throwing some light on the real reason behind her insane behavior.

Faust: "She is an intelligent woman; I know exactly what her problem is. I am sure once she understands what is gripping her moods, she will snap out of whatever spell that she is under, just like magic! What I am about to say is not some village gossip monger's spiced-up tale but is based on scientifically proven facts which will help you understand that she is genuinely sick, is suffering from symptoms of pre-menstrual syndrome also referred to as PMS for short. Why do you think woman go through PMS? Because biologically speaking, it is their last chance to get Pregnant during this cycle, which is a woman's most primal goal. And the pain is a biological signal for her to fulfill this need too! At a micro level when you see, there is one egg and billions of sperms fighting with each other to penetrate the egg. Then it is the egg that accepts or rejects. It is only when the egg accepts the right sperm, does fertilization occur. Similarly, at a macro level, a lady waits patiently for her right suitor to come and cruelly rejects the others. The right suitor too is the one, who perseveres for her and only her; Thus, it becomes a test of a woman's ability of whether or not she can live drinking the slow poison of an eternal wait for the right mate, who may or may never come; While in case of a man the test lies in his Eternal Persistence in trying to become worthy in her eyes, and when that magic moment happens, their moment of conjugal bliss lingers on in form of their children and then children's children and so on!"

Chanakya: "I know she never listens to anybody yet if you persist, do give it a try. But remember if you fail you will kill her. This will be a huge favor from a friend to another."

With all this touch of affection, he gives him a tighter than normal hug. Faust cannot help but wonder if he is bi-sexual but then smiles when this thought arises that, somewhere we are all promiscuous in Nature, bi-sexual are people who must take themselves too seriously! ...

ACT 1 A MOCK FIGHT

Husband Chanakya enters the bedroom where Wife Mayuri is sitting with an intent of starting a fight and then leaving for the next stage of his Drama to begin.

Chanakya: "I'm going to my sister's house far away from your acidic words."

He then slams the door on her, insulting her by not caring to hear anything that she had to say!

Mayuri: "After compromising with my freedom of choices, I feel cheated! We get married and suddenly we have a Partner to give or take advice from! Major deception, as whenever an either/or, "Dharamsankat' situation arises, either one of the Parties will have to compromise! I can now see this contradiction which is one of the reasons behind my Despair: Being a fully grown adult I am expected to take full Ownership for my actions, after all it is me also who will get fried in hell's cauldron for all these sins in the Karmic Court and yet being a duty-bound wife, my accountability shifts as now I am expected to do what my husband thinks is the right thing! All my trust in the Institution of Marriage is gone! For me to trust anyone again is impossible! Is not the only true relationship that binds us is Humanity and nothing else?! I am now in such a sorry state that even if my darling husband were to walk all over my rights to go for another woman, I will be only drinking that poison silently!" ...

ACT 2 - IS HE THE
DEVIL IN DISGUISE?

Every word from Husband Chanakya, pierces through his Wife Mayuri's heart, like arrows dipped in poison, sharper than a hundred spears combined!

When one is burning from insult of being scorned, the flames must go up to the merciful Father-of-All above, who then acts by at once injecting His Angel of Faith to re-kindle hope of a new life!

She takes off all her ornaments one by one, slowly, stoically changing into her thin black dress to go sulk in her sulking chamber - her bathtub to burn alone in the fire of insults that come from rejection by someone who is most trusted! With downcast eyes she says to herself, "I earned a lot of money life, not realizing that what I thought would give me security became the very cause of insecurity and a secret fear of death from the very people with who I live with!"

She has her sedatives in her hand for deadening all voices of reason when she hears the doorbell ring. Her ears perk-up. It could not be her husband as he is too arrogant to listen to her word, then who else...? Now double curious she runs fast to open the door. Now whoever is on the door no surprise that he looks doubly handsome to her! When she hears Faust friendly voice, she knows not how all her pain has vanished! He suggests they go near the pond to see if he can do anything which can bring back peace to the lives of this household. He leads her to follow to the pond that they he had built for her. When has fire and cotton be friends that they would now, so that from here gravity takes over to set the scene, for the rest to follow like chemical processes!

Faust first strikes some casual conversation with her as she sits down in her black nightgown playing with her own reflections in the water and then throwing some on the Lotus Flower.

Then, he gives her a full body scan from top to bottom, which can be decent, till it gets stuck at the obstructions on the chest and then it cannot call it decent anymore! She blushes and her head bends down with shyness, when she just gets conscious of her revealing dress, she at once covers her breasts with her hands and runs in bashfully to change into something more decent. He enjoys how she gets conscious and runs inside. He wants to run after her and enter the room and see how she looks naked, but he does not, instead eagerly waits for her to come out. His wait is well rewarded when she comes out looking stunning in her silky navy-blue spaghetti top and matching silk pajamas, when a naughty waft of wind blows opens her long hair from her loosely tied bun, making her bagala-mukhi (Swan Face in Sanskrit) features even more beautiful!

He uses flattery to make her fly just enough so he himself does not lose his own footing, as much as possible!

Faust: "Your husband must be either blind or gay to leave his charming wife alone and unhappy like this! If I ever had the good fortune of having you in my life, my life would become more colorful than the rainbow in the sky. Your moonlight like aura would have illuminated all my nights."

Mayuri: "Beauty lies in the eye of the beholder and to know that your beautiful blue eyes could see them makes me feel so much more beautiful. Then she uses flattery to make him fly just enough so she herself does not lose her own footing, as much as possible!

Mayuri: Is flattery not but a refined art of lying? Especially in cases when a lover is trying to impress the lover!

Faust: **We must understand the difference. Truth is not light or darkness, but that both Light and Dark exist!** Lying by itself is not a reflection on anyone's Character as when used for a worthy cause it is just else is in-just and since impressing a lover is ultimately a good cause I see no harm in using it in these matters of the heart!

Mayuri laughing: "And pointless to say, telling the truth at this point, is virtual suicide!"

They both sit next to each other, playing with the reflections of the moon in the water. Both forget the entire world around them with its miseries! In this moment it is only him and only her, alone only with the sounds of their heartbeats!

When he kisses the reflection of the moon, she thinks he is kissing her reflection, so she blushes. Then when he sees her blush, he blushes on realizing that the cause is him. When he catches himself blushing, a roguish grin spreads over his Face. Even if they are alone and no one can hear them, they know not why they are answering in whispers!

Suddenly at this point of time, the control shifts from their hands to their entangled frequencies to bring order to all the chaos around them! Then, as if the supernatural forces were conspiring with the evil in them, a thunderstorm appears on the horizon. Both get wet. They run in to sit next to the fireplace.

Both are sitting side by side watching the fire. Being true to the reason that he is here, he begins his counselling session with her. Sticking to his plan for a compromise between the couple at war, Faust begins his earnest effort for a reconciliation.

Faust: "Do you have the courage to swallow the bitter pill of truth?

Mayuri: "I have no choice left for me other than facing the truth! My heart's state is like that little girl's, who must serve milk laced with poison to her sheep who has gone mad and is just too nervous to do anything! Then my intelligence tells me stoically, 'look again! What you are assuming to be a Sheep is really a fox in sheep's disguise. This sheep claims that she has not gone mad, but really it is only an act! He is a very cunning and shrewd fox. It runs around barking loud, creating a fuss till it gets everything it wants exactly how it wants! This fox has no allegiance to its Master, only to the feed. If the Master will not serve its needs. I will not be surprised if the fox kills its own master and then without feeling any remorse go hunting for its next prey. This cat has now tasted blood, is now even meaner and hungrier! Really, he cannot lose as if I am living, I am paying him from my salary and if I die, he gets even more from a life-insurance policy that he took out on my name with him as the beneficiary! Marriage must be crowned as one of the biggest deceptions of all-times in giving one a sense of false security!"

Once Faust learns about the life-insurance policy, he can see the real motive behind Chanakya's victim card drama and after that his allegiance reverses!

Faust surprised: "I had come here to counsel you for a compromise with the situation, but now after hearing your perspective, I am myself convinced that despite being an intelligent woman you cannot figure out how to get out of this trap! The very time you need your husband, he is with his sister instead! What good is he to you! Divorce him! Divorce him now! For that matter, why even waste time for the entire process to finish? Just leave him this instant! Your life is under a bigger threat!"

Mayuri: "The SuperKundalini has given women a sacred door for delivering the purest gift of nature, but when the same sacred door is used for peeing, is like sin mocking the pious! Which makes me wonder if anything at all is sacred in this world?!"

Listening to the echo of her worst fears from his mouth, she sits terrified of her own shadow! Suddenly, now this mouthpiece starts looking twice more handsome than ever before! ...

ACT 3 - WHEN SPACE DISTINCTIONS VANISH TO WITNESS THE WEST EMBRACING THE EAST!

'mano to ganga ma hu, na mano to behta paani'
(When you look with Reverence you see River as our mother, else it
just flowing water)
- Unknown, A popular Hindi saying

Once the third Wheel Faust and Wife Mayuri, loose their man-made Relationship tags to become just Faust and just Mayuri, what do they do then!? Like children they start playing silly monster games! Simple. Faust is running after Mayuri, shouting, "I am a monster! I am going to eat you! Run for your life! Hahahahaha"! Taking his threat seriously, she too begins running as fast as possible to get in the master bedroom upstairs and then under the blanket - the place where she feels most safe and happens to be the precise place where gravity too is working in favor of having two beating hearts playing hide-and-seek with each other to finally come out of their hiding, as now human's work is over as the gravitational energies now take over, ensuring, the job will get done!

After all the running upstairs, he cannot resist falling on the clean, inviting bed, which she had just prepared for herself and her husband to enjoy! The sight triggers in her a bitter-sweet revelation, "Efforts never get wasted! The comedy in the situation is that all this while I was stressing that all of my Investment of Time in making preparations for this evening so I can enjoy with this man will all get wasted,   only to find to my pleasant surprise that all the investment I made in efforts were never a waste, as it will pay off, even if it is not with this man but with that man instead! I will be a fool if I give credit to myself for my efforts as something which started this evening from preparing the bed but from a time that is way before I had even met this strong-armed American man! All those efforts in getting situated in American society, learning American accent for better communication with Americans that I did thinking they were for that man, only to find that they were really for this man! Then on thinking in Eternal Timespans then possibly even before from wanting this Man from some earlier birth that that hidden desire that pulled me across Oceans, to a whole new Continent, just for this one moment of Pleasure! So, it is only fair when I say that my whole life so far has been nothing but a big preparation for this one moment of ecstasy!? Now what do I do, when I am face-to-face with this paradox: The fruit of all my eternal gains is at the tip of my tongue, but ethics on the other hand is frowning? Suspend ethics! I be damned if my foot slips now! Simple."

When he sees her more open to his suggestions, he mixes his deadly cocktail, which has never failed in any of his past conquests - Singing a romantic song with some marijuana! On seeing him light a skinny joint like him, dread comes all over her face!

Mayuri: "Why do you smoke marijuana which is illegal while all these strong sedatives and alcohol have the same effect just without any headaches of getting in trouble with the law!"

Faust: "Burn all these sedatives you have right away! How can anyone not be schizophrenic, when our bodies are more than seventy percent water and anyone who says that they do not see any link between water and emotions must have never saw the insane heights that the tides can rise to, for kissing the surface of the moon especially on a full moon! Amongst many of the lies floated in this World, this one is also false! Sedatives and alcohol are a downer, while marijuana on the other hand is an upper, meaning rises the spirits!"

Mayuri: "When Lord Shiva enjoys this plant, cannot be that bad. Why not?"

She acknowledges her consent by accepting his offer. Her honoring him by respecting his word, flatters him. Seeing the fire burning in the fireplace, he cannot stop himself from singing a song in her presence:

'a storm roars outside, a storm roar inside
Thunder and lightning roar at a distance, warning us will fall on us,
outside water is extinguishing fire, inside water is starting fire,
outside insanity, insanity inside,
close your eyes to see nothing, yet you are still seeing,
* but this time with the eye of the eye,*
that the fire you see in me for you is really the fire in you for me ...

She is sitting at his feet on the floor next to the couch on which he is sitting. She is looking for some support to get up, he extends his hand to lift her. When she sees the helping extended hand is strong but is not of her husband, in her begins a conflict! Holding a hand of someone other than one's Husband, is against cultural teachings. She wants to refuse, but still, she knows not why she accepts it. As she is putting her hand in his, a life-secret reveals itself to her at that moment: **'We all react to external situations like chemical processes! All that we can do is just let go of the past and accept whatever that the future has to offer us with gratitude! ...'**

Once both have lost all touch with this fake reality made by Human, Raw Natural Forces begin to play. The universe pauses to see this beautifully executed somersault by destiny, to see this rare moment, when the East and West dissolves all their differences to become one, when the master becomes the slave, the queen of this person becomes the queen of that person. ...

THE CENTURIES OLD IDOL OF MARRIAGE FINALLY SMASHED INTO FINE PIECES HERE!

My Body is a Temple,
It is the Stones that are alive, us humans never were ...
- *Mast Mayuri, The Intoxicated Peafowl dancing in the Rain*

Once the lustful passions have had their way, they also leave these bodies cold, to find their next victim! Their victim on the other hand, scratches their heads, trying to figure out how a sensible person like them, could also do something that only some insane person would do! Now he slaps himself for his poor execution in his role as a broker! If only he would have watched this drama as a third person and not become the first person himself... he is making a hasty exit to avoid meeting the husband at the door, while she is slapping herself hard for not recognizing her death who had come to her in the form of this deceiver who has already left her alone! She slaps her once again to remind herself of this hard-earned lesson that she seems to forget whenever it is needed the most: 'the source of enjoyment does not depend on the quality of the other partner but one's own imagination, the performance of this man is same as that man's, if not even more pitiable!

Mayuri: "I know not why I feel, as if the very first moment when the lover's eyes meet, their future is sealed?! Like moths rushing into fire with great speed, they too despite knowing their meeting will only end in pain and heartache, meet. **Now if this contrariety not the biggest cosmic joke played on us mortals, then what is? Well, the comedy of errors does not just end here, as once they consume their desires the magnetic pull with it, too gets consumed, in some invisible vortex, leaving the lovers wondering, how a sane mind like theirs could do something so insane like that?!**

Since this tragic episode also marks the end of our brief friendship, I feel cheap, like some disposable toilet paper and yet I cannot curse him as I must have seen an Image of the qualities that I look for in a husband and so let him enter my body temple, or none of all these thoughts have any substance and that I am just making too much out of some harmless self-play-joys! If I expect it to become some lifelong drama, then the fault is in my expectation! Just stomp on it and be done with it already!"

On stomping over these time-consuming thoughts, also comes the realization that there is no time to grieve at all! Her misfortune is she cannot just sit there transformed into a Stone but fight for her life till the show is still on! She quickly gets-up and re-composes herself to deal diplomatically with the next stage of this dark night which seemed would only end after it has drunk all the blood from her heart and then served in her skull to the devil in a silver platter! All her fears take shape as she begins to hear the heavy footsteps of her Husband nearing the entrance to the place of all action! ...

ACT 4 - BRAIN FRY!

Mayuri is sitting with her one knee touching the bed, while other knee supporting her elbow as her hand cups her forehead. This is not time for reflections, but action and that too now! In such a state of confusion and haste, only utter confusion is King!

Mayuri: "I get no satisfaction! When the trade goes wrong, the loss pains me and when the trade goes right, then also the gain pains me because now I kick myself for not going all-in in that one winning trade!"

A good gambler is one who has the discipline to stay within the limit, but her being a novice is challenging! Earlier during the day when she was tired of small petty wins and petty losses, she was toying with a trade that is all or nothing! Since the thought had gone in suspended mode and so this same trade is still on her screen, which is just a keystroke away from execution is a great set-up for some major upheavals! In her confusion, she is running towards the computer to start her own little drama of pretending to look busy with her usual pending office work. In her nervousness, she hits the key that executes that fatal trade that acted like the final nail on her coffin! In these times of HFT - High Frequency Trading, in a matter of a fraction of Second, the execution of all open orders happens! Being no undo choice, it takes away all her life-time earnings with this one fatal keystroke! In less than a second, from hero she became zero! Now that there is no undo choice, all her money is for-ever gone into some blackhole, that has no beginning and no end! Once an arrow leaves the bowstring, it cannot comeback! No matter how much she prays, the black monster of death, refuses to regurgitate! The train wreck has happened and all she can do is curse her own timing!

On seeing danger, a Pigeon's reaction is to close its eyes hoping that the predator too will do the same and this way will not see it! But that is just dreaming and so, then not becomes food for the predator. She too feels like being in that same pigeon's state - paralyzed with anxious! Once fear has completely overpowered her, she can feel all saliva in her mouth drying up, a burning sensation under the Skin and as if she has forgotten how to get her breath back to her body! Unable to see any escape route from this fiasco, she can now see, all those inauspicious omens, dire consequences take a real shape ...

PUBLIC STONING!

An experienced Policeman knows the Perpetrator as soon as he sees the scene. The strong smell of marijuana tickles his nostrils whispering the dirty secret, as he stands at the foot of the staircase. As he goes up the staircase, ornaments that his wife would often wear were lying scattered on the steps, telling him the trailer of a story whose heroine is his wife, but hero is not him but his own best-friend! His male-ego gets a rude blow as he knows not why he expected his wife to have either killed herself or the invader but never surrender to that other man who has no qualities in common witch could have confused his muddlehead wife's head or something like that!

Chanakya to himself: "How can this be? This woman who was so dumb that she would act like her own enforcer for the censor-board policing her own thoughts from only allowing my thoughts only, is now in another Man's arms! This event is a big slap on my mental prowess! Not just that, it also means she does not love either of us only the one who will flatter her ego the most; Yet it cannot be true either because I do not see any signs of self-love in her. Then it means, she is a mere slave to her desire that too was not hers but something which was planted in her by me!"

He continues to walk in disbelief and self-denial, till he is now at the scene of action - their bedroom, where he is now staring face-to-face with reality. He says nothing and just looks at her angrily, expecting her to explain herself by her-self.

Her face looks white and perplexed. She stammers incoherently and inadvertently extends her hand to cover the screen! Her nervous reflex action of covering the screen to hide the blunder, instead attracts his attention towards what she is trying to hide! He pulls her hand off the screen, which screamed all her trade loses flashing in bold blood red color! ...

ACT 5 - A HARD KICK IN THE STERNUM OF THE GODDESS OF MONEY, LAKSHMI!

When Chanakya sees all her money or his money by proxy, disappear in a split of a second, a cold chill runs down his spine. Then when his gaze turns towards his Wife Mayuri, a cold chill runs down her spine. Seeing her face turn white, he wants to embrace her, tell her he will fix everything, but in the very next moment he looks at the screen, then he is fire again. He takes her by her long hair and dragging her down the stairs, says, "You worthless woman! The very one Goddess of Money, Ma Laxmi, who has been the most generous with us, you just kicked her in the sternum! Now alienating her means no money, no money means you are no good either! Your ignorance of the dangerous effects of promiscuity has put an end to our Marriage! Just so you understand the gravity of the situation, sexually transmitted diseases (STD's) are at an all-time high in the world, especially here in America where you live! Now you are impure for me to live with you anymore! You were my goose which laid golden eggs every month, but now you are neither golden nor good for your dried-up eggs, you are only the source of my disgrace now! The cause of your miserable condition now is wanting something that is beyond your body's limitations so now I will help you get free of that bondage by deviating your desires to just one desire which is death!

ANOTHER PLATITUDINOUS
WANDERING JEW BORN!

Husband Chanakya: "Who are you?! don not even recognize you anymore! Just a short while ago, you were pledging your allegiances to your Great Husband Chanakya till eternity and beyond, but now in just that one night when I was not with you, you forgot everything and the insult to me does not just end here, as you were dancing and playing with a whole new Husband who has no resemblance with me for you to delude yourself into mistaking me for a look-alike! Here I was thinking that the net of religious vows we took with fire as our witness is a proven method of taming a lioness, will work again! Now I know never to underestimate the power in lustful desires! Now no one will take me seriously, including myself! My surprise is not as much over my own wife's conduct but why it has taken me so long in throwing her out! I AM NOT YOUR HUSBAND ANYMORE!!! You are a fake... A BIG FAKE! I just helped you by proving to you, because you are too retarded to see for yourself! You should be grateful to me for bursting your bubble and bringing you down to FREAKING REALITY! 'Patience is divine,' you say all the time, right? then just wait some more 'patiently' and watch what I do now! Just bloody watch!"

With these murderous thoughts swimming wildly through his mind he is now thinking of the strictest way of punishing his wife! To make his importance felt, he takes his cigarette and by using the lit end, burns the top layer of the skin situated right in the middle of her forehead, just where the Lord Shiva, The Lord of Destruction's

Third eye is found. It is easy not to miss it due to the glowing red Kumkum (An accessory worn by most Indian Woman) she is wearing.

He continues, "This burn has been strategically put at a spot where the third eye lives as when the Third eye opens it is said to burn all desires in the person. Which means you will wander around hungry forever, like the proverbial 'Wandering Jew' or the Character Ashwatthama in the Epic Mahabharata!"

She crouches down expecting him to beat her but instead, to her surprise, he has already vanished from the scene. Even after going through all the humiliation, one would expect one to let go of everything but even she does not know why she still thinks of herself as his wife and is still worried for his welfare! So, fearing that he might be doing something to hurt himself, she runs towards the door and starts banging on the door, asking him to open the door, saying "it's me! ... open the door ... it is me!"

Suddenly she stops making her own banging noise, in-order to hear the sounds coming from his Room and when she did hear she gets full of dread, as the sounds were of his leather belt touching his own bare skin! She gets even more horrified when she realizes his real agenda behind disappearing like that! He is making marks on his body to serve as a proof which will not do much damage to him but will decimate her completely! Dread written all over her face, she is now shivering nervously once she understands the real intent behind all this high-stress drama!

Mayuri: "He is trying to get me trapped in an offense which is untrue yet difficult to reject. He is smart enough to not wait for me to do what he just did! Now I wonder what surprises are packed in the next act."

Police is at the door.

ACT 6 - LET GO!

Mayuri: A step forward is stepping into an uncertain future while a step backward will put me back into the hell's cauldron to be cooked day and night and then relive a death sentence.

Police officers: Please come with us for now, you can always come back home later once the legal negotiation process starts.

Mayuri: It was he himself who had given our house a new name of - 'The Dream Palace', but now this house has become a symbol of my nightmarish life, so now re-christen this house with a new name of 'The Nightmare Palace." What were our dreams yesterday are ash today!

The police officers stand there listening to every word while not saying any of their own. These officials are trained to not do the mistake of interrupting the nervous rant from an in-experienced battered woman, as the moment she stops talking they will be losing vital information! Finally, once the rant of the frustrated woman ends, they too break their own silence and stoically say, "As police officers, we have met all kinds of fantastic minds, so for us to be surprised means, limits have been crossed! We must acknowledge that we are not just surprised but shocked to see it happen with an Indian couple whose culture boasts of divorce rate being less than one to two Percent! Keep in mind, we are not here to decide if you are innocent or guilty, that is the job of the Court of Law, or even to deal with the ridiculous reversals of love-hate unending dramas. We are merely executioners to the orders given to us. We are here to serve you with a restraining order from the court which requires us to escort you out of this House. Now the control over the later flow of events is neither in your hands or the other party's! From here on "The System" will take control over your fate in relation to him." They say words of empathy that help her feel better, "We can easily see through the cunning of your husband in how he is manipulating the system to his advantage and yet we cannot act otherwise as we are no movie heroes but are mere slaves to "The System." Yet since humanity is not yet dead and we are real heroes, we will go out of our way to help you get to some safe nearby Car Rental."

Car too is gone! Things are bad.

INVERSION OF CONTROL /
BANKRUPT WOUNDED LIONESS
KNOWS NOT WHERE TO GO

A woman who has the power to build her house with her own hands, in this suddenly with a cruel flip of destiny has no house for herself anymore!

She knows not where to go when a naughty gust of wind blew off her veil as if mocking her, teasingly exposing her bosom to the entire world. If this wind had such insolence just a night before, she would have at once, with great urgency, covered the exposed part, but now all her sense of shame and womanliness seemed to have gone with the wind...

Mayuri: "Where does Mayuri go from here now?

This man, in whose arms I was moments ago, will sure embrace me again, then by accepting me as his wife he will help me in getting back in getting situated in this unforgiving society once more."

Aggressive like a man she now assumes the role also of a Man too.

"FFFAAUUST! FAUST! FAAAAUUUUUSTTTTTTT! FAUST!!! Open the door! It is me! Open the door!" when a small two-year-old girl comes running out from the back door to see who this excited visitor is in their usually quiet home! From the front door enters a beautiful young woman who upon seeing another woman instinctively says an unwelcoming remark, 'Whose pants are on fire now!' Faust could have introduced the visitor as someone he sees as a friend and shown her respect by saying some welcoming words, but he does nothing of that sort.

She lowers her head in shame, on realizing her own hypocrisy in even after seeing his impotence she is still standing there to hear what her deceiver had to offer! Her ears still had some hope of hearing some good news which can give her a new life?!

Mayuri: "My friend Faust! I have lost everything. I need shelter till this unending dark night ends. Can I live with you here?"

Faust is silent. His silence encourages His wife to lash out, with her uncontrolled and wild tongue.

Faust's Wife: "Absolutely not! We are not running a Charity here! I warn you, even if I see your shadow seven houses away, I will have you arrested and put behind bars for stalking my Man!"

Mayuri, wonders why she feels she has heard similar words before! Then Mayuri is reminded of her Karma from that incidence with the Widow in childhood. Her head spins! If Mayuri would have heard such cruel words of disrespect towards her, she would have ripped that tongue off, but today, she gulps, drowning all the acid from her words! Her eye-balls dart towards Faust but he stays quiet...

Mayuri now looking directly at Faust: "This question is for Faust."

Faust: "My wife's wishes are above everything else!"

On facing humiliation once again and hearing such cruel and insensitive words against herself, she closes her eyes in disbelief, sheds a silent tear on herself, then on her helpless situation and lastly on her failure in recognizing her death which had come disguised as this man, who she had worshipped even more than her husband!

She leaves. After she has turned a corner, she is surprised to see the car of Faust, gesturing her to meet him at the gas station ahead. She does not want to do anything with this cheater and yet she knows not why she is obeying his instructions!

Faust: "It is all your fault! Looks like in your imaginary world, the only one married in this entire world is you and that is why you never even bother of asking me about my marital status! Still, I am worried about you. I see this fresh wound on your forehead, for which I can bring marijuana for little extra cost, just so your pain gets some relief..."

Mayuri: "Regarding your concern over my pain, whether I liked it I will still not include it in my life, simply because if there is any habit that will make me dependent on you, I will just not start it! Regardless, thank you for reminding me once again that I am neither dependent on your sympathy nor my Husband's, but on my real Husband only who lives high up in the skies! Let us stop all further conversation at this point, as feel that I am beginning to lose my respect for you."

Now that there is nothing more left to say or hear, Mayuri begins to leave from that spot when he stops her once again!

Faust: "It is not because I take some perverted pleasure in doing things opposite of what you ask me to do, but really I have a big secret to tell you which might help you get a closure over this whole event."

Mayuri holds her breath as she hears all about the way she was set-up by a drama whose director is none other than her own Husband, Chanakya!

Mayuri: "Is love not but a mere trickery of a cunning Seducer?! My whole faith in love is shaken-up! If you had come to kill me, why did you not!?"

Faust: "I came to kill you if I failed in resolving the dispute. But that did not happen. In the evenings when the dark passions prevail, a man is always the weaker one in front of a woman, especially when she is in heat! Also, when all the outside conditions become favorable, the best course of action for the players left is to respect the decision of the natural forces by just going with the flow!

When I called your husband, he did not give me any money because I failed in killing you. I lost. Your Husband Chanakya told me you too have lost all your money in stocks, so even if you were dead, he would not get even a penny, so he lost too. Your losses are just too many to even try quantifying. So, in short, in this battle of evil bloodbath everyone lost!"

Mayuri is listening to every word of Faust quietly. Once she has heard the whole story, she stopes all begging, arguments, and reasoning and instead becomes silent. She could hear her own words that she had learnt every time she fell, '**Life is a synchrony of a teardrop and a laugh. A teardrop, for that one object you could never reach. A laughter, which follows, on seeing one's own foolishness'**

NULL / STATE DIAGRAMS

I become nothing, to assimilate with the essence of everything ~
Love ...
, The Intoxicated Peafowl Dancing in the Rain
Coulda/ Woulda/ Shoulda ...

ANGER

Et Tu, Brute? Your cowardly act did not just expose all the hypocrisy in marriage vows but also has robbed from all my belief in love and humanity! The fire in me wants me to burn down your dream palace just as you just burnt all my honor and prestige that I enjoyed from becoming your wife and yet you can relax! I will never do something drastic like that, not just because the wisdom of the Rishi's blood runs through my veins but because the hope in me is stronger enough to not let my past ruin the new life which awaits me...

SELF-LOATHING

Temptation is evil! These bleeding marks on my body are like mementos given by the mercy of Lord Vishnu, The Preserver as a constant reminder that I have come too far from my ethical values! My fateful and sinful acts can only lead me to my ruin only! I want to scream from rooftops to warn all my sisters out there that, 'O sister! Be content with what you have, even if he is old and wore-out and never covet that young Italian stallion grazing in the green pastures of the neighbor's house!' How since childhood whenever I would hear stories of women caught in adultery, I would automatically degrade them to inferior individuals than us who come from cultured families only to find, I did not just become one of them but the mascot of this clan! If such a travesty had occurred in some brothel, one would not get that easily taken aback, but for this to happen to a granddaughter of a priest still does have a surprise element in it. An event that should never have happened has happened!

SELF-PITY / THE BIGGEST LOSER

How can we ever call any comparison as fair when everything is
unique?

When the Master himself turns against his loving pet, then it becomes only a number game before he himself serves his own unsuspecting, pet with some milk laced with poison with his loving smile!

In one stroke of misfortune, I lost all my investment of my childbearing years, my youth, my physical beauty! The only consolation is that humanity is not dead as the thief did leave me with a clean house! If ever there is a competition for finding the biggest loser, then you do not need to go any further. Here is your winner, who will win easily. Put all your garlands of victory around my neck.... no, not this way... you are hiding the garland of bleeding marks which the people I trusted the most, gave me!

Could neither get a baby, nor true love, but what did get in abundance is loads of bruised ego and self-loading...what I thought to be pure gold, turned out to be a fake, fake like my smile, fake like my performances! What looked like a shining Cadillac from outside turned out to be a clunker! And now I am stuck with an added bill for towing the clunker off my lot! Never again will I put all my eggs in one basket as now that the safety net is gone, I know not what will become of me!

GUILT

How can I ever blame my husband for anything at all when all the fault lies in me...? It is me who dropped the ball. It is my inability or disability that prevented me from fulfilling my share of my duty as a wife of giving him the happiness that comes on becoming a father!

Why could I not look at my oath of celibacy as mere words, like everybody else? My pledge to never marry has a big bearing on all my later choices. Why did I have to wear the coffin of my oath, in an age where people can forget anything just to move on and that too, on the name of protecting their ethical principles, their family traditions, knowing fully well that at the receiving end is my neck at the chopping block?

HUMBLE REQUEST

Listen! O esteemed philosophers and the authorities of Ethics, I shall implore the whole congregation for a deeper investigation, to ensure no one must go through what I am!

My change request: Every woman gets the man of her choice! Who will obey all her commands and fulfill all her desires just the way she wants! And if they refuse to grant my wish, I shall give-up all religions and form my own religion!

I share my secret disgrace, to dissect like a guinea pig, so that no one must suffer the way I did...

APOLOGIA TO MY HUSBAND

Hell's fire might look like ice water compared to the heat of shame; I am experiencing right now! How can I ever blame him when he just had the courage to do what I wanted to do! I am like a bird who is dependent on his master for his tender love and care; if he does not feed his bird on time and then if the bird gets tempted to take a bait from another master and fly's away to the new master's home is might be seen as an expression of fickleness in the eyes of the quick to judge world, but for my new open eyes, is an expression of desiring a mirage ...

If ever my conduct hurt you in any way, forgive me as someone rightly said, 'to err is human' and I am still at that low animal level ...

TELEOLOGY VS ETHICS

To Err is Human, to Forgive Divine
Source Unknown

Most Teleology Philosopher's shout to us, reminding us that 'one's allegiance should be to the goal and not the players and objects,' but now with my new experience I change the statement to say that indeed the allegiance should be towards the Goal, but only if the Goal favors Universal Goodness!

APOLOGIA TO MY PARENTS

The most giving relation in the world must be the mother as without her giving me birth, my existence was not even possible. The mother is the first to welcome her children to the world. Whether they turn out to be saints or turn out to be sinners, she does not discriminate, as for her loving and caring eyes only see in the person, the same little child who sucked abundance from her breast!

How like a coward, I married without consulting my own parents which! But now when the very person for who I rebelled against my parents for, has kicked me out, my situation is disgustingly printable! I know my parent's heart is big and they will accept me back too but how will I face the community! Outwardly they may not say any cruel words to me, but inwardly everyone will take enjoyment on my situation, I will become the hot topic of all gossip circles. That is why know I realize that even when the entire world turns against me, my only hope for an unconditional acceptance is my parents, because as I said before, the most giving relation in the world must be of the Parents ...

THE ULTIMATE JOY - A KISS WITH DEATH
21.10.2014 / BIG BANG / GAME OVER

Satya mev Jayate!
(Truth Always Wins)
- Mundak Upanishad

A DIVINE CLUE - GODDESS SITA

Since, I am no goddess, but just another platitudinous mortal, Mother Earth will not do me the same favors as it did for Goddess Sita, by parting and then swallowing her, as mentioned in Epic Ramayana, all that is relevant for me in it, is my clue out of this labyrinth! When in her case, after Goddess Sita's Husband left her, she did not go back even when there was a chance for her to go back! Now that this clears all my confusions, it is impossible for me to back, without losing all left-over self-respect! These huge doors, which when seen by the eyes of Bride Mayuri were the doors to a dream palace, but now when seen with my new aware Wife Mayuri eyes, are doors to a nightmare palace...

To solidify my resolve to my own fickle mind, I pledge today with Heaven above as my witness, 'I, the daughter of Father Aakaash and Mother Aditi, am never going back to that "nightmare palace again!'

Overwhelmed with deep sorrow, I get in my car. I can see how this event must be the last final limit! A door from which anyone who came will have to go through is the only door left open! Then is not death a beautiful exit for ending a life that is only going to get increasingly painful? My mind is swimming with destructive thoughts, the more destructive they get the more my foot presses harder on the accelerator, as if with its fearful speed I am ensuring it has nowhere else to go but plunge into the depths of the abyss! When the light from my grandmother left her body, I saw her body simultaneously expel excreta too from her body. Now I have experienced such an action every time I use my body to give me ultimate body pleasure! Then is it not fair to say that an embrace with death must be another form of the ultimate joy? ...

THE BIG BANG

OM *tryambakaṃ yajāmahe sugandhiṃ puṣṭi-vardhanam*
urvārukam iva bandhanān mṛtyor mukṣīya mā 'mṛtāt

ॐ त्र्यम्बकं यजामहे सुगन्धिं पुष्टिवर्धनम् ।
उर्वारुकमिव बन्धनान् मृत्योर्मुक्षीय मासमृतात् ।।

- Mahamrityunjay Mantra Rigveda
(OM, O the three-eyed one, we give sacrifice to, the fragrant, the vir-
tuous, the supreme being, the giver of nourishment, wealth, perfection,
just like urvarukam (a kind of cucumber) when ripe detaches from its
holding easily, similarly I too free myself from death without any diffi-
culty to salvation)

Mayuri's vehicle is no longer in her control. The vehicle has crashed into a strong Banyan Tree ,with a strong transcendental sound, setting all supernatural forces in motion! It is like the third eye of Lord Shiva - The face of SuperKundalini for overseeing destruction, just opened, expressing His anger on seeing The Super-Kundalini Inder's favorite devotee, Mayuri lying helpless in this dying state. The poor tree suffers silently, unlike People who would have chased her all the way up to the hell's fire till they get a compensation for stress and trauma caused to them by the accident!

The sky roared with thunder and lightning, as all the birds in the sky begin to fly erratically as if what they just witnessed is something that should never have happened and yet has happened. ...

PHASE FOUR OF LIFE: WHEN THE SOUL IS KING

For a believer life is Heaven because there is nothing accidental, while for an atheist life is hell because he is the reason behind everything that went wrong!

AN INTERVENTION OF THE SUPERKUNDALINI TO BRING ORDER FROM A CHAOS

The Lord Inder, The Demi-God of Natural Forces, is sitting in an Assembly, surrounded by all his advisors consisting of the best heads together to come-up with the best diplomatic way of informing Mayuri that, she has died by mistake before her time, which means she has to go back but since it is their fault, they feel they owe her a personal touch by giving her the pleasure which comes only by seeing the Lord's Lotus Feet!

Looking at the beauty in Lord Inder's face, tears of joy were covering Mayuri's face.

Lord Inder: "One of my favorite humans, Mayuri, we all are here to tell you that the special job for which you had to take birth, is still not complete! Due to an un-anticipated mistake, you will have to go back!"

Human Mayuri: "Lies, my Lord! My enemies must have poisoned your ears against me by giving you incomplete information, as whatever work I had to do, my co-worker who works with twice my speed is working on it already! There is nothing more left on Earth for me to see or do!"

Lord Inder smiles his mysterious smile at her!

Lord Inder: "I am not referring to these toys, which are doing an excellent job in distracting humans from their real duty of learning to do things the right way, else their illiteracy will become the cause of 'Pralaya' (Sanskrit/ Catastrophe in English), which will destroy

385

this beautiful creation! You may think you have seen everything, but really what you have seen is less than a drop in an ocean! The reason of choosing you, is not just because one of your many names is Grandma Baby Mayuri or because of your talking skills but because you have the right balance of experience needed of the East and the West, the right amount of exposure to the fire, needed for coal to transform into diamond, which is needed to fulfill this special task."

Human Mayuri: "Like every other incomprehensible riddle of yours, I am at a loss to comprehend this riddle of yours too!"

Lord Inder: "When the right time comes you will understand the meaning behind my words and even if I were to disclose it to you, is of little use, as it is a limitation of a human form that prevents mortals from ever grasping these special top secret high-level concepts. So, without any more conversations go back to Earth and resume your life after this brief but important pause and with my blessings: rejuvenated!"

Mayuri: O Devraj, the King of all Demi-Gods, if I am indeed your favorite then will you grant me a wish?

Lord Inder: I do not trust the cunning in you humans one bit, so first tell me, what is it?

Mayuri: "Please promise me to come to me periodically not because every pore of my body rejoices in your presence, but because when I am in need for direction, I can ask you directly."

Lord Inder: "I will not come, not because of the common assumption of Human that I must have a stone where the heart lies, but because it is absurd asking someone who is already there to come. (He smiles His killer smile of all smiles). All answers are in you, all you need to do is listen! The only advice I have for you is to be patient and develop more trust in the Eternal's ways! "Bin maange moti mile, mange mile na bhheekh (An age old saying in Hindi, meaning, 'often we beg and still we get nothing, while other times when we are not even expecting anything we end up getting pearls.'). A lot of time has already gone in conversations, so now go back to Earth where a new life awaits you!". Listening to the Lord's words, suddenly Mayuri realizes she is in presence of the one she has ever loved and then tears of joy cover her face and before even confessing her love to her true love, the Lord has already vanished along with all her memory of this Event! ...

INJECTION OF AN ANGEL
TO THE RESCUE

With an embrace of the kiss of lips, she awakens ...
"I found my seducer; I found my deceiver!
I found my seducer; I found my deceiver!
I found my seducer; I found my deceiver... "

Profound expressions indeed, teaching the World, the two most appalling opposites giving the world an image of eternity! Father Aakaash and Mother Aditi, who had dropped everything to come to America for being next to her, stand there mesmerized for being one of the few Parents who get to see the birth of their daughter for a second time within the same lifetime! All her vital signs that confirm life in a body, are flashing a bright green on the signboard screaming to the world her victory over death! Her eyes are shining like the sun, body glowing, as if she is the bride and fairies in their chariot, pulled by colorful peafowls and reins made with ivy vines had descended straight from heaven to the earth, to dress their Lord Inder's favorite for her bridegroom! Tears are dumb, they know no difference between pleasure and pain, thus expressing both extremes of emotion the same way in the form of a teardrop, leaving any sane mind, wondering over their own state of mind if they were out of happiness or sorrow!?

All doctors, nurses, and other staff, crossing all boundaries of human form divisions, unite to join the family and other well-wishers, in rejoicing over the confirmation sign from The Merciful that the mercy of the Infinite is Infinite, by singing and dancing to hymns that are now playing on full Volume over the Air waves in the Hall! All start sharing different stories of car crashes and how Mayuri is one of those few fortunate ones who just came out of Fire alive! Her Father Aakash cannot help but wonder if her coming back to life is a form of validation of the statement from the Scriptures that when someone has some important unfulfilled telos still left to do, person could will oneself back to life!...

HYPOCHONDRIACAL CURIOSITY
THAT KILLED THE CAT!

Even when people are rejoicing, their inquisitive minds are already racing to find, more about this secret unconventional method that this young doctor used, who looks more like some Doctor Frankenstein's incarnate, bringing the dead back to life! The family are too overwhelmed with delight over their daughter's victory over death to give any negative thought towards the means that the Doctor used, who is feeling so overwhelmed with anxiety over being caught for a cure, which can destroy his whole career life:

"When I entered the room, Mayuri was lying comatose alone in the room. When my eyes fell on her face, the words of a poet starting ringing in my ears, 'With an embrace of the kiss of lips, she awakens....' In my mind started a conflict! If I am successful, I win the highest honors but if I lose, I lose all my investment in getting a medical degree and possibility of a dark future awaits me yet damn all red-tape that has killed the doctor, I risked my all, to breathe life in her with the help of the most potent fluid possible on Earth, which The Superkundalini itself has blessed us men with! Without being Judgmental just look at it as an experiment which worked, how like the wizards pull rabbits out of their hat, I too pulled this miracle out of my hat! Long live the force of curiosity! Unfortunately for me, before I could even celebrate my victory, all the life signs on the board started flashing wildly startling everybody, including me and I got caught red-handed!"

Father Aakaash (breaking the silence): "We are elated beyond limits that your unconventional method did breathe life into a Coma
Patient; however, my fear is that because her natural defenses were
in a very lowered state, her subconscious was also more naked to
suggestions. For you it is more about the victory of your experiment, but we cannot declare it a complete victory until we get a
better picture of this experiment over the psyche of the patient too.
Since, you are instrumental for her second-birth, chances are that
she starts developing feelings, quite similar as a wife does for her
husband! I fear that the authorities, might get busy in acting
against you, which might even be overstrict to serve as a deterrent
for the rest! So, it will be in the best interest of all parties involved
that we check the patient closely, not just for her physical recovery
but also her Psych!"

Doctor NoName, now composing himself, says:

"First of all, accept my apology Madam, for not even knowing
your name and still experiment with you without your permission,
even more for not being able to hide it skillfully. I took all preven-
tive measures to protect my brown skinned girl's pride and dignity
and yet our dirty little secret just blew-up in such an in-your-face
fashion, that I now understand that there are some unaccountable
variables in an equation that can raise their ugly head anytime!
Something I never thought could have been done by me, has happened by none other than me! I am myself questioning my own
sanity for having acted with such careless decorousness! I too agree
with the request of watching the case as the time progresses!"

Now, with an even greater inquisitive look on his face he cannot
help but ask Mayuri a private question. "Oh, forgive me if I appear
too nosy, as I am still curious to know how you got this black scar
in the middle of your forehead." Mayuri's memory of the curse
turns the color of her face to a pale yellow. Reading the discomfort
on her face and the air of sudden silence in the room, he waves off

his own question by diffusing it by using humor: 'A poet so rightfully once said to his beloved, who had a scar on her forehead that I say to you, 'even the Moon has a dark spot on its face and yet it looks pretty, same is the case with you also', I say the same to you too..."

The patient is looking at the doctor with a wide grin as a child who looks around, not yet knowing the name of the relationships, just a feeling that she is in a secure place! Then, looking at the young doctor she wonders why he looks so familiar, as if they know each other from ages, even if this is the first time, they have met...

Mayuri: "Who are you? Looking at your age you could be a son that I never had, as a son if I ever did, would be your age... Then in that case, can I adopt you, given that I am more-or-less your mother's age?"

Doctor: My name is Sarthi educated from Nalanda, India. My loved one is call me with various other loving names too, but we will go over how I got them in some other conversation.

Mayuri: How can I ever attribute my misfortunes to people graduating from Nalanda, when one killed me while the other brought me back to life! Your name is beautiful! Your last name Sarthi in Sanskrit means Charioteer! I feel you will show me the path to Heaven! However, your name confuses me as the first name 'Soren' is Danish, and the last one is Hindi, but you are from India, please solve the mystery behind it.

Sarthi (laughing, showing all his teeth): Thank you for the compliment. Regarding the secret behind my first name is simple. Philosopher Soren Kierkegaard's enlightening writings had a considerable influence on my mother's life, so as a symbol of her affection toward him, she gave me this as my first name.

Mayuri: Just when I thought nothing could surprise me, you come and wake me, that too, not with some light shaking, but a soul-shaking tremor! How beautiful is your body and a soul that is even more beautiful! How can anyone not worship your enigma? How can anyone not want you? Every dark cloud has a positive aspect and meeting you must be the silver-lining to the whole tragic episode which put me on this Hospital bed in the first place! Just like the man in Khalsa History, who ran through the streets shouting 'Guru ladore, Guru ladore' (Found my Guru in Punjabi), on finding the true Guru amongst dozens of fakes, I too want to run through the streets, shouting "I found my enigma, the man who is worthy of spending my whole life in decoding his enigma!"

Mother Aditi: Slow down! You are also making the same mistake that many do! Any person who saves a damsel in distress, the saved-one begins to see Him as God, while the savior is just another mortal human, infected by the same diseases as any of us in this Materialistic World! He just happens to be the right candidate for this situation to be able to **execute The Creator of All Creator's, will.**

As wise people always say, any decision made in the state of giddiness or in depression, turn out to be most likely wrong! When one is happy, he ends up giving too much and when sad too low, while the decisions made by a balanced mind often come out to be more in the ballpark.

Next, regarding Mayuri's brilliant comment, which shocked everyone in this room. When you said you are 'like a mother to him;' the answer lies right there in your question! Like is not equal but equivalent. It is a proven tool in the armor of the manipulative mind, who cleverly switches the term interchangeably to suit its own agenda! ...

THE LEAP OF FAITH

One of the most dreadful moments in anybody's life, must be when an unexpected news of that one, with who you do not just share the same blood, but also memories from the golden years of childhood together, is now battling between life and death, which happens to be Chandrashekhar's experience now! His state is such that, he does not know if he will be able to inhale his next breath now that he has reached the point of hyperventilating! The anxiety from all the uncertainty surrounding around the incident is unnerving, still he does not let emotions overpower him as a lot is resting on his shoulders, like completing all formalities needed to see his sister from Death ...

Since he is no doctor, so there is no point of him being around the patient, but at the place where he is needed the most - the billing Department, so that is where he heads non-stop! On meeting the billing agent, he ensures them that they will not hesitate in using the right equipment needed, even if it be expensive as losing his sister's life is a loss that he is not willing to bear!

Another Angel-injection now appears   in the form of a Nurse for aiding Patient Mayuri. She is a beautiful Indian girl named Chhandani from New Delhi who is visiting the country for completing a short training course for Nurses. She has a beautiful curvy figure with long thick, black, and curly hair from the same place as Chandrashekhar - The Heart of India, Delhi! Most importantly when she walked in, she is wearing blue jeans, just the kind that works wonders for him! Who says we need to make complicated floral arrangements for love to happen, when loves happens in that one instant of time, when he looks into her eyes, while she lowers hers, binding the two under a spell of Kam Dev (The God of Desire)!

As he goes by speedily, a doubt arises in her, if he just degraded the brief kiss between their eyes as some mere glance! The feeling of losing him, puts her mind in action for producing some trick to transform her desire to a reality.

Chhandani: "Most good love story has an enthusiastic beginning. Something must happen and a mini drama is already taking shape in my smart mind!"

Quick as lightning, she does a backbend and somersaults with a leap of faith and lands straight into Chandrashekhar's open arms. Seeing the beautiful co-ordination between his instincts and strong arms balance and the beautiful reward, he smiles!

Ecstatic over her victory and being in the domain of her future husband Chandrashekhar, a husband who will never let her fall, she takes the drama to the next step, by pretending to faint in his arms. He at once puts her on an empty stretcher lying on the side. Unthinkingly, he puts his lips on her lips to transfer air in her so she can come back to life! Since all good things must end, his enthusiastic but brief CPR session too ends, when they hear wild sounds of emergency sirens coming from Patient Mayuri's room!

Chhandani at once jumps on her feet, he could now see through her trick and so winking at her and straightening his shirt he says, "More later"! While she is still dizzy on the wine of his passion she whispers in his ears some sweet words, "My Wizard first kills with his eyes and then breathes back life through his lips!" ...

She thinks he will praise her for her boldness but since for him it is an insane move, he scolds her, "What if I was even a fraction of a second late, then you could have had a head concussion. Then instead of you nursing these patients, you would have become the patient!"

Chhandani, (laughing): A foot forward with faith and failing is not a betrayal of faith, but precisely the lack of it. Its mere carelessness!

Grabbing his jacket, he says shaking his head in disbelief, "How strange that we are from the same hometown and yet we do not meet at a place where the likelihood is high but oceans away where the likelihood of meeting is the least!

Chandrashekhar: I had promised myself to stay away from girls, put a blindfold on my eyes and had challenged love saying, "let me see how you will enter in my Heart now, because they say love enters through the eyes, but now I find a new route for love that goes through the lips and from there, straight to the heart!"

Leaving all love talk that never wants to end, he begins to leave when Chhandani at once straightens her hair and clothes to also go after him saying, "Do not go anywhere without me, I'm also coming wherever you go!" ...

KALBHAIRO NAMO -
A SYMBOLIC FUNERAL

'Kalbhairavo Namo,
Kalbhairavan Namo,
Kalbhairavan Namo...
(Kal - Dark time
Bhai - Fear
Ravan - Destroyer
Namo - We salute you) - Vedic Literature

THEN I GOT MY SMILE BACK /
THE RISING OF THE PHOENIX

Yes, I can also be wrong,
Now that one of the strongest energies in an individual - Lust is no
longer being wasted in chasing a mirage, I feel light, just like a prisoner
must, who after living in darkness all this time, spending each day in a
dark, dingy, and cold cell that was heavily guarded with seven gates,
locked with heavy locks, is finally getting one's first peak of sunlight
must feel, is precisely how I feel now ...
- Chhandi The Smart Warrior Princess

THEN I LEARNT SUBJECT TANTRA SHASTRA / QUANTUM SCIENCE

SuperKundalini is not not alive, People are not not dead
I am not not friend; People are not not enemy

Mayuri to Brother Chandrashekhar: The Universe is me! The similarities between the way that our Solar System is organized and the way that the the smallest unit of matter in the Universe - Atom is structured is the same! The Sun is in the center of the Universe, just as the nucleus is in an atom and not just that, the Planets revolve around The Sun in the Universe, while in the Atom, the Electrons too revolve around the Nucleus the same way in elliptical orbits. So, does it not imply that, we are the Universe in a nutshell, that I am just another platitudinous attempt of the Seducer of Seducer to experience reality as experienced in this Avtar as Just Mayuri. ...

Brother Chandrashekhar:
So, in simple terms, this is how I understand the view from Quantum Science. Mosquitoes are almost invisible flyweight creatures, there movements are like a dance to some nerdy electric pulse around their Victim, where in one moment they are on the left and almost like in the same moment on the right and this left to right jumps remind me of the 'Quantum Leaps' which the Electrons do from their Orbit to another and just like the Schrodinger's Uncertainty Principle, where the Observer influences the

outcome of where the electron will be, we as Observers get confused about the direction in which the mosquito is. Like these leaps our focus too jumps from "now-here-to-now-there"! This is how the scan of a scatter brain's mind might look like. To remedy this situation, the ancient meditation techniques are great for getting the patients Focus back to laser point precision levels. After regular practice one will be able to master this art and begin to focus on the current task much better. Since the individual's current task while meditating is only breathing, one begins to enjoy just that! Since excess stress is a sure recipe for disaster for the individual by being in the present all the anxieties of the Future or Ghosts from the past cannot overwhelm us anymore! ...

THE RAY OF HOPE

Faith, is like jumping into a high-risk investment,
without the fear and anxiety that comes from uncertainty
component...
- *Mast Mayuri, The intoxicated dancing Peafowl in the*
Rain

Mayuri to Brother Chandrashekhar: Who better than you, who is not just my brother, but also one of the most successful Hedge Fund Portfolio Manager from New York City, to answer this fun question which just popped in my mischievous mind?

Chandrashekhar: When I never reject anyone seeking my advice in my area of expertise, there is little reason for me to not let my own elder sister not take advantage of this offer? That's silly, just ask!"

Mayuri: "Ok then here is my Question? What if I were a stock with a symbol, trading at the Nasdaq, NY "Citay", and given that you know me well from being my brother, what would be your rating action out of these three - buy, sell, or hold?"

First Chandrashekhar holds his head up, with his index finger touching the forehead, in a Socrates thinking pose, which elicits laughter in the room.

Chandrashekhar: "Since, it is a particularly good question, I did not rush to answer it as this would have spoiled the beauty of an incredibly beautiful question. Do not think that the reasoning behind my statements, is that you are my own and so I am trying to say things just to encourage you, as what I am about to tell you is backed by scientific metrics.

Since for you are appearing from the life's ditch, the risk metric algorithms, always look for these bottoms as from this point, the downside growth is little as there is little room to grow, while the upside from here is unlimited, as there is plenty of room to grow! Thus, only a fool will have the courage to go short now when all the damage is done; since you love talking in Infinite terms, betting against you has the potential of bankrupting anyone who dared to go short now, as that would spell nothing but virtual suicide for him! Therefore, my message to Mr. Sortie: 'you are digging your own grave because, If you dared to short means you could never understand the destruction in a Tornado; If you dared to short means you never could understand the strength in the proud Himalayas that stand tall after millions of years of environmental stress; if you dared to short, then it means you could never understand the madness of the waves tirelessly trying to kiss the moon; If you dared to short, then simply you never understood the Fire in a Volcano;

So, your symbol is 'Hope' and, anyone who invests in you, is someone who knows the power in Hope!

Your symbol is also 'Courage', meaning only the one who knows the power in it will invest on you!

Your symbol symbolizes 'Will', only the one who knows the power in it will invest on you!

Your symbol stands for trust in 'Miracles', only the one who knows its power will bid!'

Since I am a believer, I would go all the way to buy your stock with all the Investment money I have! Go all-in! Even if it means breaking all the corporate rules that say, 'diversify your portfolio, etcetera.'! I will break all those rules, leave no stone unturned in making this move! It is the most prudent thing to do for the success of myself and especially my clients whose success is of more importance to me than mine!" ...

MIRACLE SCIENCE

Mother Aditi: "A Miracle is like a Science that is a mockery of proven Science.

Whatever Science says is true, Miracle Science comes and says that the opposite of it, is also true...

Another way we can define a Miracle is that, when chaos is King, it is a form of intervention from the Creator for saving His Creation's life from sinking into a chaos..."

Doctor Sarthi: "All talk about Miracles is nothing more than an idle Person's bored mind's way of empty entertainment or in short, a baloney!"

Father Aakaash loves to learn through a good debate. He too contributes by coming out with some new facts.

Father Aakaash: "As the Danish Philosopher Sarthi Kierkegaard - 1855 once said:

'A miracle is not the suspension of natural law, but the operation of a higher law.'

This statement makes me see miracles with much more respect!

From my experiences and research on this topic from the Vedic Literature I too have come to my own conclusion:

"The Eternal Laws is greater than our Creator even. The only way that The SuperKundalini intervenes is like a magician does. Miracles are more like the Lords vanishing trick. Just like a magician does God too makes objects appear when they are not there or make them disappear even if they are there!" ...

THE BEST-FIT ALGORITHM

Dear Mayuri's Diary,

When I saw, how in my worst life crisis, when everyone had betrayed me, the one person who in spite of not being supportive of the cause, respected my existence by risking everything to go to the end of the Earth to get the medicine needed for my survival, was the person with who I not just shared blood ties but also shared many childhood growing memories ‑ my brother, I shed a silent tear! ...

I did not take the route of adoption, because it is not the cries of a child that I craved but the praise a woman always gets on becoming a mother! I know not why that even after seeing that I am fighting too hard in trying to get away by putting a square peg at a place where the need is of a circular one, I did not respect my body's limitations. It is only after coming out of this toxic situation can true happiness is not in getting things for which you are not qualified for but in expanding your abilities, respecting the boundary conditions! Now I can see how running after a Mirage was like having a noose around my neck, the more I run towards it, the more I hang myself! ...

People get married and start calling themselves Family. Wrong! The right definition of Family is two best-fit separate individuals completing each other symbiotically, linked with children! When traditional definitions proclaim, it is trust between themselves that binds them, is either self-delusion or hypocrisy! This safety net, or in other words Family, are God-gifted gains. Thus, trust between a parent and child must be higher than outside strangers, trust between the siblings even higher as the choice is completely The Creators gift and finally most trust should be in The SuperKundalini who run his complex algorithms, for choosing for us the best-fit womb for us from which to take birth from!

Now I can see how these Great Rishis who wrote mythologies, wrote giving ideal values for people, which when followed work like chemical processes for domestic harmony. The work of these Rishis is genius. I salute it, however when I see their own lifestyle, their preaching is the same for everyone but the way they live their own lives is completely opposite! So, the one who were to put full faith in the Rishi, obeyed every word faithfully, became the great King of the People, but not realizing he just killed that Rishi in him with his God-like powers! From this observation, I conclude that the smart way of living is to still use these guides but more as a vehicle for initiation. Keep practicing and then go further with it so I can experience life to its fullest...

LADDER FOR A LEAP -
INVESTMENTS NOT GAMBLING

ROLL THE DICE AGAIN

Chandrashekhar: When even staying on the sidelines/ putting money under the mattress is not safe due to the monster of infla-tion and other clever financial instruments such as demonetization, when becomes Government Policy, can easily devour the whole value of the currency, then it only makes sense to always look at every investment as another gamble!

Now, you might suspect my sanity or start seeing me as your en-emy, when despite knowing the fact, that the stocks were one of the main causes behind your bankruptcy, I recommend that you roll the dice one more time! The reason I want you to stay in the game, is that something that has the power to take you down from riches to rags must also have the power to take you back up to In-finite Gains! Just try to look at it this way: stocks are like playing with Fire. Just like fire when not tamed can devour a whole forest, and on the other hand, when in the hand of Guru who knows the Nature of this Beast, the same fire can serve this Person as an obe-dient slave, burning just the way the master wants, making deli-cious meals for the whole family.

Thus, do not blacken the Force, by doing so, you are committing a fatal mistake, like throwing the baby with the bath water! ...

LADDER FOR A LEAP - SELFLESS LOVE

THE SILENT KILLER

Keyword is Still.
Not like a dead body, but like a Tree,
as the former is dead, while the latter is alive...

Doctor Sarthi (wondering aloud to himself): "My Mother should have forewarned me about this most dangerous killer of all in a woman's arsenal - silent lips and talking eyes, but unfortunately, she did not. Now I sit wounded! When I was sitting next to her, I sensed the nervousness and anxiety in her voice, so I told her to not say a word for a few moments, not knowing that those silent moments would prove to be the most dangerous of all, as now the weapon of assault has shifted from words to eyes and needless to say that when in the battlefield the enemy is a doe-eyed woman the man has been proven to be the weaker of the two! I felt completely naked as she showed me no mercy in her rapid-fire round and stopped only after I fell on the ground unconscious! In those silent moments, the way her eye's lowered when I was scanning her with my eyes, the way that she smiled mischievously when she felt her victory over me, then when she ran away coquettishly leaving me alone with my thoughts, she killed me! Now I stand wounded by the same arrows that I sent towards her."

Mayuri (wondering aloud to himself): "Since the Director of Directors of all directions, has blessed me with a second chance for life, it must have introduced this new actor in my life to enable me to let-go of the past, in-order to embrace the gifts of future! I know not why every time that I look in his eyes, I feel as if, since previous births he has been coming as a special mention in the most important chapters of my life! ...

CHILDREN BEHAVE!

I am so busy finishing-up my sandcastle, that even if death were to come now,
I will say with my most enchanting smile: 'one minute, just one more...
-                    *Mast Mayuri*

One would think that any new scientific breakthrough panacea, which will help all mankind, even if offensive to the Moral Police, will get rewarded, but however in this real fake world, which did not happen! Instead, the medical board is busy flipping through their rulebooks, for finding ways to stop the name of the Doctor getting glorified due after violating their Moral code constitution! Fearing a radical religious mob's wrath, they choose to suspend the doctor instead and that too, indefinitely!

On hearing this news people cannot but wonder if what they are seeing once again is just another platitudinous love-story that will meet its tragic end before even starting! ...

EMBRACED A CLOUD

News that has a good impact on the future, does not bring out as much emotional responses as fear based that have bad effect on the future! That is why, Nurse Chhandani brushes-up on her diplomatic skills before delivering this bad news about the Doctor being blacklisted from his job. So, wearing her best poker Face Nurse Chhandani lets Patient Mayuri know with gentle words which would help minimize the blow but, in this case, since even minimal is like a drop in the Ocean, Mayuri lay flat on the floor from a fainting spell! Nurse Chhandani at once rushes towards her with a glass of water which might help her come back to this world, but Mayuri angrily throws the glass towards the wall! The very thought of her being the cause of the downfall of someone who is the cause of her coming back from Death, makes it unable for her to swallow anything down her throat, not even water!

Mayuri: "Here I am happy thinking he is like the moon; his shine is for everyone so no one can take this happiness from me only to find that he is no moon but is more like a cloud who vaporized the moment I tried to embrace it. The same source, which was the source of my happiness then, is now the source of my misery instead! It is injustice and what hurts even more is that I am the cause of it!"

As these thoughts are running through her in background processes, her eyes lock on a meditation endeavor of a Yogi editorial lying on the table.

Mayuri: "After being brought-up in a culture, that had been declared free but was still not free from the Colonial Hangover, I had always mocked these saints, labeling them as Backward would ignore them, but now I know not why I am reading it now. As I am reading, every word is penetrating every pore of my body, injecting in me Hope that is telling me that I am not helpless, that the powers required to reverse this injustice are in me, that by using the power of Yoga I can arouse the Divine Goddess in me who will then bless me with the wisdom needed to deal with this situation! "

A smile emerges on Mayuri's face. ...

A MEDITATION ENDEAVOR, INSPIRATION BAGULAMUKHI (SWAN-FACE) GODDESS

O M SW HA

DAY 1 - SOUTH

When I close my eyes, I can hear better,
When I close my ears, I can see better,
That is why I have now decided to meet people wearing a blindfold
and earbuds so I can understand them better... ahehehehe

Dear Mayuri's Diary,

First a bow down to Bagulamukhi, one of the ten higher science Goddesses from the Vedic Literature before I start with anything!

A loud frightful scream let out by me in the middle of my sleep, awakens me towards my own denial towards, all the fear in me, in facing the hidden fears inside me! Makes me realize, about all the fear part in me, due to my committing to this Meditation Endeavor, as at stake is my sanity! In spite of being wise enough to not risk my sanity over anything I know not why I cannot stop myself from jumping into this Labyrinth that draws me towards it and then just like fire draws moths I too cannot stop myself and just like them who even after seeing all the dead bodies of their friends strewn around, cannot stop themselves from meeting their fate of death and dissimulation, I too am unable to stop myself! Now I could just enter blindfolded but because one of the side-effects of this endeavor is also that I appear wiser so makes sense if I start using my wisdom already to set me up for success. Using the concept behind a vaccine, I too decide to expose myself to the areas that I fear but deal with them in micro-small doses.

In my first challenge, to appreciate the value of my eyesight, I try to do things wearing a blindfold! Then I must find my way from the start to the center to the middle. The adventure does not just end there as now you also have to go back to the point from which you started. To make things even more interesting the paths are not static but keep changing dynamically. Yikes!

The Drama is to start from ten in the night and end at five in the morning. Plan is to finish hundred and eight chants of any mantra in the praise of the Goddess of choice. I had already made the preparations needed for setting up a separate room as a Temple. The preparations include a lot of cleaning and de-cluttering. Since I too believe with Philosopher Sarthi Kierkegaard's saying that 'purity of heart is to will one thing,' I also give-up all my other obligations so I can fully immerse myself in this one endeavor. This way I can enjoy every moment, seeing myself as a third person making this slow but steady movement away from Maya (Sanskrit)/ Mirage), towards the Eternal Truth!

SECRET-OUT - THE MOST SUCCESSFUL IF NOT ALL RELATIONSHIPS ARE THE ONES WHO ARE SYMBIOTIC IN NATURE!

Successful Political Structure for Co-existence - Both Bacteria and Virus should have freedom to exist at their own terms ...

After a few days of minimizing all my social commitments, I begin to see better how even if we complain about relationships and friendships being a big drain of our time and energies, they are still valuable! We must learn to interact with each other to fulfill our day-to-day survival and procreation needs. Thus, we can say that all successful relationships found in nature are symbiotic in nature, starting from a child's conception whose survival is dependent on the mother's womb, else it is not there...

SECRET-OUT – EXPERIENCE REALITY FROM ALL SIDES IN ORDER TO DEFEAT ALL ADVERSE CONDITIONS!

After staying out of touch from my friend circles, many have taken umbrage and already left my group, but I do not let it stop my march forward inward, as these same people who have boycott me now, will come back when I become active in the scene!

I am now getting a better understanding of how best our bodies can take the most advantage of the outside sources of fuel for augmenting our inner aura, for awakening the divine energies in us! The basis of all life is breath. Plants give out oxygen during the day and so does the great ball of fire energy, Sun.

Since, the right-side nostril helps us inhale the oxygen while the left side one helps us exhale it and since the right side of the brain oversees the functioning of the sympathetic system, while the left side manages the functioning of the parasympathetic functions in our body, we need to send breath Energy to both the systems, so a good way must be to expose my body to the Sun to gain its heating effect in energizing my body and then at night to the Moon to gain its cooling affect in relaxing my body by customizing my knowledge of Breathing Yogic Practices to my Body Composition. The big inhale – the bright day followed by the big exhale – The dark Night. In other words, a Breath Cycle, in other words life itself – OM ...

SECRET-OUT – THERE IS THE POWER OF SHIV, THE DOCTOR OF DOCTORS INSIDE / WHEN I GOT MY JOY IN EATING BACK!

Just the thought of having to go without my amazingly tasty and delicious meals laden with oils and spices is sending chills down my spine already! To tolerate hunger for someone like me who has never even dared to fight with hunger for even a day, can prove to be overwhelmingly challenging to say the least and yet after getting confidence from reading similar experiences I keep moving forward with my fight with nothing!

Shame on me! For never giving this critical issue even a single thought and continued to sin without any remorse! I have been eating Meat all my life, but now because I have not eaten any of it from a good amount of time, suggests to me that I am weaned enough from all the addictive substances in it, to give an un-biased opinion. This is my balanced evaluation: The main reason that I will not forsake eating meat completely is that when God has given us canines for eating meat it must be because God wants to keep that choice open for us, teaching us that for meeting survival needs if there are no good alternatives one can eat flesh of other beings. There are many instances in nature, like some animals like scorpion eating its own children.

The main reason that I will forsake eating Meat, is that ever since I began to look at things from the perspective of energy, my perspective gains more weight as it now captures like an X-ray machine the inside story!

Whenever an animal is killed, the body of the animal is now a snapshot of all the Energies experienced at the end. Since they can see un-natural death for themselves coming, they must experience anxiety and fear hormones run through them, which means, when we consume the same flesh with trapped fear hormones, we too are bound to reflect what we eat. Then when we consume it, we introduce the same negativity in us by proxy.

No surprise then, that the multi-trillion Meat Industry wants us to see animal flesh as the only source from which we can fulfill our daily protein requirement, while the truth is that animal protein is not even a complete protein! Also, harmful Virus and Microbes spontaneously generate only on animal meat!

As much as we would like to believe that we can defeat any vaccine with a vaccine, we cannot, as the Virus will then mutate and then we will have to waste more efforts and money in producing another vaccine.

Thus, the only way out of this unending ennui, is to adopt a vegetation lifestyle and start a revolution that will help regulate the practices followed by the meat industry!

Much to my surprise after being on a diet of coconut milk mixed with its pulp and about one to two dates here and there, I am experiencing a burst of energy like never seen before! I now realize that all this while I have been eating more out of fear of losing muscle mass and other lies! As a result, even if my body has not sent any hunger signal, I am still eating non-stop!

Busy Lifestyles has robbed me of all the real pleasure in eating. As a result, I am doing a bad job in chewing and even worse by stuffing my body with all kinds of food with negligible nutritional value, just to keep the screams from my hungry stomach in check! I am now in control over my hunger and not the other way around!

On pondering over the matter more deeply, I can find a link to my own experience that happened with me, just me a few days ago.

I had a severe headache and had ended up eating some foods that I am allergic to, but because of my recently acquired knowledge from Yogic Principles that teach us to accept pleasure and pain with equal respect, I too decided to not run for any external help till my face cannot hide my pain anymore. Since I am aware that a lot of body recovery process happens while sleeping, I made a conscious effort to sleep. Next early morning around four o'clock, I had a strong urge to get up as I felt a running diarrhea has said without my permission and the fear of ruining all my luxury bedding helps break my deep slumber. I was sitting on the toilet bowl seeing death close to me, then an urge to throw-up made me run to the shower area. There I just fell on the floor, but my third eye kept seeing myself! Without me making any effort, with one automatic reflux thrust like action all contents inside came outside! For me to dismiss this magical moment as some accident, would have proven to be my loss only, as in this incident lies a proof for me! That the power of Shiva, the destroyer of enemies lives in me, that there is a doctor in me and who is actively working to restore my health! At that moment of feeling the presence of Shiv, tears of joy erupted and covered my whole face!

Then I realized that when I am taking painkillers, I am only treating the symptoms and not the cause and what good is that when the power of Shiv, the doctor inside me has the intelligence of killing the cause of the pain, from its root itself!

We never had to teach our body how to do its job in digesting the food, which means there is a secret power center, an Intelligence in us who knows all about how our body functions and can so if it knows this it must know that also, knowledge of healing the damaged parts. Then it also suggests that this secret divine power has the knowledge of ways to fulfill all our deficiencies!

Thus, all that I need to do is to listen to my body and respect it is limitations, giving it enough time to recover on its own!

SECRET-OUT - SACRIFICE THE WEST TO GAIN THE EAST!

True happiness is when both the right side and the left side are united without trampling each other's uniqueness.

I am awake early to do my sun salutations. I catch my eye-pupils red-handed darting again and again with great speed towards the Internet device lying beside me revealing to me a dangerous addiction which works very slyly and devours most of my time and focus - My Gateway to 'Maya', in other words to all my social connections from my past, Present and the wannabes who want their presence in my future, via all these great social networking websites! Thank you, the Goddess of Wisdom, in me, in helping me discover this costly mistake in time as here I am trying to go east(inward)while this addiction is strong that it has the potential to ruin all my effort by putting me at the opposite end instead - the west (Outward). Since I can devote my body's resources towards enjoying only one side at a time, I will have to sacrifice one to gain the other. By no means am I down-playing the importance of relationships but more often than not the time when you need their support, even when they want to help you they cannot as they might not have the required skillset for to fulfill your need, but when you are working on your inside the possibility of a higher return on time investment is high as then we are not relying on people with their schizophrenic tendencies but on the super powers of The Superkundalini! I see how as my ability of taking on more stress, increases, automatically, like magnetic forces, we too start attracting the right people from whose company we both can help the most, symbiotically! I use the important lesson in it, towards helping me in forgiving all people who left me when I thought I was still weak to bear the loss, as now my aware eyes can see that what I assumed to be my insult was a huge favor, as it is only because they left is that I am still alive! How would it have killed me? As the one who left me is because that person was indeed the stronger one and so for me to piggyback on that person to also enjoy the joy that comes by only flying at those levels where the Lungpower, is still not ready for those levels, I would have died instantly! Now I realize that all these social connections were taking me away from my trust in the divine God-like powers in me as they were like crutches that people gave me thinking that by preventing me from falling, they are helping me, not realizing that they just robbed me of a Heaven-sent opportunity of developing the powers needed to survive any fall of the kind! Thus, I sacrifice west to gain the east, while the west-west, I thank for keeping the Yoga Flame alive by showing the world some unmatched jaw-dropping performances!

DAY 13 - NORTH

As I am at the last day of the endeavor, I check my mails and to my surprise there was a mail from the medical board lawyers!

This helped bring my focus back to the main reason I started this, the worldly survival concerns be fixed!

On seeing the contents of the letter confirming my victory, I know not why I am having a hard time accepting that all this is no co-incidence but a blessing in the form of these favorable conditions which will help get what I prayed for!

At this point, I leave all further analysis of this topic to invest my energies towards conquering new frontiers ahead! ...

INDIA. HOME.

Welcome, welcome, welcome!
Even if my stepmother has pampered me,
Showered me with way more than I ever expected,
Yet I know not why, my eyes still look longingly in my birth-mother's direction...
Welcome, welcome, welcome!

THE FORBIDDEN SIN - LOVE

What Is Love?
A sacrifice of letting go. a duty of flying away...
- *Mast Mayuri, The Intoxicated Peafowl dancing in the*
Rain ...

A WET GOODBYE

After long busy days in the Hospital, Chandrashekhar and Chhandani finally get a chance, even if it is to say their good-byes!

When Chandrashekhar's virility and Chhandani's entangled feelings of love meet then, it only becomes a matter of time, before the intoxication levels from the wine of lust reach prohibited levels for driving, that can only have un-intended consequences!

She says her dry goodbye and begins to go back. As she is walking a fear, an anxiety grips her, and she begins to wonder about the cause behind the unrest.

Chhandani thinking: "Good things go quick! A Groom is also a commodity, in the end! If a good bid comes from some other party, he could be gone. All this while I have been under the impression that trickery is evil but, most of my friends who used it by cleverly extracting promises, exchanging rings, indeed got the man they wanted, so I see no evil in using the same tricks when the cause is a noble one and what more noble than marrying a man who possesses all the qualities of a good father and if we get married with Vedic Rituals then our union might even continue for several lifetimes!"

Once this thought comes, her feet cannot stop, till they lead them to him! Leaving all her womanly hesitations, she does not let prying eyes disrupt her run towards her sweetheart... what if he has already boarded and the doors are already closed for all the passengers... now she spots him walking alone in the runway towards the cockpit of the airplane... she recognizes him from is his back ... seeing her love, her pace hastens even more... the run seemed would never end but it does... her efforts get rewarded when she embraces him from the back and then when he turned around to see her face the surprised smile on his face, gives her happiness worth millions!

His body is now hard as a rock... he asks her to go into the bathroom and wait for him... she obeys with a shy smile and goes towards the male restroom but un-intentionally bumps into another male-friend who had also come to send-off Chandrashekhar ...

The male friend thinks, she must have made a mistake, so he starts telling her directions to the female bathroom, which she already knows ... she stammers, manages to say some white lies that, will save their secret from not being a secret anymore... standing in the men's bathroom anxious thoughts grips her, what if she were to faint right here in a men's bathroom, or what if he changes his mind and does not come! But then she smiles as she relaxes with the thought that that, how can he not come, when torturous are these affairs of passion! ...

DAMN THOSE YOGA CENTERS

After experiencing one of life's most pleasurable moments, even if it is in a bathroom, all one can wonder is how one was going North but ended up South?!

Chandrashekhar: "Damn those Yoga Centers! How, could all those hours of practice over self-restraint, best-practices learnt from the top-most gurus in the field of Yoga, fail, all washed down the drain in front of the desires of a lioness in Heat!? All this doe-eyed beauty had to do, is give me her most enchanting smile, as then I lay done for!

I never do anything that break cultural rules and yet, it is me who did it! It is like that cautious man who looks left, then right and then left again, still gets hit from a helicopter flying over his head! This very instant I promise myself; I am never trying these celibacy poses ever again, they beautifully work every time, except when they must deliver!" ...

MEMENTO PATTERN

If I get you, I reach my Salvation
If a woman still complains, after her lover
honors her with the ultimate gift of love,
the gift for which most women would kill for, must be a witch of the
highest order

To Dear Chandrashekhar from Your Chhandani,

At first, I did get anxious when you simply vanished in thin air without leaving any trace after showing me wonderful dreams! Now a liar I can forgive, but never a thief!

You took my heart and left with me with a memento, which will now never let me forget about that incident! The seed of your deed with me has already taken firm roots in this fertile piece of land - my womb. Once this little sunflower gets wings, then be sure it will seek you wherever you may be, will take you a prisoner, tie you with the ropes of my string like braids of Parranda (an Indian hair piece) and then bring you in-front of me, your victim, to decide the best punishment for you!

I am sitting wearing the same clothes, listening to same music you put that evening when our relationship jumped from something to everything! Quick to jump people might judge our union as impure! Indeed, we did err by not taking any vows in front of eternal symbol - Fire outside but we did have the fire burning in us! I do not see how this form is in any way inferior from the other choice.

Just because we did not get our marriage certificate or take our vows in the presence of Eternal Fire by Vedic Laws, still how can our union ever be impure when the highest form of purity is the outcome of this action?

As a woman, I too am blessed with the divine virtue of patience. Just like an egg in a Women's body does not go anywhere, it waits for the male's snake to come, a true feminine beauty waits for the proposal from the man. Still, because of the circumstances I give up my nature, transform into a man and propose to you for marriage. If you let the moment pass then, there is little choice left for me, other than to marry this other man who is wealthy beyond limits, even if old.

He is willing to give the child in my womb his name and fulfill all the monetary expenses needed to bring-up a child. He himself cannot have any children due to medical problems that often come with old age!

The similarities between him and you are so high that I often mistake him as some husband-by-proxy of mine! I do not fear that old man, but the cunning devil that sits in me too! My emotions are like wild ocean waves now, are vulnerable and might take any path that offers least resistance. Here is where I need you! Save me before I take a step towards a path that does not lead to you! Now do not test my patience anymore. Just come now, following the heartbeats of your Baby that is developing in my womb and save me from disgracing the essence of life - Love, save me from my evil thoughts ...

Your forgotten would-be wife?

Chhandani

To Dear Chhandani, from Chandrashekhar,

I can fight anyone for you my darling, but this is an old Richie Rich's golden stick that you are threatening me with! This can make any man wet his pants!

All jokes apart, the reason that I could not respond to you earlier, is not as much because I was busy in changing my sick sister's colostrum bags but because of another sinister reason behind my late response was for you to realize the risk involved in trusting anybody, especially most of us men folk of today, who are like hungry wolves looking for their next prey most of the time!

Please do not make any hasty decisions and then regret later! You are still incredibly young, do not think that after one the desire for another will not arise but if you lock yourself with someone who has less energy you are only jumping into a very toxic scenario! Just trust me when I say that I have the skills and degrees needed to reach the top and fulfill all my family needs!

I am a Khatri warrior's blood in my veins, and I am not one of these cowards who will run away and blame others for their actions!

I will start on working on planning for a formal marriage ceremony with you, that will follow all rituals and traditions set by the Vedic Laws for our benefit.

Your proud Going-to-be-Husband,
Chandrashekhar

SECRET EPITHETS OF LOVE - LETTERS / PROBLEMATA

To Dear Sarthi from Mayuri,

Subject: The Illusion of Space

I took my friends advice and stayed at the west coast while leaving her on the east coast, thinking that the space distance between us will make us forget each other in three or four days but now I want to shoot that liar myself as nothing like that happened. And instead, what has happened is the exact opposite! I laugh now when I see the folly in this assumption, as the light of our love can never stop burning as when it is night for me, it is day for you so when I sleep, it burns in you and when the cycle reverses it burns in me and thus like a ring it keeps on burning even after we die, after all we are all eternal beings...

YOUR MAST MAYURI, THE INTOXICATED PEAFOWL DANCING IN THE RAIN

To Dear Sarthi from Mayuri,
  Subject: Dark Horse
  I feel like the chess woman who wants to break all the rules and jump like the dark horse and capture the king, but she cannot because she is no horse, she is the pawn who can only walk the straight line, for short distance only. And if she ever tries to cheat by acting like the strong horse there is a big chance of her getting caught because as I said before that she is no dark horse. Therefore, if only when she makes peace with her own identity, bears the cross of her own limitations with a smile can she spend the rest of her life dreaming of her king, else the system will take-over, declare her mental and take away her right to be seen anywhere close to where he lives, comes, and goes and if was in their power, they would gladly even put a restraining order on her from meeting her king through dreams!
  Yours,
  Mayuri

To Dear Sarthi from Mayuri,
  Subject: Humiliated like A Dog barking without any response...
  Poor me! I was peacefully sleeping with my face under my blanket when you wake-me up with a start on seeing you sitting on me. Now did you not just commit the greatest sin of awakening the serpent of lust in me and then disappear without fulfilling them.

Now my condition is pitiable as can be as now I feel like I like a dog who is barking uncontrollably at you all night, but you still not respond! I feel humiliated, low in front of my eyes and yet know not why I keep taking the humiliation from the one person I want to show the beautiful side of me!

Is this a good thing to leave someone who loves you in such a wretched state?"

Your patient,

Mayuri

To Dear Mayuri from Sarthi,

Subject: Your medicine: Just Listen!

You thought all those letters that you sent me are out of love for me and only me. Wrong! Me being your well-wisher want to help you come out of this delusion by the awareness of the real secret behind these actions! Once you are aware of the real reason behind your actions you might be able to get a better hold on your actions. One reason is that middle age for a woman is particularly challenging because of all the hormonal changes that are happening in the body behind the scenes. When a woman reaches her menopause or pre-Menopause her situation can be seen as a person, in front of who is a Mountain called old age for which she will need to prepare herself to climb it with these knees that have already begun to show signs of wear and tear, while on the other hand is optimism which wants her to grasp onto whatever pleasures which only a youthful body can have! Being a part of this materialistic world where everyone is taking part in a mad rush for increasingly sensual pleasures, she sinks in despair over the choice she has – to eat whatever that comes her way even if that food will have a toxic effect on her! Such is a cursed life fit only for the mountain birds who must rely on carcasses that are stale and have a nasty smell! One of the main reasons that you are in this same situation now like these mountain birds is due to your fault of violating the Laws

set by nature for a woman of marrying at the right time, when her
body is ready to receive the gifts from Mother Nature!

The best way to get out of such a hellish life is to focus on discovering your Telos and then be true to it!

The answer is in you, all you must do is **listen**!

Your true Well-wisher,

Sarthi

~

AGE-OLD MYTH SURROUNDING THE DREAMS BEING A VOICE OF GOD FINALLY BUSTED HERE / INTERPRETER FOR COMMUNICATION BETWEEN DIFFERENT DOMAINS

My worst enemy is my own soul! Why? Because it is blind and demands from me the most absurd, forbidden actions, while my senses can clearly see how once executed, this society will disown me and never let me live as an honorable member...

Mayuri to Brother Chandrashekhar (in context of Doctor Sarthi): "Since the syntax of the language that a man follows versus the one that a woman does, is not the same, it suggests that the gap can result in confusions that sometimes create feelings of tender love and care, but more often we see repulsion from misunderstandings! So, therefore what I need is a dependable interpreter who can convey to him the right intent in the things I say and things that I do not.

Brother Chandrashekhar: "Caution, dear sister! Fooled once, it can be dismissed as a mistake in innocence. Fooled twice you should stay on Alert. Now, if you continue to do the same mistake again, you deserve the severest punishment! Sadly, you are now in the category for severest punishment. Now you cannot afford to go wrong, as this will mean you will lose whatever little you have left! You cannot afford to err this time.

So, if this man in question, has some thief hidden in him, it becomes your duty to evaluate his integrity first. Do not become a victim to another deception! Let me remind you of your origins, which started from the humble lanes of Paharganj in the city of New Delhi, India!"

Sister Mayuri: "My energies have been sapped completely, I just now want to lead a life watching others play, as an old lady standing on the sidelines cheering and booing the players in the arena, but I am unable. Why? Because what is a clue to the mystery of life? Dream. What is love? Dreams content. That is why. Dreams must see pictures drawn by the eye of the eye, voices coming from the ear of the ear, say with the tongue of the tongue. They are not bound with any limitations of what is proper, and what is improper. For me to have dreamt of my hero, not just once but multiple times, tells me just how strongly I want him!"

Brother Chandrashekhar: "I can see how interpreting dreams can lead to many misinterpretations. What you saw is what your body demands. Dreams are like a blind man, who can see colorful images as an opportunity to feed their hunger! You say you love him, but it is toxic lust for someone who happens to be in your hunting grounds and the dreams see in him an opportunity, which your conscious mind does not see!

You have been single so long, that the lust in you has started controlling your actions, is conniving with your mind to capture this only man you are interacting constantly with. These same emotions could easily develop for any other man who would have been in your playing field."

Father Abnash: "Is a dream not but just a dry run of a scenario/possibility of an outcome, a kind of help in seeing almost like in a movie format so you can then know how that life would be if you chose that choice, like a parallel Universe! If you enjoyed that journey then you know is worth pursuing, else serves as a good warning about the kind of dangers that lay ahead if you chose to pursue this one instead!?" ...

THE POWER IN SURRENDER TO HIS WILL

Learn to find pleasure in pain, from a woman while giving birth,
savor every moment of it,
as the rule is not that the law of averages may prevail,
but to be more precise will ...
- *Mast Mayuri, The Intoxicated Peafowl Dancing in the*
Rain

To Dear Mayuri from Sarthi,

Subject: How I conquered an Addiction

My coffee machine broke. Now all I can think is coffee and all I need is coffee! This made me realize it is addictive nature. Then I wanted to control my addiction. Then I realized that you are a good person to ask as you have proven you can control by going from writing to me long letters from all day to zero! This observation arouses my hypochondrial curiosity and must get the answer to it! Have Mercy on me O Mother-of-all and reveal to me the Secret behind your Success! How does someone achieve discipline! How did your frail hands move a mountain? Please solve this puzzle for me, else I will die of curiosity!?

Sarthi.

To Dear Sarthi from Mayuri,

Subject: The Secret to self-control - Complete Surrender to His Will/ Hoi soi jo ram rachi rakha (Only that will happen which Shri Ram, from Ramayan by Shri Tulsidas, has scripted)

When the very reason that I am alive is your curiosity, then there is no way that I can be someone who discourages you for this attribute in your nature! For that matter, it becomes my ethical duty, to answer all your questions earnestly, as your conclusions have the potential of making discoveries that will help the whole mankind!

My answer to how I achieved success, in controlling my urges for the man who I love even more than myself, is this: The instant that I could see my mistake the same instant I could fix the insanity! The mistake is that all of us tortured people go begging to the tyrant for mercy not realizing that he is not even the deciding authority, that there is nothing in his hands. Once you begin to see things more closely you will be surprised when you see how all events work the same as chemical processes! So, I have concluded that no need to divert our energies in altering or controlling the outside conditions, especially when the variables involved are next to Infinite, instead we strengthen our selves from all sides so that the Enemy cannot take us down from any side!

If what the scriptures say is true about us being eternal beings who have taken several births, then that suggests that there is nothing to worry about, as time is just a myth, death only a rejuvenating kiss, fire never dies and hopefully also with it, the fire between us too! ...

Mayuri

~

MEETING OF MOTHER-IN-LAW AND DAUGHTER-IN-LAW AS RIVER GANGA AND RIVER YAMUNA!

WEDDING ACCEPTANCE

Meeting Of Mother-In-Law and Daughter-In-Law as River Ganga and River Yamuna! How did this Miracle happen?! Well.

What Is love? A sacrifice to let go. A duty to fly away. What better supporting evidence for this saying, than a mother's Love for her only Son!

In this take-over session between Daughter-in-law Chhandani, and the mother of the son Aditi, Chhandani stays extra careful in ensuring that, her dress-up, mannerisms and speech are elegant and formal!

Knowing the impact of the proverb, 'first impression is the last impression', Daughter-in-law Chhandani first touches her mother-in-law Aditi's lotus feet. This method works like slam-dunk. It helps diffuse all tension of ownership battles, as this gesture conveyed that Chhandani respects Mother Aditi, the being who bore pain to give birth to a being who is now her caretaker/ Husband! Mother Aditi feels so respected that she instantly, lifts her from her feet and embraces her with a heartfelt joy! Chhandani then sits next to Ma Aditi.

Chhandani: "Ma, you gave birth to a man with character, nourished him with your milk of knowledge and wisdom, which makes me deeply indebted to you! I know very well that the reputation of the relationship between a daughter-in-law and mother-in-law has suffered a lot over ages, but it is time, we both be the role models who will restore this relationship back to some respectable levels!"

Chhandani feeling pleased with her performance smiles. Ma Aditi too smiles back. She tells a little mother-in-law and daughter-in-law joke which further lightens the mood.

Ma Aditi: "The story says that Queen Sita preferred to go for exile because of her love for her husband, but the grapevine says that she rather be without any comforts of the palace, than go through torture of living with three mothers-in-laws!"

All share a good laugh when they understand the irony part in the joke.

Ma Aditi continues with her charming smile: "You mentioned earlier that you are indebted to me for bringing my son to this world and then even more, for bringing him up as a Man of Character. It is true and yet in a way it is not, as I am just a caretaker of this property! Now that the real owner of this property has come, the test of my love begins. This property I have cared-for, with my blood and sweat, nourished him with my own milk! I got attached to this property so much so, that even if we are two separate bodies, I treated it as one! But now I must rip it off from my body by myself and then hand it back to its real owner! Yes, my heart is bleeding, my tears will not listen to me, my sorrow is immeasurable and yet respecting love, I too sacrifice my own selfish desires of binding my son to my bosom all my life, passing the baton to you! When he forgets me, I will be happy knowing that you are taking good care of him, that you are indeed the woman for him!

My blessings are with you in becoming successful as a good wife which will make you also a good mother and thus gifting me also the happiness which comes on meeting the grandchildren. I must have done many charitable deeds in my past life, to get a daughter-in-law like you!

You have won my heart. May you always prosper and be blessed with many sons and grandsons!" ...

WEDDING GAMES

Laaton ke bhoot baaton se nahi mante
(These scoundrels only listen to the language of kicks, talking is a
waste of breath!) - An Ancient Indian saying

Chandrashekhar addressing a small gathering of both families, in a religious engagement ceremony: "Now that all the hurdles in getting the bridegroom and bride together have been crossed, I am in favor of a simple and nice wedding which will serve as a good opportunity for both families to mingle, to become a bigger family! Let all our loved ones too share and become a part of our blessings and joy!"

Being a traditional Indian wedding, after all the prayers and promises of allegiance with the sacred Fire and The SuperKundalini as the witness have been done, the custom also demands that the Groom put a garland of acceptance around the bride's neck, and then the bride does the same. Now this seems like a simple task, but there is a major lesson of the victory-in-surrender-in-love-games in this little custom too! As to put garland around the taller bridegroom's neck, the bride will have to take help from him to complete the task, as without him bending his head in front of her, she cannot fulfill it without taking the risk of toppling all over him, revealing to the whole world her impatience of embracing him, thereby embarrassing her whole family!

Now when the bride Chhandani looks at the groom Chandrashekhar, expecting him to bow his head, all young men from his side start shouting for him to not bend his head as otherwise, as an omen says that if he bends his head now, he is likely to keep bowing his head to all her wishes for the rest of his life!

With this concern, starts a new round of tough negotiations! While all negotiations were coming to a standstill, someone from the girl's side shout's that the bridegroom must bend his head now, as the auspicious time is now and if not respected, the marriage will not bring much joy!

When the bride hears that, she panics and instinctively punches the bridegroom hard in his stomach and lo-and-behold, he bends his head as a reflex action. The bride does not lose this opportunity and at once puts the garland around the Groom's neck! Then she giggles shyly over her victory and everyone including the looser Groom's side start to laugh heartily! The Groom Chandrashekhar, smirks with his mischievous smile and laughingly says "Beware darling, I will make you pay for this, by having you pay me back with the gift of love!" Understanding the innuendo hidden in his remark, she blushes. Seeing her blush, he feels a warm tingling current run through his body from the head down to the toe! ...

LADDER FOR A LEAP:
BIRTH OF AN IMMORTAL DAUGHTER /
THE LAST HEAVY NIGHT

THE REJUVENATING KISS - DEATH

To Dear Mayuri from Sarthi,
  Subject: Like a phoenix rising from its ashes
Since, this news that I am now about to deliver you, has to do with your Past, I would like to begin with cautioning you. Memory is the thief who steals the "current moment" from the Present to give it to the Past and a **brave** person is one who fights for a cause and not for winning and has the courage to walk away from the battlefield, once the war is long over!

It takes a lot for me to be surprised, but this new piece of table-tilting news got me! My specialty is not in delivering news in a diplomatic manner, yet is my burden, so pardon me if without putting any positive or negative spin to the news, I plainly convey you the news as is:

You are **pregnant.**

Also, the report mentions that you have also contracted a **vene-real disease** which was never, till you got pregnant. I can know see the need of educating people on safe intimate touch! This is one of the main reasons that most cultures promote monogamy or else a harem of tested people versus a polygamous society without any restrictions! The whole taboo nature associated to this topic is understandable as the moment I started to talk about it with you, I could feel an awkwardness come over me, so I will not be surprised if you too feel the same way.

I had a candid conversation with the Man responsible – Faust, and it looks like he is not in a good mental state himself due to many misunderstandings that are now serious enough to destabilize his Marriage.

Since he too can see all the risks involved in a Woman of age, who has medical conditions, getting pregnant now is neither safe for the baby nor the mother, he will co-operate throughout the process of abortion, all the way from start to finish.

Beyond this brief communication, he refused to comment any further.

From your doctor,
Sarthi

...

DEMONS BACK TO HAUNT

The whole medical staff see this news of the pregnancy of Mayuri a serious Game-Changer, as the dark shadows associated can wake all the sleeping Serpents, jeopardizing her recovery as once again she can be pushed in the same pit of desires of fulfilling her unfulfilled desires, which she also sees as one of her ethical duties as a woman!

As everyone expects, the sleeping serpents of the past have begun to turn in their graves showing signs of new life.

Sarthi is tossing and turning in his bed, thinking, "To live with her with this knowledge, is impossible, yet being with her brings me immense joy! This episode in the past, cannot be seen as a past, as this past is really a present, which is carrying the seeds of the future. ... "

Faust is tossing and turning in his bed. "I want to sue that wretched priest with his silly forecast! Should have had more faith on my own virility, than her proclaimed barrenness! Being one body, sailing in two different boats at the same time, is impossible! Thus, I am seriously considering having a surgical castration for myself and for her to go for an abortion! This episode in the past, is not a past as this past is a present, as this past is carrying the seeds of the future! Earlier I had said to myself, I will pay her spiritual debt back grandly, in ways that the world cannot fathom, only to find my Lord Jesus Christ squirming in his grave over my unique ways of paying as, yes, I am indeed paying, just in ways that are beyond anyone's comprehension, including myself! This episode in the past, cannot be seen as a past, as this past is really a present, which is carrying the seeds of the future. ..."

Mayuri too at her end, is tossing and turning having silent conversations with The SuperKundalini. "O Lord Bhawan Shiv, am your chosen sink, through which all the poison of the world must flow, so the world can see, just how much of pain a Taurus Bull can take?

Just how deeply Faust has penetrated me, is evident from the fact that, even if he belongs from another dimension of my current existence still, I know not from which mysterious well inside, these tears keep coming, as every teardrop has his name on it! Dear Faust, you have helped me see the true cause behind my actions, as is clear from the fact that despite knowing all about your promiscuous ways can become a big health problem for me, I still jumped in the fire with you!

O Sarthi, just how deeply you have penetrated every pore of my body, that too at a time when even the smell of men would repel me, makes me wonder if you are the one for me! You put a life-energy in me, which makes every pore of my body jump with joy!

How similar my condition is with the Bowdoin ass, who was hungry and thirsty at the same time. Despite having Hay on the one side and Water at the other side, he died, not because the stereotype that an ass has little to none thinking abilities, but because it could not choose one over the other before its time was over, same as my time for starting a new life of domestic bliss!

This episode in the past, cannot be seen as a past, as this past is really a present, which is carrying the seeds of the future. ...."

A DIVINE CLUE SWIMMING –
WINNING, MY WAY!

*I am in the gold mine of contentment,
as everything I do, I do like a child does,
play without expectations ...*

Dear Mayuri's Diary,

Eureka! I think this episode from my childhood carries in it, a simple Observation, which once understood can end all the confusions surrounding the complex topic around our Teleological goals!

Observation: The scene is my swimming pool. Every time when I would go for swimming, I would see my fellow peers, always trying to find shortcuts to beat everyone in some invisible race going on in their heads, while me on the other hand, like a fish in water would instantly become water itself! There was no envy for the topper, on the other hand, I was consciously slow!

While I was swimming in the water, I realized that joy is in the experience of the act itself! Pleasure is in splashing water around oneself, in pedaling one's slender arms back and forth, in kicking one's beautiful legs, in feeling the sunrays kissing the body, then I feel it will not be far-fetched, when I say that it is only at that moment that the individual is alive!

Once this realization dawned in me the game reversed! What good did the winner of the race achieve, when he lost the whole point of a race - to have fun! Then does it not also mean that the moment I fulfill my desire, I also end all the fun associated with the Journey!

Then ultimately, is it not the loser who is the winner? ...

A NEUTRON

Complete like a neutered cat,
has nothing, needs nothing...

A Life must be content if it is like a Neutron - The component of the smallest particle making any matter the Atom, which has the property of neither attracting nor repelling anything! When any individual is in this state, must tell us that, these people are on track in meeting their Ultimate Goal, of an embrace with their first true love, the ultimate Lover, whose love for us, is the only constant that stays with us faithfully as we jump forms one Eternal Life, to another. ...

ANOTHER PLATITUDINOUS PARADOX

Mayuri to Parents: Being a Taurus woman who was born at noon, when the Sun's fireworks are at its fiery best, suggests that, that fire element of Sun is more dominant in me, that it will never let the fighter in me, show it's back in the battlefield, but now, I know not why I am getting cold feet! Does this contradiction then not beg this question to be explored further 'Is not in the acceptance of defeat, really where victory lies?'

In vain, I delude myself over my age! Painting furrows on my face, covering the whites in my hair with fluorescent red colors, in a hope that my lover always sees in me a sweet sixteen nymphet! The rebel in me will not let me to continue with this deception, which is only deceiving me and not others! Then, these painful symptoms, that every woman must go through when nearing the pause to her reproductive years, further confirms to me that, my transition period has started, where I say farewell to my youth and embrace whatever the next leg of my life-journey has in store for me, with class!

Since lust is also an energy and being an energy is in-destruc-tible, means it is still there in me, even if dimmed, still screams at me asking, 'why not quench our thirst for each other, this way our thirst will vanish with that night, and this way the whole affair can end without any major disruptions?" Which puts me at crossroads again of choosing between the two options I have: either I prepare my body for starting a new family life and wait or accept my defeat and move on?

Mother Aditi: From all my observations of you from childhood, I know that from having a Taurus nature in yourself, you are stubborn like your sun-sign - a bull! Always been having doing things your own way, but this time just try to think with an open mind. Here is a very well-guarded secret that I am going to share with you:

All talk of Marriage being the start of a new life that will fill every day with sensual pleasures, while really it is all a clever marketing gimmick meant to tempt these gullible and in-experienced Youth into Marriage! Movies and romantic novels are the tools which help propagate this lie. If the couple are aware of the real definition of Marriage, they would never do it! **Marriage has nothing to do with intimate moments between a couple, but instead is a duty, a very demanding duty which requires hard sacrifices, not sacrifices of worthless things which have lost all value for you, but of the object that you love more than anything! You sacrifice your time and energies for the upbringing of the children to become self-reliant individuals!**

Father Aakash: This time, I want you to not think about how your life would be if you had a child but think about the kind of life you will be giving to your child! A child might become a source of entertainment for you for some time, but in the long term become wearisome, not for you, but for the child! Think about the life of the child for a moment. Every time, he sees other children with their loving fathers, then he will experience the pain of not having any father figure in his life. And when one's child is in pain, how can any good mother not feel doubly miserable, especially when she is the root cause for the child's misfortune? It will make life a living hell for the child, and the mother too!

Now picture the scenario which is golden to you but has been eluding you so far! You give birth to a child and then begin feeling victorious over your win of finally getting the title of 'mother,' but

476

what is there to feel victorious about, when birthing is not even an art, especially when every household is busy multiplying exponentially like cats and dogs? The art lies in the parenting! It is only when you have been able to bring-up your child with values which will prove beneficial to the Universe can we call it a victory for the Parents, can we call a woman successful as a mother! It is this victory which differentiates an unsuccessful mother from a successful mother. Therefore, being a good mother is no child's play! It is a demanding duty, which requires every ounce of one's energy!

This is an immensely powerful paradox which is beyond the awareness level of most people to be able to ever grasp its meaning! ...

FORCEFUL TERMINATION OF PREGNANCIES - A NECCESARY EVIL

To Dear Mayuri from Sarthi,

Subject: Life is a form of Life Sentence!

In Garbha-Upanishad in the section on the stages of the embryo formation, it mentions that it is in the seventh month, that the 'life'/ 'jivatma' in Sanskrit enters the womb, till then the various body parts keep developing, meaning, till the seven months the embryo is still like clay...

If one is looking to find an example of selfish-love relationship in nature, look no further we have the winner already as, it is between a mother and a child, as what is in the eyes of the judgmental world an expression of the purest form of love, is in now aware eyes an expression of the most selfish love in nature! Wait! Put your stones down and first listen to my edification, then only with an equivalent mind decide, if I deserve a punishment or be put on the highest pedestal!

Here are the posits for your consideration, which led me to this edification: 'How is it, that despite knowing fully well that life is not a bed of roses but thorns, is not a blessing but a curse, the kind mother not be kind enough to drown her own child as soon as the child is born? Okay, we except the excuse from the benevolent mother, as she admits she has a problem with self-discipline, then also is no excuse as why she then not gets her tubes tied to prevent any misfortunes? No, she does not, because of the reasoning that I just told you. She is selfish.

Hence proved, the relationship between mother and child is a good example for selfish love in nature instead!

The monstrous paradox in time-cycles is that, unlike Satyug - the Age of Truth, where procreation is an act pleasing to The Super-Kundalini, same act now in Kalyug - The Age of Darkness, is an act of selfishness, an act which is not in favor of love as life in this age, is a life sentence of having to live as slaves in the prisons which we make ourselves and for ourselves!

Farewell,

From Your well-wisher Dr. Sarthi.

To Dear Sarthi from Mayuri,

Subject: Reply to Life is form of Life Sentence! / Consent Letter

By getting pregnant at this later stage of my Life and changed unfavorable conditions for any children to thrive, I admit that a serious blunder has happened! Just as the beauty of different chapters in one's life can be best experienced only when you have the matching energy demands, trying to enjoy motherhood will only be draining and exhausting under these conditions! The product from a body that is aging and suffering from many medical conditions might not produce a healthy product. I disrespected the demands of Time then, so now Time is punishing me instead!

Despite knowing that giving you consent for an abortion is the right thing to do under these circumstances, still I know not why these tears will not stop! They are flowing like some flood dam that just broke! This decision is one of the hardest decisions that I ever had to take in my life, and I would never wish it on even my worst enemy to have to go through, what I am going through right now!

This decision of an abortion might put the pro-life activists' angry, but keep in mind before passing any judgement, know that every case is different, that only the one who will pay the price is the one who should have the final say in the final decision. The people who never had to face such a situation, can preach all night long, but before you judgmental people start passing your judgements, keep in mind, that when it is them on who the lightening falls, they will be in for a big surprise on finding that their actions are the exact opposite of whatever their advice is, as there are very few of us who even know what the right thing is, what is the true price we pay other than just Dolla Dollar Dolla!

The vein masses might mistake this ending of my chapter with Faust as a disgrace to love, but in the court of love above, we will get a mention in the Roll-of-Honor, for doing the right thing, under the given circumstances!

Farewell,

From Mayuri.

After long deliberations, with a calm, rested mind, Mayuri picks up her pen to write to the man, who had long gone, but still whose fragrance is lingering with her - Faust.

To Dear Faust from Mayuri,

Subject: The World is a one big Lord Vishnu Katumb (Vishnu's Family)

If only you would have seen the entire world as a big Vishnu Katumb (Lord Vishnu, the Preserver's Family) and not just your blood and wife, I know not all the many more mountains you would have conquered then!

The divorce laws are unfair here, as they give absolute power to women and that is where the cause of the problem lies as it is a proven fact that absolute power absolutely corrupts!

Please try not to stress over your children's future as your children are also individuals that come with their own destiny that is separate than yours!

I know it is a stressful time for everyone, but have Faith, like other storms, this too will pass and soon enough we all would have forgotten all these hardships and started seeing new dreams for new goals already! ...

From A well-wisher,
Mayuri.

FULFILLMENT OF ANOTHER PLATITUDINOUS TELOS

Asäto ma sat gamayá
Tamaso ma jyotir gamayá
Mrt_yor ma amrt_tät gamayá
Om shaanti shaanti shanti Om
(From lies went to truth,
From Darkness went to Light,
From Death went to Immortality
Om Peace Peace Peace Om)
- Ved shastr/ Vedic Literature

Sarthi smiling with his most enchanting smile: "Once you sign this one final piece of legal document, you would have freed me of not just a financial and career ruin but also my mental sanity! For this debt, I am willing to be your slave forever, do whatever you want!"

Now after a long time of living in solitude, her intuition is more in-sync with her actions. She closes her eyes and then detaching herself first from the situation, views it as a third person.

Mayuri (After a long pause): Shame on me! For not being able to empathize! Like a movie I can see, this young man hiding his nervousness! His whole career is dependent on this one signature on this piece of paper, from this woman who is still in grip of her unfulfilled desires and can blackmail him into doing whatever she wishes! The young man is in a weak position to say no, as doing so might infuriate her, so she might not co-operate anymore, which will mean instant career suicide for him!

Now that I can empathize with your situation better, please just first relax! Now that I can see the real cause of my dance like a maniac around a man who is not a fit in my new life-path and goals, is this serpent of my hidden unfulfilled desires that was deceiving me into believing it is just innocent love making me write all those love-letters which had nothing to do with love, but a trickery of unfulfilled desires attempting to trick you into submission! I did feel the disconnect between my new path and your path and yet kept deluding myself into believing a lie, all driven by these hidden forces! Now that this awareness has helped me be more in-sync with my intentions due to you, I feel immense gratitude towards you! Thank you, for being instrumental in helping me come out of a lie!

I want to show you my gratitude and for that, despite knowing you will be willing to pay me any amount of money in return for this paper, I will not charge you even a penny for it! Not because my desires are still strong toward you, but for helping me get free from the bondage of your charms, and of my secret desire for pro-creation, which is toxic for any pre-menopausal woman with many prior medical conditions!

Sarthi: "Phew! I too feel relieved now! I had asked my mother for permission, and she had flatly refused! Let us change this bitter topic to something sweet now!

I am curious to know, tell me what is keeping you so busy?"

Mayuri(laughingly): "Preparing to give Birth."

Sarthi: "Give birth? Please stop talking in riddles with me any-more and just answer me directly!"

Mayuri first laughs, and then becomes serious as she gets to the irony part of his statement:

Mayuri: "You do not have to remind me of your curious nature, because in a way, it is only because of this property of curious experimental nature of yours, that I am now alive. Since one of the major teleology's as a woman is procreation, I fulfill it by giving birth to this beautiful daughter who is in the form of this Book which will live forever, will enlighten all Future generations with all the knowledge embedded in her. Now you must want to know the answer to 'what kind of knowledge'? Since, even after the fact that the other name for love is life, it is one of the biggest tragedies that we live so little and are stone for the most part! The more I see cities after cities full of impotent humans, the more I realize the need for this literary work to clear most doubts on one of the most misunderstood Topic in the whole world! So, to bring back life in this dead world that is hanging on the brink of destruction, this literary work is critical for injecting divine values in people which will help bring these dead people back to life!

There is still a lot of work left to finish, so please do not think I am being rude when I ask you to leave now! ...

LADDER FOR A LEAP - LISTENING TO THE IMMORTAL SONG - LOVE FOR OUR FATHER / THEN I SHED MY OLD SKIN TO TRANSFORM INTO MY NEW SKIN OF A BHAKT / LOVE-, INSPIRATION FROM BHAKTI YOG

Even then smallest particle of matter is infinitely beautiful because it
has the stamp of 'Made by the Infinite' on it,
All my actions try to favor,
my love for the Eternal...
A song is like a heartbeat,
arousing the feet to dance to the immortal song-love,
played by the magic flute ...
in this form of meditation I find, I found the sweetest of all nectar ...
-   Mast Mayuri, The Intoxicated Peafowl Dancing in the
Rain

BHAKTI YOG

Dear Mayuri's Diary,

I had started my sun salutations every day and started looking directly at the The Center of the whole Universe Activity, The Sun, only to find my vision is getting blurry and if I continued this way, I could go blind from a condition, often referred to as Sun Retinopathy!

Suffering from Sun Retinopathy revealed to me a life-altering secret revelation! The Creator of this whole universe does not want us to solve His own enigma, but for us to live!

The purpose of life is to keep flirting with death! Here, by default victory is always yours, as if you win over death, you will gain confidence, else if not, you are still victorious, as now death be forced to finally take you in his strong arms and embrace you!

Just stop all this fear talk every time when standing at the crossroads of life altering-decisions, like wondering if there is something better and brighter for us that we overlooked, that whether we just jumped the gun in haste! Instead, I find that all I need is to just listen and see, not right and left but right between the eyebrows, where the third eye or in other words the Ajna Chakra is!

On sitting with the back straight and looking at the monitor screen on Ajna Chakra, with closed eyes I begin to just simply see as a silent witness to whatever the thoughts are. As I keep going scene by scene of the issue, this "movie" tells me, that the process of elimination of all the wrong doors is already taking place by some invisible, mysterious forces, which are already active in creating situations that will make the doors nor meant for me to shut-off automatically on their own! This is a sign that I have been waiting for! Now that I know which door is for me, all confusions vanish, as a smile appears on my face, as I now see the beauty in the opportunity which this open door holds for me, under the current situation!

Even if my bruised ego wants to take revenge with all those people who closed doors on me, I do not bother! I choose not to focus on dead ones, but instead re-focus all my energies towards jumping over all the possibilities that this golden door has to offer!

Now that all doubts are cleared, my first step on this path must be one of the most beautiful of all steps, as this step is a sign of respect to that Eye of the Eye, so now my eyes can see what they could not before.

This first step is the sign of me having enough faith in the Lord, to now just let go of the anxiety which comes from uncertainty of the Future and then simply follow this light coming from the end of the tunnel! ...

A CENTURIES OLD SCAM OF GOD FINALLY BUSTED HERE!

For a true believer life is Heaven,
because there is nothing accidental about the way things unravel,
while for an atheist life is Hell,
because he is the reason behind everything that went wrong!
- Mast Mayuri, Intoxicated Peafowl Dancing in the Rain

Dear Mayuri's Diary,

Most people who believe in existence of a God, are mostly people who believe in complete surrender to the Almighty's quirky ways, I respect their belief but since it has been my focus of study for a good amount of time, I feel I can say a new theory which can help us grasp better just how God fits in the overall picture!

First, like clockwork every time that I start my Project with taking the God's name, I have failed miserably, however with the ones, that I have done following the steps just as the 'Guru,'/ the technique behind God made creations, I have tasted success!

Thus, the beauty of my Project is not dependent on my brain power of creating new things, but in my ability to reverse engineer, what is already existing in its natural form!

With this awareness my eyes can now see, how is using our love for our Creator and our ancestors to push us masses into darkness!

How must God work then? Truth is present in an encapsulated format, covered in layers of secrecy. Just as our digestion processes, the whole flow process, and the knowledge about what to eat and when, is all hidden. This suggests that the way God helps or hinders our plans, is by using this powerful tool of knowledge. I feel that when The Guru of Gurus wants us to succeed, the Guru does it by exposing to us the knowledge we need to make things work as designed, else when we are not yet ready for the Guru's blessing, the blindfolds of arrogance will prevent us from getting to that knowledge. ...

AHAM BRAHMASMI IN SANSKRIT / I AM THE CREATOR OF MY UNIVERSE

Here is introducing the two mighty contenders for this epic battle I am
constantly fighting:
my own Vices vs my own Qualities!
It must be the most challenging war in my lifetime, as both the Enemy
and Friend are me only
and yet are an incomprehensible riddle to me itself...

As the proven Scientific Law of Conservation of Energy says that Energy can be neither created nor destroyed, only transform itself into another form. And what is our body? An encapsulation for hosting our life-energy. Thus, all principles that are applicable toward energy, must apply to me also! That also means, that the true me is still wandering around from one form to another! It also means disposal of dead bodies need special attention. Since we are dealing with energies, I have found Garud Puran a reliable source for finding out the right way of dead-body disposal.

What do I need to do to sharpen my third eye so I can see right from wrong? The way is by feeding the divine properties in me, by sharpening my understanding of Mathematics so I can better find the design patterns that God created things follow. All that knowledge should help me find my mistakes better and by doing all my everyday activities in the right way, slowly those techniques will become my second nature and this way I will be beating the old me with a new me day by day! Building beautiful Rome did not take a day, so did my unpleasant habits too, blaming it on ignorance is not a good excuse. By using the weapon of faith in the techniques used in the creations by The Creator of All I have a feeling that I will be successful in meeting my eternal goals.

At the time of Sagar Manthan, when the world was going to drown from drowning in poisoned water, then Lord Shiva drank all the poison to save the world, similarly this is time for my Sagar Manthan. To save my soul I too will have to drink all the poison in my body! Which poison and how it got in my System? This poison comes from my failures, not the ones that I tried and failed, but the ones I stopped trying, or never tried; this poison also comes from those victories which fell in my lap without me even having the adequate skills for it.

LAST WORD

Never thought this Time to end will come,
but like a most dependable friend,
Time came as promised,
not a moment late or soon ...
Now enough chatter!
You do your work, while I do mine!

A PRAYER AT END OF THIS ENDEVOR, FOR EXCEEDING EXPECTATIONS, AS I LAY NONE IN THE FIRST PLACE... AHEHEHE

Satyam Shivam Sundaram
(Truth is Eternal, Eternal is Beauty)
- Upanishads

Thank you SuperKundalini, for always giving me with both hands, much more than my efforts ever called for. This time when you are pleased with me and want to give me something, then bless me to have the courage to choose that choice, which will always function as a fertilizer for the divine forces and pesticide for the evil ones residing in me." ...

RAIN OF FLOWERS

OM -The sound of the vibration made by the destroyer of Darkness:
The Father of all Fathers - Sun

Lord Inder along with all his Ministers assemble to honor this mortal Mayuri for saving this world from drowning into a sea of despair by gifting it with this beautiful daughter in the form of this Upanishad that will help humankind for all generations to come!

All the nymphs, fairies, and all entities around begin to dance to the tunes of soothing music and while Mayuri smiles on seeing a rain of flowers from the sky, done by her true love for his true love on the famous verses 'purnamada' from Isha Upanishad (Sanskrit):

Om purnamada purnamidam
Purnaat purnamudachyate
Purnasya purnamadaaya
Purnamevavasishyate
OM *shanti shanti shanti* OM

_____ :-)

s-cube

Another attempt of experiencing an alternate reality of The Seducer of all Seducer itself, in the form of this Avtar of your Author Inderpreet:

www.ingramcontent.com/pod-product-compliance
Lightning Source LLC
Chambersburg PA
CBHW022042020426
42335CB00012B/497